PENGUIN BOOKS

GIRL, UNDRESSED

Ruth Fowler was raised in North Wales and graduated from Cambridge University. She has written for *The Village Voice*, *The Observer* (London), *The Guardian*, *The New York Post*, *Wired*, and other publications. She currently lives in Los Angeles and works as a journalist and screenwriter.

Girl, Undressed

On Stripping in New York City

RUTH FOWLER

PENGUIN BOOKS

Previously published as *No Man's Land*

PENGUIN BOOKS

Published by the Penguin Group

Penguin Group (USA) Inc., 375 Hudson Street, New York, New York 10014, U.S.A.
Penguin Group (Canada), 90 Eglinton Avenue East, Suite 700, Toronto,
Ontario, Canada M4P 2Y3 (a division of Pearson Penguin Canada Inc.)
Penguin Books Ltd, 80 Strand, London WC2R 0RL, England
Penguin Ireland, 25 St Stephen's Green, Dublin 2, Ireland (a division of Penguin Books Ltd)
Penguin Group (Australia), 250 Camberwell Road, Camberwell,
Victoria 3124, Australia (a division of Pearson Australia Group Pty Ltd)
Penguin Books India Pvt Ltd, 11 Community Centre,
Panchsheel Park, New Delhi – 110 017, India
Penguin Group (NZ), 67 Apollo Drive, Rosedale, North Shore 0632,
New Zealand (a division of Pearson New Zealand Ltd)
Penguin Books (South Africa) (Pty) Ltd, 24 Sturdee Avenue,
Rosebank, Johannesburg 2196, South Africa

Penguin Books Ltd, Registered Offices: 80 Strand, London WC2R 0RL, England

First published in the United States of America under the title *No Man's Land* by
Viking Penguin, a member of Penguin Group (USA) Inc. 2008
Published in Penguin Books 2009

1 3 5 7 9 10 8 6 4 2

The experiences recounted in this book are true. However, names and descriptive
details have been changed to protect the identity of the individuals involved.

THE LIBRARY OF CONGRESS HAS CATALOGED THE HARDCOVER EDITION AS FOLLOWS:
Fowler, Ruth.
No man's land / Ruth Fowler.
p.   cm.
ISBN 978-0-670-01939-7 (hc.)
ISBN 978-0-14-311565-6 (pbk.)
1. Fowler, Ruth.   2. Sex-oriented businesses—New York (State)—New York—Employees—
Biography.   3. Stripteasers—New York (State)—New York—Biography.   4. Women—New York
(State)—New York—Biography.   5. English—New York (State)—New York—Biography.   6. New
York (N.Y.)—Biography.   7. Sex-oriented businesses—Social aspects—New York (State)—New
York—Case studies.   8. Striptease—Social aspects—New York (State)—New York—Case
studies.   9. Marginality, Social—New York (State)—New York—Case studies.
10. New York (N.Y.)—Social conditions—Case studies.   I. Title.
HQ146.N7F64 2008
306.7092—dc22 [B]   2007040509

Printed in the United States of America
Set in Fairfield Medium   Designed by Francesca Belanger

Imagine me; I shall not exist
if you do not imagine me.

—HUMBERT HUMBERT

THIS WORLD YOU'LL GLEAN from scraps of words, debris of the past carefully gathered, lovingly preserved in whimsical gauzes of tissue-paper memory torn up and painfully recreated on these pages—this world won't feature the New York you all know and love, vacuum-packed and delivered to your tastefully decorated abodes via HBO. It'll slip in shockingly few apple martinis at Pravda while eye-fucking the male model at the next table. And there'll be a sad lack of shopping expeditions to Bergdorf's to punctuate each chapter's end (though not through want of desire). It'll make you reevaluate everything you ever learned about New York, for while Manolos may be featured, they're certainly not the star attraction, and while there *is* sex, it's not on the third date. Yes, there's at least one millionaire, but his obsession with toilet paper and strip-joints ensures that he's no one's Mr. Big—except, perhaps, mine. You see, while I spend quite a few hours frittering away the time with my bourgeois English friends in Marquee, rubbing shoulders with Manhattan's A-list crowd, I also hang out with those people you just don't listen to very often: the illegals, the immigrants, the people in low-paid, cash-in-hand jobs.

I'm one of them.

1

First song, dress on

IT SOUNDS LIKE an obvious statement when I say that girls don't grow up wanting to be strippers, but you'd be surprised. Most people—civilians, that is—seem to think that even in the cradle we were wrapping ourselves around a greasy pole and grinding our hips to Britney Spears, while our crack-addicted Mothers painted on their faces prior to standing on the corner of the highway trying to pick up new Daddies for us.

No, the truth, the reason *why* we're strippers, is invariably more boring, more grounded in nonexistential needs like money—and pragmatic concerns, like money. It's all about the quick fix of money, like that hasty illicit cigarette outside when the boss isn't watching, covered up with a gargle of mouth-wash. Our mouthwash is our own mantra, repeated over and over in our heads, *It's not forever.* I think we keep coming back because standing on that stage, posing and preening in the mirror, turning and arching so the light strikes our luminous, smooth skin, is the only time we don't think of things. You know—*things.* Guilt things. Hopelessness. Boredom. The fact that Old Venus in the corner always says, "It's easy to get into, impossible to get out," nods her head, looks down at her breasts, like two bizarre antennae placed upon a sagging thirty-five-year-old body, and you're thinking, is that *me*? Does that refer to *me*? So we don't think. I know I don't. I put every effort into making my movements deliberate, controlled, seductive, self-absorbed . . . and on the rare occasion I do catch my own eyes in the mirror onstage, I don't even recognize them, encased in pandalike makeup, huge, defiant, ferocious, daring my other self, the self I was before all this, before Mimi, to argue back, to walk offstage, to have the confidence to say, *That's not me anymore,* and mean it.

When we get drunk, the regrets come out, the dreams and ambitions cloaked in cheap polyester, stretched taut against skin hidden beneath layers of Mystic Tan. "I'm a good girl, really I am," sighs one. "I'm a good Jewish girl. I'll make a good wife." She takes a drag of her cigarette and I think to myself, *I'm not a good girl. Not really. Not anymore.* But I sure as hell would like to be.

Second song, dress half off, top slipped to waist, grasp pole

I was always the boring, studious, well-behaved child. Quietly ambitious, personality the ghost of good grades, my rebellion was confined to the occasional cussword and a failed drug deal (age sixteen) that resulted in the purchase of dehydrated morels and the contents of a Tetley tea bag. At Cambridge University I was one of a minority of students who attended what was known as a comprehensive school—government-funded state education—and as part of an even smaller minority from the wilds of North Wales, I was a certified novelty. People noted with amusement my short, accented vowels, and my impressive capacity for gin with respect. Cambridge is flat and barren, set in the bleak Fen District of East Anglia, and the absence of the mountains I'd known all my life left me with a hollow feeling, a sense of being exposed, naked in that bitter northeasterly wind that always seemed to blow no matter what the weather. I believed them—the university—in their glossy prospectus that claimed poor kids went there from state schools, and Northerners, and even brown kids. But to be honest, most of the people I made friends with sounded like the Queen, had gone to the same boarding school, and all fucked off to London every weekend to go clubbing and avoid the bad assortment of student DJ's mixing drum-and-bass music in seventeenth-century cellars. Pubs. Cambridge has a lot of pubs.

I was one of those types who always wrote for the student newspaper, whose plays were put on in the local theater, who was on every committee, who left with a first—the UK equivalent of a 4.0, a magna cum laude—because the token minorities must get firsts or thirds; there's no acceptable in-between for us dilettantes of suffering.

The day after graduation I left the country, driven onward and outward by a fire in my belly, a consumptive hemorrhaging passion in my soul. Something deep inside was longing to get out, far away, see it all, live, breathe, be different, make a difference, eat to excess, drink to excess, love, fuck, scream, cry, hate—to excess. I think I surprised even myself when I didn't sign up at the corporate milkround and get a job with Merrill Lynch, or go to law school, or work for the government, or do any of the things that good Cambridge graduates are meant to do.

I went to Argentina. Got a job as an English teacher in a private school, taught Shakespeare to squat hairy teenage boys sporting masturbatory sneers upon their spotty features. I hated the work, was frankly confused by polo, loved the country, was paid next to nothing. I would take the train from the suburb of Hurlingham, the apex of English expatriate existence, into the center of Buenos Aires every weekend, bypassing the dusty, empty stations whizzing past. In one a llama was tethered to a post, nibbling at the dirt ground, the legend TIERRA DE NADIE scrawled above it across the exterior of what seemed to be a decrepit public convenience. *Tierra de Nadie*—"No Man's Land." Land of Nobody. Land of Nothing.

We were all so hyperbolic in those days. We were Cathy from *Wuthering Heights,* impassioned and annoying and always right, by turns tragic and ecstatic, riding the peaks and scoffing at the troughs of living. A friend from university who lived off espresso and Marlboros, her huge, beautiful eyes bloodshot and yellowed with adrenaline and nicotine, would stare at my sensible well-fed demeanor with incomprehension when I'd knock on her door to deliver some essential nutrients. "You need to sleep, Sarah," I'd murmur, glancing around at the pages of writing littering her floor, the dog-eared books, two smoldering cigarettes upended in a moldy piece of toast. "I don't sleep," she'd correct me. "I can't *sleep* when I have so much going *on*." She'd wave her hand around the filthy room, a slim, pale, manicured hand clutching a cigarette. We had nothing "going on," but we expended our energy and our higher-than-average IQs into whipping our intelligent little minds into a state of excitement and expectation and drama and tragedy in order to make our normal, dull lives a little more worthwhile, a little more suitable for writers and actresses and famous people. Fame. We wanted to be paid for fucking around all day drinking coffee, smoking cigarettes, and typing one-fingered sentences about ourselves in our thinly veiled autobiographical novels.

Leafing through old journals and postcards preceding my arrival at that stage, what I notice in the empty words scrawled on onionskin paper, e-mails polluted with mistypes, is that this time was driven by a fierce, defiant passion. The correspondence from this time are coruscating in their heartfelt naïveté, their devotion to "having the guts to follow one's heart" (although being a Northerner I did not, I assure you, use the third-person singular in speech). Examples: Kathmandu, Nepal—e-mail home revealing to my resigned parents that I wasn't going to do the PhD, instead was going to travel more, do some humanitarian work, become a political activist, write a novel and a play, live in the Himalayas, and campaign to free the Panchen Lama: *"I'm staying longer and sneaking over the border posing as a tourist. I plan to wear my 'Save Tibet' T-shirt in Lhasa."* Alpe d'Huez, France—postcard to a friend in London: *"I've never drunk so much beer in my life. Snowboarding is awesome and the guys are hot! Is Dave still seeing that American bitch with the big tits?"* Antibes, Côte d'Azur—quick e-mail littered with the typos of the alcoholically depraved: *"i knwo nothig about boatts but the crew ive met donr seem to either so ive takenthe job sailing across te atlantic"*

A chance encounter in a bar in the South of France, too many beers imbibed, too few people to make me stay behind.

The bar was empty, the air thick and warm, intoxicating after the thin, calloused atmosphere of the ski resort. He sat in a corner, caught my eye, and laughed along with me when a drunk Australian fell over a bulldog belonging to the bartender. He bought me a pint, said he was a captain. More likely he was just another ski bum making money by cleaning rich people's boats. Friends from Alpe d'Huez had told me Antibes was the place to be, that now was the time to get the best jobs, the best boats, the best money. Antibes—the European center of the luxury yacht industry; a small, cobbled gray-stone town with winding streets leading to secretive courtyards surrounded by tall, pastel-colored shuttered buildings, airy, expansive views of the glittering Côte d'Azur. The port dominated the pretty resort with its rude display of grotesque wealth: huge sailboats and yachts owned by rich people, chartered by rich people, an industry fed by rich people as they flitted around the world on tax-evasion schemes, paying sunburned hobos posing as professionals too much money to drive their boats, scrub the decks, lay their leopard-print pillows out in feng shui order on the mezzanine, prepare five-star cuisine, and (in some cases, literally) wipe their arses.

It was late by the time we left the bar, we were a little drunk, and I still wasn't convinced he was a captain. He went back to his boat, supposedly, I went back to the crewhouse, and I didn't see him again. He sailed for Barcelona the next day. I stayed on in Antibes, and as the days become lighter, longer, warmer even than that first glorious evening back in the caress of the South, more travelers—Brits, South Africans, Americans, Aussies, Eastern Europeans—arrived hoping to seek employment on the boats. I applied for jobs as a chef by day, drank beer at night with other people like me—broke and selfish and unemployed and young and hungry for life. We had nothing to lose, and, indeed, did not care even if we lost that, so long as on the way we felt the sting of our own existence. By the end of the summer I had a packed résumé of employment, several thousand euros, an impossibly high alcohol tolerance, and a considerable amount of sea miles. In Barcelona one evening toward the end of August, I met him again, the Captain, over prawn crackers and Foo Yung in a shoddy Chinese restaurant. I was with a group of boat crew, all of us taking a course on fire safety for our insurance papers. He grinned at me and through the gap in his front teeth rolled a cocktail stick around with his tongue, grotesque and comical. "You met me at the right time, luv. Need a bloody chef to cook for me and the crew when we sail the boat across the Atlantic in October. Reckon you could do it?"

Glance down at heels, up into lights,
arch back, slip leg through slit

I imagine Mimi as a parasitical spirit, a placenta feeding off my experience, siphoning from my awakening to life, groaning with the bellyache of eating fruits not yet ripe enough to pluck but all the more delicious because of their illicitness.

She waited patiently for her revolution, timed it to perfection. Midway between America and Europe, in fifty knots of wind, strapped into the cockpit of the sailboat to prevent the waves from clawing me back out to sea, doused and drowned and slapped and bruised by the ocean. I'd give you the lat and the long but I can't remember it. You'll find it if you look hard enough though, somewhere in the logbook of *La Bella*. Even in the midst of the storm, when there were other, more pressing concerns at hand, like breathing, surviving, not capsizing, she saw her chance.

"All you talk about," he roared across the wind—the Captain, that is, and I could see him shaking his head in exasperation, in admiration, in amusement and pain—"is yourself. *Me me me me*. I'm going to call you Mimi."

Logged, down with the wind angle, the tides, and our position. There and then it all coalesced and it all changed. Up until that point it had been the clever kid gone awry, broken-hearted, stumbling away from home to where the booze was cheap, the drugs were plentiful, and the sex was shared, all sticky, indiscriminate wrestling bouts of it. A cracked, flawed version of me, ready to splinter and bleed. And now, Mimi. Two syllables, just in case you didn't get the self-obsession the first time. Two pairs of letters coupled snugly, no room for any more. Indestructible and self-contained.

Life changed after that. I guess it's like calling the devil. Find the right name, you draw him out. Although this wasn't an exorcism. This was more of a baptism.

Palm connects with brass, grip tightens,
glance up into lights, away

I have my ritual when I come in. The ritual of anesthetization.

Dressing room. Quiet, empty. My body's calm, flexible, glowing from several hours of yoga. I look in the mirror and the face looking back is scraped clean of makeup, unblemished skin, a soothing rose tint of health. The dressing room is dark. I slowly walk around, then screw the lightbulbs into their sockets around the large makeup mirrors until a fluorescent glow drains the last vestiges of health from my appearance. The face looking back in the mirror now is deadened, skin translucent, dark rings encircling the eyes. I stare into the pupils and light a cigarette, and my chest heaves in repulsion, because I don't smoke outside this place, and coming in involves conditioning myself to be the person who works here, and this involves smoking, another drug to deaden the feelings of outside. The ritual of anesthetization. I stare into my eyes and then I have that curious feeling of looking outside myself, at myself, and it disturbs me, because I don't want to look too deep. Down the stairwell into the kitchen. I help myself to the busboys' coffee. Bitter and strong, the buzz kicks through the yoga haze. Milk. Sugar. Walk upstairs again. I take a cigarette from a discarded packet, light it, take the coffee, and settle into my usual position, the old, tattered sofa in the corner of the dressing room. It faces a full-length mirror.

Looking into this mirror I can see that the ritual is starting to work.

I move into the main body of the dressing room. I put on foundation. Clinique. Light-reflecting concealer under the eyes. Dark, smoky brown shadow over the lids. Thick black liner. Curl the eyelashes. Paint over them with mascara, own brand, cheap crap from Duane Reade. There is an order to everything, and the careful orchestration of that order is the balm to a chapped and fractured soul. The coffee and the nicotine buzz are fading. Girls come in, laugh, chatter. There is one thing I have consistently found about strippers in New York. They love dogs. If you ask about their Chihuahuas, their pugs, their runty little lapdogs, you will slot in like you belong. After months of diligent enquiring about their pets, I belong, and I throw out a comment or two, eye myself in the mirror. Today I am wearing a tiny white schoolgirl outfit that barely skims my ass, neatly divided in two by a white-and-red-spotted sequined G-string. I have waist-length blond hair, $21.99 from Ricky's around the corner, clipped into my own shoulder-length mop so the acrylic and the real blend seamlessly. Sophie walks in. Her Chihuahua is suffering from a slipped disk where the annulus fibrosis weakened or tore, resulting in a bulge or protrusion of the nucleus and annuli that exerts pressure on the nerve. Old Venus comes in, breasts erect. Her dog is having jealousy issues with Lila, the champagne manager's dog, after the two were introduced over an extended drinking–marijuana-smoking session sometime last week. The ritual of asking about their dogs soothes me, acts as an analgesic, and the music over the Tannoy speakers kicks in, which means the club is officially open, which means I can go downstairs and order a drink and sit at the bar and let the alcohol soak into my body, leak out over my system, and blot out the goodness like india ink. My legs sink gratefully into the comfortable familiarity of rigid plastic shoes that, after continual wear, are perfectly melded to the arch of my insole, although it is more likely that I myself have melded to the curve of hard plastic. Giulio, the manager, is behind the bar. He has black greasy hair combed back off his face in a Guido-*Sopranos* style that would be ridiculously caricatured if you saw it on a character onscreen, but for reality it is fine. He smiles briefly and says

"Yes" before I even open my mouth to request a free drink. It is another one of our rituals. He knows it as well as I.

The blast of the AC slaps my porcelain skin, deliberately cultured to maximum whiteness to emphasize my supposed English complexion. The early days of fake tan are over for me, as I learn to accentuate what makes me different from the legions of Rubenesque Brazilians. The bartender is a dark, busty Puerto Rican girl with a Bronx accent who likes me. We talk and laugh about the other bartender, a white girl with a large nose and no sense of humor. I can't remember their names, even though I've worked with them four times a week for seven months. She can remember what I drink though, and as she tells me about her dog she drizzles Ketel One over crackling ice, adds a wedge of lime, soda water. The first sip is pure vodka, and my stomach clenches involuntarily. Over the empty chairs is the shadow of the DJ in his booth behind the stage, purple and black and red. My hands are shaking. Ketel One, crackling ice, a wedge of lime, soda water—my drink of choice refined over eighteen months of trial and error and inadvertent alcoholism. Red Bull and vodka and I was awake for weeks. Beer, headaches and bloating. Cocktails, vomiting within hours. Wine and I had constant blackouts. In the beginning, when I started stripping, I drank very rarely, an odd shot, more likely a Diet Coke. I still think of this with awe. *I drank nothing.* I worked without medication, without the deadening of the senses, the deadening of oneself, the real. I worked fully exposed to the illusions of the club without my blanketlike embrocation of alcohol and Mimi. I earned very little compared to what I earn now.

I'm sitting at the bar, drinking my third Ketel One and

soda, and I'm still talking to the Puerto Rican bartender, and I have no idea what I'm saying. I doubt she knows what *she* is saying. It's a ritual we perform every day, a request that today be like yesterday—no surprises, money, drinks, bed before four a.m. if we're lucky.

There's no one in the club besides us two. Then the blond girl with the sweet face, the puppy fat of a teenager, walks down the stairs. She sits on the stool next to me and puts a gentle hand on my arm, a plump hand, soft, tender, pigletlike.

"How long have you been dancing plis?"

The question, phrased in the halting imperfection of Eastern European, surprises me and I answer without lying, which is unusual.

"A year. I started working as a waitress at Foxy's, and then realized I could earn more money as a dancer, so I became a dancer."

"A year? But you dance so well. You are the best dancer in this club. You are very flexible onstage. I want to dance like you but I do not know how."

I digest this without blinking. I am a good dancer. I'm probably the best in this club, this small club. I have mastered the art of not giving a crap, so crawling across the stage wearing only dental floss panties and a look verging on the orgasmic has become effortless, reflexive.

"It took me a year to learn. How long have you been dancing?"

"Two weeks. I was a waitress in Foxy's too. And then I came here. But I think it will take me a long time to learn how to dance like you. You make very good money, yes?"

I take a sip of my drink, Ketel One over crackling ice, wedge of lime, soda water. Everything visibly relaxes, an exhale, a sigh. I'm nearly there, rituals complete.

"Promise me something," I say, and my voice is urgent, insistent. "Make your money here, but don't work longer than a year. Save your money and then fuck off. Don't stay."

Her brown eyes blink rapidly. Soft eyes, soft skin, soft rolls of baby fat around her plump waist.

"Maybe I will go back to my country in a year. And you? You are going to leave?"

"Yeah. Soon."

My stomach lurches, and I turn abruptly, walk over to the bathroom, squat over the toilet taking care not to let my dress trail on the floor, and then violently and efficiently expunge the contents of my intestines into a toilet stinking of piss, traces of white powder on the floor, sopping rags of pulped tissue paper around shards of glass, and the sour, stale smell of old alcohol, cheap perfume. This, too, is my ritual every night. I wasn't born to this. I did not intend to be this way. I have a good degree. I am training to be a yoga teacher. I have ambitions to write journalism and screenplays and fiction. I care about global warming and the crisis in the Middle East. I am a kind person, the kind of person who stops when an old lady falls in the street, who likes animals and babies, who still believes in love. Had I taken a different route I could have had a comfortable life and career in London. I am the last person you would ever expect to be a stripper, to live this life, to anesthetize myself every night so my bowels drip out of my body rather than press unbearably on the nerve, like protruded annuli.

In the mirror, the person who walked into the club and began the ritual of anesthetization ninety minutes previously is gone.

I smile. It's going to be a good night.

Hand slides down the slim indentation between breasts, over stomach, rests on dress, half off

I gorged myself on life, and then one day, on vacation from the last boat I ever worked on, five years after I'd graduated and started traveling, three years since I first stepped on a boat, I woke up alone on an avocado farm in Guatemala. A half-finished novel by my side, lips tinged with cheap red wine and the kisses of someone's husband, chest hurting from the altitude, I knew that it was time to stop. There's no grand explanation for it. No epiphany. Just a void that could no longer be filled by the procrastination of travel and the thrill of the new. I sat drinking coffee on the chill of the mountain-side, watching smoke puff lazily out of a volcano, and felt immensely sad at the thought of halting this incessant move-ment, of becoming familiar and intimate with a place, hav-ing a relationship with location rather than a one-night stand. I went back to London, not a little scarred. I was different certainly, when I came back—you must understand that. I liked the nickname I'd picked up on my travels, mulled it over in my head, rolled it around on my tongue like a savory treat, an aperitif, a delicate bonbon, a snack that fails to satisfy. *Mimi.*

On the tube, the interminable Northern Line, buffered

from the winter cold by the stale, hot air, I realized England was not The Place. As soon as I'd stepped into the London Underground, slapped with the rancid roar of bad-breathed commuters, I wanted to get off. But I was on the interminable Northern Line and realized with a lurch (which could have been nausea, or could merely have been the motion of the train), that staying on this line could be more detrimental than the years of squalor and traveling and life bulimia.

I got off before I hit Edgware or High Barnet or Morden or any of the multitudinous stops in between. You might ask how that's possible. You might not give a proverbial shit, but I'll tell you anyway. It's quite simple once you get the hang of it, this leaving business. You think of a destination, you book your ticket, you pack your bag, you leave. Once you're in the habit of leaving, those around you will get used to it too. Your parents, if they're like mine, will just give a *humph* down the phone, get back to a cup of tea and the telly, clucking disconsolately at that expensive education at the taxpayers' expense gone to waste.

Leaving, ah, I can leave! No money, no savings, no overanxious parents, no ties. Leaving is easier than staying, staying where the rent and the tax and the living and the struggle to keep ambitions flourishing costs money that you just don't have. Leaving what you don't have is the most exquisite feeling on earth, for when you leave what you don't have, you can only find it. *Leaving*. That's one thing I am exceptionally gifted at, something I have always managed to do without failing, something that has invariably provided me with a bed, and food, and money when there was none.

Arriving? Well. Now, that's something *entirely* different.

Third song, dress off

Perhaps you're wondering what went before this, before my mid-Atlantic baptism, before that fateful trip to London, preceded by five years of solipsistic wandering, before the decision to up and leave for New York. Perhaps you're wishing for a more ardent and thoughtful biographical recollection of my life, something a little more than the recollection of a depressing trip on the London Underground. Perhaps a few sweet childhood photos of myself, to contrast with the glossy, hard set of a corrupted mouth as I swing, eyes a-flash, around that damned pole. Sorry, no can do. It's not my job. Both memoir and biography deal with making a whole out of parts, pretending the gaps have been filled in, what's on the page is absolute veracity. But as far as I can recall there are very few of either genre that deal with the literal process of making someone up, composing yourself anew, becoming someone entirely different to who you ever thought you were, literally editing and forming the person who's writing the words. And that's the ridiculous task I've been given. *Mimification*. It's Mimi who has become inextricably bound up in New York, in dancing—in truth as much as in fiction. She's me, but she's more than me. She's the movie me, minus the credits; the novel me without the chapter endings. She's the story bleached of inconsequential detail; the rash I get if I use scented bubble bath, sitting in the Laundromat on Second Avenue waiting for my washing to dry every Tuesday, or the time it takes to pee. When Mimi walks, acts, moves, it's with a soundtrack in the background, the essence of me, distilled and pure, so me she's more than me, she's nothing like me. "You're sure this is true? You're so *different* in real life." Me? I'll fade into a corner with strangers, blush if called upon in company exceeding two, whereas Mimi . . . *Oh Mimi,* the men sigh, their mouths burrowed in my hair (fake), their dicks twitching with longing, *Oh Mimi, Oh Oh Mimi.* She's me, I swear; I'm her and this is our story. You can tell when she takes over, you really can, although we do, at times, become indistinguishable. But really, it's *her* dragging the other me on that dirty, downward spiral to the bottom of a slime-covered pit of iniquity and sin, a rumpled, thin figure sodden with drink and lolling on a Manhattan side-walk, still painted like a doll and smelling of stale smoke, of pheromones, of a night dancing.

2

I **WALKED THROUGH DUMBO** on that first day, sick with trepidation, a sense of the inevitable, acutely sensitive to the approval of averted eyes and glutinous glares. The Hasidics looked away, the Hispanics hissed, low and snarling, suppressed animal lust leaking out like a punctured tire through teeth snaggled and brown and cloven with poverty. *Gooood* Bless You, siphoned through those broken piano keys with a low whistle, an ache, a twitch. God Bless *You*. I looked like a woman of low morals who would serve IBs and traders midday Budweisers in an underground cell in Midtown. Or maybe I just looked like I possessed a vagina, let's not be too optimistic about the discernment of the men who hiss at you, or the men who pray to Yahweh. Hands clenched tight, manicured fingers digging into pink palms, nearly at the subway, nearly at the club. I glanced at the face of one of the men, one of the men who hiss at you, dark-skinned and leering, his face creased into a sea of a thousand wrinkles. I couldn't see his eyes, because they were hidden behind thick lenses. But in the reflection of his glasses I could see the girl Mimi, now evolved into a bad imitation of whatever a stripclub serving staffer was supposed to resemble. I looked like I should work there. I did, really, with the badly dyed hair, the poverty roots, and the makeup applied with a shit-shovel. Let's hope the boss saw it that way. Let's just hope so.

Broadway, Midtown, emerging into the blinking, gaudy fetidness of Times Square, lurking winos, commodified perverts, and musicals featuring tired homosexuals filling in the crow's-feet of disappointment and age with thick, poisonous makeup and repulsively cheerful song. Broadway. And while we're here, what the hell's going *on* with Broadway? I'm not a New Yorker and even I can tell there's something fucked up about this winding non-avenue slicing through the grid system, an oleaginous concession to the obese red-state tourists in their white socks and whiter sneakers, the white cotton of their captioned T-shirts strained taut against jiggling man breasts, mammaries grown huge through emasculation by junk food, Fox News, frotting. New Yorkers would never tolerate an area like Broadway condensed, so they planned it to snake elusively through Manhattan island like an aorta, explode into the premature ejaculation that is Times Square, an angina of planning, before it pisses off west again farther north and disappears with a sneer into the Bronx. The stripclub is on Broadway, lily-white Broadway, white trash Broadway, built for the Hanks and the Juniors and the ladies released from their Middle American bakefests to see Letterman (*see* him!) and swoon.

I lit a cigarette before I entered that cavernous mouth oozing the promise of titties and ass like halitosis. The doorman nodded at me in a disinterested way, and the exhausted blond with the enormous breasts and the mouth like a slit throat—wet and crooked and shiny against cigarette-paper skin—overtook me with a sigh and pushed through the dark glass doors as she flicked a lip gloss–stained Parliament stub into the street. I watched her leathered face stitched by no money, bad decisions, and several abortions get swallowed up by the club without even the simulated pleasure of a little mastication. There followed a brief moment of . . . triumph? vindication? a little gloat of pleasure perhaps? remembering Paula of the 34D chest from Year 9 Drama, with that derisory snort directed at me, directed at the skinny nerd who, at fourteen, was the last virgin in Year 10, still wore an M&S training bra, and never (I swear *never*) even shaved her legs. *No wonder she never got laid* the playground whispered, venom borne on breath tainted by the prejudice of snakebites consumed in the kids' playground on the council estate just off Ivy Crescent. So *this* is where all the cool girls ended up. *This* is what happened to the bitches, the easy lays, the girls with the perms and the right trainers and the Kama Sutra sex lives predating their menstrual cycles. This is where they *arrived*. I always wondered about those girls. When you're fourteen and sad, it was no consolation, the assurance that they'd be, in the end, knocked up and fucked up. Even *that* was cool, cooler than anything *I* could do, destined for university, destined to be a clever white bitch. Even aged six I was a weirdo with my hair like bugs' tentacles waving fondly above the shoulders of the other little girls. *Mam, please don't put my hair into three plaits; all the other girls laugh at me and say I'm a freak.* At twenty-six it's some consolation to know that they ended up in a stripclub. Until you realize that *you* ended up in a stripclub too.

Lily appeared in front of me.

"Hey you. C'mon, I'll take you to the boss."

Girls writhed on a stage, pocked with two poles. Girls writhed on men, fewer clothes. A line of limp and lethargic waitresses yawned and withered in the brutal assault of the AC. Dingy corner, slab of a man, guffawing and guffawing as a girl's hand slips lower, lower, lower—down his bulbous stomach, a button undone so the white hairy paunch stares at me obscenely, the umbilicus bleeting, futile, like a drowning man. *But this doesn't come yet,* I should stay in line, step by step, counting it out as it happened. Arrive New York, find job, move from Astor Place to Brooklyn, lose money, lose hope, then . . . I would prefer chronology, from A to B, because it would be easier, yet the truth is that chronology does not exist anymore. The past preceding the stripclub is corrupted by the knowledge of what came afterward, and try as I might, I can't disentangle it, find a straight-up, easily digestible truth that can be explicated by the glories of the linear. I'm sorry, I really am. I wish I could make it easier. I wish I could make it easier for myself too, but it's corrupted, like I said. It's a plastic audiocassette with the shiny brown tape tangled and knotted and ruined. Even if we managed to untangle it by the grace of God, played it, it would sound distorted, creepy, and wrong.

The card is flimsy, thin, nondescript. An off-white speckled like a robin's egg with tiny circles of yellow and blue and pink that you can barely discern until you pull it into sharp focus, study the clean stamp of the gray lettering. It's so *nothing.* So irrelevant. But when you don't have one, with your name neatly typed in capitals below the white shadowed letters SOCIAL SECURITY and the nine-digit number responsible for punching you into the American system, you start to think that somehow being deprived of one equates to nothing less than social *in*security. Not even social insecurity. Nonexistence.

However, when you're on an Air India flight to New York, squashed up next to a huge Bengali lady called Bunny, nonexistence is the farthest thing from your mind. Questions of legality, bureaucracy, employment, money, the slight niggling concerns of transporting your entire life to a city you have visited for a grand total of forty-eight hours and in which you have absolutely no friends—for someone who has traveled for five years, who has survived solely on her ability to be a cheeky gobshite, who has absolute faith in her ability to turn up somewhere broke and make good—these concerns don't really feature. Sure, it'll be difficult. There'll be discomfort, but I know I can take it. How hard can it be, after all? Illegals are people without education, who can't speak English, who no one wants to employ. To get a green card, presumably all you had to do was show up, get a job offer, and then show the paper to Immigration. Worries, concerns, anxiety—I feel *some*, sure, but to be honest, they're obliterated by my infallible confidence in a Cambridge degree, a pretty face, and consequent employability.

I stood in Baggage Claim gazing outside at the snow dancing agitatedly in gales of wind, the sky a midnight blue at nine P.M. Heaved my luggage gratefully off the conveyor belt, struggled toward the exit signs, the gaggle of waiting cab drivers with Brooklyn accents, Jamaican faces, New York attitudes. The airport is *tierra de nadie*, no man's land, a nonplace, a transition. Airports, boats, trains; curled up against a dusty backpack, spine lodged against a rigid plastic chair, unbrushed teeth, empty Styrofoam cup sticky with dredges of coffee. The first time I boarded a flight on my own I thought people could tell that I didn't belong. As if traveling was a snooty sorority for the dreadlocked globe-trotter, a frat house for the first-class hobo, something that excluded a small Welsh girl who'd never even been to London alone. But no one knew. No one could tell that I was out of place. Forever after I associated airports with something better, something more. Airports were where I took off my skin of comprehensive schoolgirl, Northern accent, bit of a nerd—taking it off, hanging it up, walking away.

The automatic doors outside Baggage Claim swing efficiently open to expel those who have successfully navigated Immigration, clutching tickets and pristine visas and fake addresses and false promises to return home after two weeks and a scrawled cellphone number hopefully clutched in a nervous hand. The snow swirls in and taxi drivers queue up for their fares, ignoring the listless, anoraked men clutching paper signs with names scrawled on them in blue Sharpie. Wind smacks faces, crawls into hair, into nostrils, ears, drags you away from monochrome airport existence and tinny announcements and soggy egg sandwiches wrapped in crisp cellophane, and it's drawing me in, already, New York, even if the sting of the cold is like the back of Mam's hand and the whistling in my numb ears is suspiciously like her menopausal squawk. I turn back for a moment and meet Bunny's eyes, warm and twinkling raisins, and I could swear she flashes me a deep, warm smile, as palpable as if she'd enfolded me into that grandmotherly bosom, a wink, and I turn away with a gulp before I can cry. I leave the stale fug of JFK behind, step into the cold, and pull out my map to find out where the hell I'm going to be sleeping tonight.

New York, that light factory of foreign voices and stinking gutters and steam wafting from paving slabs and shouts and people hurrying hurrying hurrying and someone shouting loud *Hey girl, get on over here and talk to me girl* and a crazy lady lying in the doorway asleep with a thin trickle of yellow ooze dribbling from her slack mouth while the world passes by in designer heels and prêt-à-porter labels. It punched you rudely in the face along with its peculiar scent, that hot, sharp stench of people, death, shit, garbage, life, sex, betrayal, fear, death. New York fucking stinks. I love it and hate it, all at the same time. Loved it the first time I came here on my way home from a ski trip to Oregon, age twenty-two, sleeping in a bunk bed in a hostel in Harlem, wandering round clutching a subway map, navigating from street signs and pure luck. I knew I couldn't leave. It wasn't a sign. There was no bullshit opening up of the heavens and a messenger from on high telling me my fate lay in Manhattan. No, we make our own fate, our own luck. I made my fate by staring out of the window of an airport shuttle bus three years earlier and resolving to turn myself into a New Yorker.

The bus drops me off outside an apartment complex on Astor Place. "Nice address, baby," says the driver, a huge Jamaican guy. I have no idea where I am. I drag my suitcase into the shiny brass lobby, locate the elevator, up to the third floor. The guy I'm staying with is one of those friends of friends of friends, the ex-boyfriend of my sister's boyfriend's friend. I have a grace period of four days with this stranger, four days to find somewhere to live, a job, a future. I have about seven hundred dollars in my bank account. I ring the doorbell. Steps. Door opens.

There will always be a part of me, or Mimi, missing on the page. An episode omitted, a careless phrase forgotten, an important detail elided. Mimification is a process that afflicts every biographer, autobiographer, memoirist, as we censor ourselves unconsciously in the retelling of the story, salvage the scraps of fact and memory and conjecture, mold them into the words that make up an image of a person, an era, a fleeting, insubstantial moment. We'll scratch our heads in bewilderment as we try and trace our path backward, hunting for an elusive, haunting fact to cram into our chronology. Closing my eyes now, attempting to remember, I am haunted by the present fleeting backward, reaching out to the past with outstretched hands like a lost and cruel lover, as if the past will make sense of the present. But once it's on paper, it's undergoing the change, the Mimification, the rendering of fact into story, into narrative, into—dare I say it?—some form of fiction. And yet fiction, I feel, would be so much easier than this repackaging of the doubtful truth into the definite, this deliberate attempt to make it digestible, to make memory toe the line, leave a neat, well-tended garden path leading to the present. But then there are some things that even now astound me about the truth. I go back, recheck against diaries and e-mails home, notes, memory, yet even fiction cannot assuage their impact.

I have four days to find somewhere to live, a job, a future. Seven hundred dollars in my bank account. And I do not yet know how to use the Manhattan subway system.

If you are Indian you head to Jackson Heights; if Dominican, Washington Heights; Russian, Brighton Beach; Polish, East Williamsburg; Kazakhstani, Nigerian, Bengali, Lebanese—there is a place for everyone, everyone in their place in New

York. You turn up, flash your passport, stare dolefully into the camera, proffer a flight-swollen index finger to the little glass screen, left first, then right.

What's the purpose of your visit? Promise you're here to visit your married sister and her newborn baby, *two weeks, just two weeks only,* and then it's off to the nearest payphone, clutching that thin jacket closer around a shuddering body, unfurl the crumpled paper, avoid the man outside with that *stench,* a stench you don't find in Mexico City, in Calcutta, in Istanbul, in Dhaka. A stench of poor white man, white man poor and begging in the slums, indicating that there is something wrong, something very wrong in this peculiar and frightening city, and as you put in the tarnished quarter carefully preserved for the purpose all the way from wherever you were disgorged, you turn your freezing, disoriented back to the cacophony of chanting issuing eerily from the rocking figure, the white beggar with that stink YES-NO-YES-NO-YES-NO-YES-NO and you wait for the phone to pick up, the phone to pick up, so you can surround yourself with accents like yours, people as poor as you, as desperate *yes-no-yes-no* you seek your own kind because as soon as you arrive *pick up* you realize it was a mistake to think you could have just slotted in without going through the pain *yesnoyesnoyesno* the pain that no one bothered to tell you about when they said that America was the Promised Land.

But when you are white, British, educated, a possessor of four fully functioning limbs, and not (especially) retarded, you are a misnomer, a blip, a mistake, a joke. One cannot employ white people to do the job of dark people! Go seek your own kind! Of course I never intended to go about things the difficult way. I send off the résumés, call and schmooze, network and e-mail. Yet class, privilege, luck, and money divide me from seeking "my own kind." Where are my kind? On Park Avenue in crisp tailored suits, sipping aromatic teas in spacious lofts in TriBeCa, shopping for dainty Steve Madden shoes in SoHo, lapping up an expensive education at Columbia? My own kind don't want me. Don't I know how hard it is to get a working visa since 9/11? If you don't work for a bank, *furgedd it!* A writer? Job in publishing? Oh sure, Condé Nast works on a purely meritocratic basis. *How naive you are, little girl, how naive.* How naive I was to think it would be easy, that I could play New York like I'd played most of my life, with a bit of charm, a bit of cleverness, a bit of persuasion, and sheer stubbornness. But it's not enough. I head to the other end of the spectrum within days, shrunken and shocked by the rejection from "my own kind," determined, however, to work cash-in-hand until I can scramble to the top of the pile. I find my *other* kind, slum it for a while, hey, maybe I can write about this too. But what's this? What are they saying? Go! Get out! What is *she* doing here? What is the purpose of her visit, this strange visa-less Caucasian creature seeking employment in establishments that are the preserve of those who lack, not of those who derive from a perfectly efficient First World country on friendly, indeed *loving*, terms with God's Blessed Land.

When you are white, English, educated, and without an H-1B visa, you're a reject among rejects, caught in no man's land, land of nobody. You find that you must seek employment with those few whites who filter through the visa system because of pigheadedness, because of stupidity, because of laziness, because it's easier not to bother plowing through the reams of paperwork required by the process of getting legal—that and the fact that they didn't have a hope in hell of fooling USCIS into thinking they would contribute anything useful to this country. You must bond with them, stave off your illegal corner of England from those *selfish* Mexicans, snapping up the coveted cash-in-hand jobs like greedy toads feasting on flies.

Buon Giorno restaurant, Spring Street, Soho. Monique turns around, her face set in an ugly frown, her arms crossed and hugging herself from the cold that crept into the restaurant through the cheerful glass windows looking onto a snowy Spring Street, through the door that opened and banged shut every five minutes. She stares at me briefly, unsmiling, and then barks, "Hey English, don't get the fuckin' cawffee. Why you think we have a fuckin' busboy?"

Waitressing. The art of subtly patronizing people who want to humiliate you. That intricate tango of social niceties, complemented by an encyclopedic knowledge of the wine list, the dessert menu, the aperitifs, the *plat du jour,* and a willingness to embrace varicose veins in later life. Waitressing is considered an accomplishment in New York. Not *quite* ranking with bartending, that brigadier of skills, that valuable addition to the dowry ("plays pianoforte to an exceptional level, an expert needlewoman, fluent French, excels at croquet, and mixes *superb* mango daiquiris"), which was esteemed to the extent that expensive and time-consuming colleges offering courses devoted to the tireless explication of its mysteries had sprung up on every Manhattan corner. Yet procuring a serving job was considered a step on the way to becoming an illustrious bartender, and *everyone* knew bartenders earned more money than traders and brokers and Donald Trump, *because they paid tax only on credit card tips and worked, for the most part, under the table.* Who needed a degree? A bartending job, combined with self-proclaimed genius in the acting/directing/writing arena, was all one needed to ensure financial, social, and occupational success in the Big Apple.

Whoever had perpetuated this myth had done it well. In each dining, drinking, or catering establishment in the city, a thick wad of discarded résumés with Photoshopped pictures of winsome, sinewy youths (Hank from Bend, Oregon, graduate of the Sommelier Society of America Certificate Course; Julia from Pensacola, Florida, Certificate in Cocktail Mixology, GPA 3.9) lay covered in lint and mothballs and splodges of liquor congealing the type into little pools of blurred, sticky ink. Once upon a time the restaurant industry was monopolized by slurring, accented, long-lashed illegals, and now it was the preserve of the starry-eyed hopefuls. It was a lucrative business. And with the current post-9/11 air of paranoia that America was being besieged by furrerners, it was hard, very hard, to find a job without the requisite papers.

If you *did* find a job, it's probably because no self-respecting American teenager saving up for their semester at the Strasberg Institute would work for the kind of wages you were willing to work for. The lack of a single U.S. citizen in the only restaurant that would employ me should really have started the alarm bells ringing.

"Benji," I ask slyly, turning to the obscenely tall busboy as Monique, the Bronx bitch behind the bar, shoots us a menstrual look of hate. "How do you get your checks cashed?"

"Ah," he pauses, sways slightly. Benji is stoned. Benji is always stoned. The ritual of doping oneself up with THC becomes a necessary one when trapped in a tiny Italian restaurant working for tips with a rottweiler of a bartender six nights a week.

"I am on the water polo scholarship, so I have the student visa. But I am not allowed to work. So I have the checks made out to my American friend. He cashes them for me and gives me the money. Why? You do not have the Social Security number or the green card?"

"No."

"English girl, let me tell you something. You think anyone in this restaurant has the green card? Giovanni? Franco? Tina? The Mexican chefs? You must make up the number. No one will know. The United States, they do not care. With this Social Security number, we can pay the taxes, but we cannot claim the tax returns. They make the money off us. Do not worry. Now, I go to smoke the reefer. Do not tell Monique where I am gone."

He disappears into the night. The door slams shut behind him in a flurry of snow. Monique rolls her eyes and slips me a glass of wine in a coffee cup with a pursing of her lips, a shrewd look of sympathy. I could feel the pace of New York filling my veins with adrenaline—deadlines, timelines, everyone in a hurry—it seeped into my body and saturated the flesh, started to become part of me, like a tumor, like pregnancy, like the veins threading through my skin. I felt normal. Practically, theoretically, factually, I was an educated white girl with everything going for me, simply working in a restaurant until I could get a "real" job. But the weeks to find that job! The look of tired disdain as my résumé was thrown onto the sticky pile, the same one separating me from the Hanks from Oregon and the Julias from Pensacola! I was different from them, I felt different, and the closed look on the manager's face told me this immediately. You began to feel that your edges were becoming a little less defined, a little less clear, indistinct, fuzzy, blurred, and uncertain. People saw the white clear skin and heard the clipped consonants of the English, but that privilege was canceled out by my liability as someone lacking the necessary paperwork, thus turning me into a threat to national security. The quiet solitude of the restaurant and an empty bar came as a relief. I was paid nothing but tips, but it was a relief, not being a liability. It was a relief, being with people who understood what it was, more than I did, to be a nonperson, to find that solid earth was becoming unsteady, unfamiliar, with the unmistakable, almost resentful air of stolen goods.

You seek your own kind. The Mexicans from the restaurant lived in a studio, all six of them, in Astoria, a decent neighborhood. Benji was in Greenpoint, sharing a room with two other Hungarians, a fourth soon to arrive. I sought my own kind but I couldn't find them. They weren't in the cheap accommodations you find on craigslist, that's for sure.

"For what you wanna pay, you ain't gonna get much more than this," the super says, scratching a rotund belly protruding from a dirty wifebeater. He points to the mattress in the corner, next to the girl with the blank face and the pupils seeping like bruises into the iris, hematoma eyes too damaged to hint at the real damage inside. "You want?" presses the man, bored. It appalls me, a shared bare room somewhere in Queens. I feel nauseous, realize I'd have to stretch my budget a little further if I didn't want to live like those girls. Those girls like me who had been led to where I ended up, with promises that were not entirely spurious. I found my own way there.

I found my own way there, but I assure you I tried to make it work the other way, the *right* way. I tried those other jobs, I tried the lawyers, I tried, *I tried*.

The "loft conversion with room to rent" is an attic full of musicians, cats, plants, and junk, situated above the headquarters of a Jewish newspaper titled *Der Blatt* in the heart of the Hasidic community in Brooklyn. The spare room is a painting studio with a damp futon underneath a Jackson Pollock reproduction. There are no bills—utilities are silently dredged from the unwitting Hasidics downstairs, even AC channeled up in the summer through an inventive series of pipes, hoses, and holes. The apartment was a parasite, a heaving mass of writhing, middle-class, Ivy league–educated Jewish musicians, and one Southern blasphemous artist all feeding off the Hasidics.

Raoul answers the door. Raoul is an artist from Kentucky. He's handsome, young, curious steel gray hair, an amused mouth. Kind face, cruel eyes. He doesn't seem kind.

"There's people in and outta here all day. It's driving me crazy. I gotta have me some kinda normality, you know? I gotta have me some order in my life. But everyone here is nice, they're good people. Except me."

He pauses, takes a deep drag of lemon zinger tea, and then spits it rudely back into the cup.

"*Fuck,* dude! Someone *ashed* in my *Zen garden*."

He points to a pot of sand with a cigarette butt protruding elegantly from its midst.

"Fucking hipsters."

A drum beat starts up from somewhere in the depths of the apartment.

"Fucking musicians. There ain't no peace in this fucking apartment, but it's cheap. Whadda you do for a living?"

"Oh, I'm a writer. I'm trying to get a job on a magazine. I just arrived in New York . . ."

"New York is gonna eat you up and shit you out like some big-ass dog on *Smooth Move*. New York ain't a fuckin' playground, English girl. You think people are your friends—they ain't your fucking friends. You gotta be strong to make it in this hell-hole of a city. Rent's six-fifty a month, includes utilities, no deposit. When you movin' in?"

"Erm, tomorrow?"

"'K." Raoul drifts away, sparks up a Parliament Light, stands silently gazing at his decimated Zen garden. "Hey, I gotta plant you can have to put in that room. Make it more like home, you know?"

I stand, uncertain.

"Thank you. I really appreciate it."

A new cacophony sweeps through the apartment and engulfs us. Raoul shudders and turns away, back to his room, still holding his cigarette and the lemon zinger tea. He puts the cigarette in his mouth, stares at my chest, absently scratches his balls, reaches up to retrieve it again.

"Yeah, well. It's already dying."

Every morning on the corner of Marcy Avenue the women line up, a tired uniform of blue jeans, a mix of Eastern Europeans and Hispanics. They look at me as I walk past, another fucking hipster kid snapping up real estate and pushing the Hispanics farther out, farther out, and forcing the Hasids closer, tighter, more suspicious, together, these American gentiles with their bare shoulders and cheek to go into the Kosher store. A car or a van drives up, halts, a hand beckons, barter, a price struck, a woman, two women, sometimes three, climb in the back. Cleaning, cooking, shopping—name a price. At midday some still linger, crowds depleted but still present, leaning against the mesh, ignoring the selfish roar of the highway beneath, still alert to the slowing of a car, money, a job. Once a lady never came back, and they found her body in a dumpster someplace. The next day I see some women crying. The day after that they stand on Marcy Avenue immune to the intrusion of the wind, the cold, the traffic, the snow, as if covered by ash from Pompeii.

Back in Buon Giorno.

"I'm telling you, girl, this fucking black guy was humping me senseless for twenty-four fucking hours. I got a standing ovation from the doormen in my building the next morning. I'm on the fifth fucking floor."

Tina the bartender's eyes light up with a fond glow as she launches into the tale of how she celebrated her thirtieth birthday by screwing a fifteen-year-old quarterback on the mistaken assumption he was nineteen. A quiet guy from Massachusetts chokes on his margarita. Tina turns her plump, sagging figure toward him menacingly. He retreats rapidly, leaves a dollar tip.

Benji wanders over. He resembles Lurch from *The Addams Family*, the disconnection between brain and body accentuated by the vast quantities of THC coursing through his system. Seeing nobody on the street, Benji scrambles to the back of the restaurant to retrieve a joint and dose up on ganja once again.

"So then I went to this bar, and Richard kept playing with my fucking nipples, and this tranny bitch was trying to talk to me, and I was just coming like a fucking tidal wave in the middle of the dance floor, and there's this old black dude who sits at the end of the bar, and every fifteen minutes he yells 'GIMME A WHOA!' and everyone goes 'WHOA!' But then he wasn't there, so I turned 'round and said, 'GIMME A WHOA!' and everyone was like 'WHOA!' . . ."

My phone beeps. A weird little text from Raoul. I'd left him my number on a scrawled-up napkin pushed under his door when I moved in to the empty apartment that morning.

The city is sad tonight.

Tina looks at it and snorts derisively.

"Well I ain't fucking sad getting screwed like a bitch by my new twenty-year-old boyfriend. Hey, I tell you what happened when he was fucking me from behind the other day?"

I settle into my curious new routine, a half-person routine, because I am, at this stage, somewhere between who I was, who I will become. A home in Brooklyn, with roommates I smile at but don't talk with. Afternoons spent writing articles, pitching newspapers and magazines, sending off résumés. Nights spent avoiding the lash of Monique's tongue and attempting to suppress the lurid images evoked by Tina's detailed and generous descriptions of her sex life. But three weeks have passed, and I've received rejection after rejection in my inbox, and forty-five-hour weeks at Buon Giorno are yielding little more than a hundred bucks a week and a constant headache. I need that Social Security number. I need that visa, that sponsor, that investment banker who wants to marry me. I need to get away from Buon Giorno.

"This place is *fucked*. Is *fucked*. I need to get high."

Benji disappears outside. The door slams. Tina briefly looks up from her book on method acting, and then resumes drinking and reading, abandoning martinis in favor of Jack Daniels. I help myself to a glass of wine, sit in the corner, and wait morosely for customers who don't turn up. What the hell am I *doing* in this city? One of the chefs joins me, Fernando, from Mexico. *Those Mexicans are short, ain't they?* croaked my grandma once, shortly after making the observation that Saddam Hussein was such a *handsome* man. *You think they have dwarf blood in 'em?*

"Hola rubia."

"Hey, Fernando. Quiet night."

He nods glumly, sticks a grubby finger up one nostril. He retrieves the contents, glances at it briefly, relegates it to the chef's whites along with remnants of an avocado and the blood of a *bistecca*.

"How long have you been in the U.S., Fer?"

"I think, maybe eight months. I am saving for college. I want to be journalist. I earn money, then I go back to Mexico."

"You have a green card?"

He looks shocked. Shocked enough to stop his game of Hunt-the-Booger.

"*No! Por su puesto, no!* I come over the border; we run across one night. But they pay OK here. Four hundred dollars a week. *Bueno.*"

In the kitchen Alejandro and JP were giggling. "You fuck American woman? You fuck her? Aawwww! *Las americanas son putas! Fácil!* Is easy to fuck them. Is easy. But to find one to marry, is difficult, *amigo.*"

I walk in and it goes silent, embarrassed, because they are different, they know that, and even if I am working in the same place as them, I'm white, and they know enough to be quiet when they see my skin. Their interactions are probably limited to other Mexicans—or the occasional "Fuck you, ass-hole" from a snarling and disdainful *princesa* as she walks along the street repulsed by the hiss, the longing "Mama*cita*"— the confusion as to why it's so hard to meet these Americans, even the Hispanics are too American now, all too American for Mexicans who don't speak English and live six to a room and can't even get employment at Taco Bell now that the government is cracking down on illegals.

10°38'N 61°31'W

Trinidad was our second port after we sailed the Atlantic, after I'd been baptized Mimi. There our crew applied for a visa, because for some reason the U.S. would not let you into the country by sea without a visa, even if you were from the "special" countries—the ones they liked, the ones whose citizens seep seamlessly into American life and pump the economy full of funds and companies and investments and white people and bad sitcoms. There was a visa for everyone coming to the

States, the Captain whispered to me: a visa for tourists from Third World countries, a visa for anyone who enters the country by sea, a visa for someone who comes into the country merely for business meetings, a visa for studying at college—a visa, even, for women who have been sex trafficked into the country. The guilt visa, that one is. The visa everyone wanted was the H-1B, the "green card" leading to permanent residency and then citizenship. But knowing the chances of gaining that were futile, everyone went for the next best thing, something that would merely let them enter the U.S., just let them in. We stood in line, me and the Captain. They sent me back because the picture wasn't right, a gray background, not a white, and I stood in the heat outside the embassy, clouds pressing on my temples, squeezing, until a Rasta sidled over and took me to the store to get it done correctly. There they would also print out the papers for you, the references on headed letters, the bank statements, the assurances neatly packaged in specious bureaucracy, fallacies, hopes as insubstantial as cotton candy, sickly and full of air. I went back and queued under fluorescent lighting, among blue plastic chairs, and the Captain and I were the only white people in there, and everyone else had on their best clothes and their best hopes fading quickly under the *swoosh-swoosh-swoosh* of the ceiling fans and the sweat pooling under armpits, the heat intensifying like the disappointment, and we needed the visa, but it wasn't the kind of need they had, and when we came away from the window with the nod of approval we knew we would get, we felt ashamed and left quickly before we could witness the clipping of the wings, the ritual of rejection and rawness.

· · ·

Benji blusters back in, looking slightly blue and frostbitten, a crazed, paranoid look frozen onto his enormous features.

"The *bells*. I hear *the bells*. Can you not *hear* them?"

I go to see an immigration lawyer not long after arriving in Manhattan, a name passed on in e-mails to desperate Brits like me. *Try this woman, she got me my permanent residency, that one sucked, don't use him, you want cheap and smart, hmm, hear that one lost Dave his appeal against deportation.* First visit free, options placed on the table, white, educated, employable? Take your pick!

She traces my future with enthusiastic semaphore, a tiny white skeletal hand in an oversized jacket, a gray cubicle in a Midtown office. Tarot cards drawn in the air: She plucks one, another, another. They all say the same thing, a simple image cloaked in the pompous frivolities of legal language: "An H-1B, also known as a working or sponsorship visa, requires sponsorship by a company that has to prove that the job has been openly advertised as vacant for over eighteen months and cannot be filled by a U.S. citizen, but they will need to apply for next year now. The deadline is in April, and the processing takes six months, or you can get the other visa for people like you . . ." It was a Rubik's Cube of language, even for me, in my language, with my people. *No wonder there's so many Fernandos in this country* I marvel wonderingly and gaze out the building at what I later learn to be the Chrysler Building. The lawyer's tone changes, softens slightly. "Really, the best option is for you to gain employment with, perhaps, an English company based in New York and get paid in pounds. There are special visas for this. You're a writer, you say? There's a visa called an 'I visa' for foreign media workers. But it won't let you work for an American company, even freelance, and to be honest, I can't tell you the chances of getting a job as a U.S.–based correspondent, but I've heard from clients it's pretty difficult—it's not something you walk into. Other than that, if you could prove that you excel in your field of the arts, perhaps with a publishing contract, then you could get a J visa, which will put you on the path to permanent residency . . ." Prove your worth and we'll take you. Permanent residency—that was the green card, the green go, the *Yes, we'll take you, no more filing for dumb work visas and fucking around with Immigration. Stay a bit longer, pledge allegiance, and we'll even let you be a citizen, the genuine article.* Such a long, long path. I was beginning to realize I should perhaps go home. Back to England. I leave and go to work at the restaurant. Later at about one A.M. I take the J train back to Brooklyn, walk home to the loft apartment in the snow, stay up until dawn writing and worrying. I shiver when I think of the apartment in Queens. I want to call home but I don't. It's not in my nature. I wasn't brought up like that. I do things on my own, always. Before I hit the street there would be someone, something, some job, some bed. I sell a piece to a newspaper a few days later and the money helps. But no one wants to employ me, not even the English companies, and the money from waitressing is just not enough.

"I'm livin' in a cardboard box for a week. People are really diggin' this shit at the moment, the limitations of mental space represented by physical boundaries . . ."

I sit with Raoul in the kitchen, sipping lemon zinger tea and listening politely to his latest performance-art piece.

"How will you take a crap?" asks one of the musicians aimlessly, emerging from the bathroom and disappearing swiftly into the makeshift recording studio at the back of the loft.

"Fuck you hipster," says Raoul.

The apartment did not have natural light; if we had been able to siphon that off too, from the Hasids downstairs, doubtless we would. Instead we subsist on a diet of eerie gloom filtered through candy bar wrappers clogging the infrequent skylights. Like plants deprived of chlorophyll, we start to curl up in that apartment, grow yellow and turgid and soft. There's a sense of unease like a dissatisfied sigh, an unarticulated desire, ambitions starved of talent, egos deprived of audiences. "How's your writing coming along?" demands Raoul inscrutably, and I can't tell if he's seriously interested or not. "Finding working in the restaurant with them Mexicans is giving you divine inspiration?" He smiles blankly, a little cruelly, and there's a baffled silence. I don't tell him about the article I've written about immigration. It seems prudent not to, for Raoul scares me with his flashes of temper, his volatile personality, his attention to me that seems, in turns, almost resentful. He was the only one in the apartment who talked to me. "Those hips," he'd growl, and look at me unpleasantly, and I'd look away and move into my room before he could press up close behind me, as if by chance. "Don't trust no one in this fucking city," he had said when I first moved in, gazing out of the skylight above my bed, watching a fresh wave of snow start to fall. His scrotum hung obscenely through the leg of his boxer shorts, I remember, the delicate trace of the raphe, that scarlike fusion line, clearly visible as it snaked, ugly, and gross, between his legs. I had looked away, annoyed. *Don't trust no one*. Maybe it had been a warning about himself. We talked, we assumed a semblance of friendship; he often wandered into my room when I was writing and threw himself lackadaisically on my bed with a cigarette in hand. I did not trust him, but I was lonely and wanted to. I smile at Raoul uncertainly, lopsided, and don't answer his question, instead take a drag of my cigarette, worrying as I did about how to pay the rent, thinking to myself that maybe I should look for a new job and quit the cigarettes, wondering if I could sell another article and then deciding simultaneously that giving up smoking might be a little extreme, even for this situation.

I'm beginning to feel the change. I had taken the precaution of writing my article under a pseudonym, my nickname, the other me, Mimi, keeping the "real me" far away from the narrative that was unfolding. It was exciting to be someone else. A relief. As if by imagining myself as Mimi, this fictional creature called up in a storm, I would become her, and whatever happened to me in New York was inconsequential, something that couldn't touch or scar the person wrapped underneath. But now—the now I am writing in, the *real* now—now I am someone else, always someone else, another-else tagged on to a someone that is assumed for the day, the hour, the man, the mood, so that even if I wanted to reach beneath the layers and rip them off, I doubt that I could. I change it up sometimes. *What's your name?* they ask. Mimi, Kitty, Lily, Michelle. Pussy, if I'm feeling perverse. *What's your real name?* Diamond, Desire, Escarda, Chanel, Mary, if I'm feeling *really* perverse. But never my real name. It's not like we'd cry if we told you. It's not as if the revelation of our real names, the hint of an identity pre-stripping, brings back technicolor images of weird Uncle Herb, the seductive allure of puppies and kittens, *promise not to tell Mommy,* a squalid motel room. The telling of the real name, it's nothing to do with that. You won't extract it from us like a rotten tooth, crumbled and black, a dark secret suppressed by the embrace of our shame with a cocked glance, a sigh, an erect nipple. Real names. Telling of. It's just not *au fait.* It's just not *done.* It's just none of your damned business.

After a while, the fake names become more real than the real, become indistinguishable from the real. Feeding off truth, the fake overwhelms truth, a monstrous tick grown juicy, plump, resplendent, and terrifying.

I am sitting in a café in the East Village, sipping steaming gray coffee made bearable only by the addition of souring milk, a sprinkling of Sweet 'N Low. I don't know what it is about New York, but their coffee is disgusting. I have drunk coffee in India, in China, in France, in Italy, in Guatemala—god, even in England the coffee is an improvement upon this tortured extract, bitter and black, a bile, a diarrhea of drinks. But swallowing this is easier, preferable, to cracking open the hard, sugar layer of forgetfulness in which I have concealed these memories in order to make them more palatable. Now I find that sugar coating is frowned upon, and instead "the truth" is preferred. *Spit it out, get the narrative flowing, stop all these interruptions, it's confusing! We want the story!* Sod off, it *hurts.* It feels easier if I do it this way. I was never one for ripping off the Band-Aid.

Next to me a Bangladeshi is composing a letter to USCIS—the United States Citizenship and Immigration Services, formerly the Immigration and Naturalization Service. I know he is Bangladeshi because he is talking to the men who work in the café, who sell magazines and candy and baconeggandcheeseon-arollwholemealwithsaltpepper and gray coffee. The letter says he is recently arrived in the United States on a B-1/B-2 standard tourist visa for citizens of countries not on the Visa Waiver Program (that is, Third World countries where the citizens are more likely to want to emigrate to the prosperous States), but now his wife is pregnant, and alack! The credit card he was using to finance the trip is maximized to its potential! There are no savings on hand, no kind relatives to help, returning to Bangladesh—an impossibility! There can be only one solution. Mr. M. Nasirullah must be given a green card! Or at the very minimum, some kind of working visa/visa extension/ability to stay unbothered in this green and pleasant land! He grunts in satisfaction as he types the last sentence with a flourish, one finger tapping the keys, slow, deliberate, and then he leans back and sighs, and we both sit and stare dolefully at the buzzing screen. *You have five minutes left, please purchase more Internet credit at the cash register.*

My thoughts slip idly to Lily, as I sit here stingstingsting on my tongue, Mr. M. Nasirullah's hope drizzling through attempts to forget and isolate and conceal that part of my life. It stings the present like that hot black bile on my tongue. It takes me back. I have those moments a lot. When I'm not in the club and I'm not smiling bright and false and stupid and answering stupid questions with stupid answers in my stupid Mimi voice, I'm sitting blankly, alone, reliving the past again. The fog of memory rolls in, damp and emphysemic.

I call her Lily because Lily is one of the names I use for myself, sometimes. I like it, like the pale, insipid quality of that ghostly white, delicate flora, the flower of death. I'm magnanimous, I know, extending my generosity to her, when really I gave her little else but this: a new name, on top of the superimposed identity of "illegal" that circumstance bestowed upon her. Lily was tiny and beautiful, sleek black hair, DD boobs bought by her boyfriend for her twentieth birthday. She was my friend, I think, and she drifts in and out of the story, my story, but she never has a starring role, because we found each other's presence unbearable, eventually. *Things OK? Dating anyone? We must have coffee, we must have dinner, we must meet up, talk, chill out.* But we don't. We only met because we had our Social Insecurity in common. She told me her story, and it wasn't like mine, which is threaded with alternatives, options not taken, bad decisions, split-second life-changing moments. It wasn't Mr. M. Nasirullah's story, but it was of the same genre, the same "U" rating, the same general theme. The United States of America, new life away from persecution/poverty/war in homeland. To find more poverty, more adversity, struggle, pain, and for what? After twenty-three years no green card, no pledge of allegiance, no voting rights, no passport? No hope? The norm. The norm. What is the norm? It's New York, this movie set of drunks and bums on gray streets littered with packaging and cusswords and a glance down, inside, away. Then it was Brooklyn, trapped in Little Poland with the musicians I never saw, never spoke to, a seemingly impossible situation, stuck penniless in New York, etching out a painful living with the odd article, waitressing for tips, unable to gain *real* employment, the appropriate visa, but still hopeful. I was still hopeful then, because after all, white English girls don't have it too hard, do we? Nothing bad really happens to *us*. We're of Jane Austen ilk, where the worst that can happen in life is old maidenhood and not getting Darcy. My point is, my point is . . . these gray people, tinged with color, will fade in, and fade out, but pay attention to them, please. I owe it to them, to Lily, because I didn't help them, and I know they needed it. I met the people, who had it worse than me. There weren't all sex-trafficked gazelles from Eastern Europe, doe-eyed Colombian maidens, heavy breasts laden with rich creamy milk ripe for the suckling. Half of them, like Lily, came because they had no choice. Half of them came because they wanted something more, something more than *tierra de nadie*. And we stayed—I stayed—because we felt, all of us, sadly, peculiarly, as if there was nothing, really, to go back to, as if here was as good a place as any, as if here, no matter how hard it was, divorced from the weight of the past, we could become whatever we wanted to become, whereas if we went back, we might only be failures.

I walked down the Bowery, on the Lower East Side. Past the mission center full of Christians and do-gooders, enjoying the anonymity, eyes that slipped unseeing past this body drowned in shapeless brown, averting the gaze we actively cultivate, tease out like a splinter in the night. I felt bitter. I want someone to do good by *me*—fuck the bums, the tramps, the retards, the crazies. What about those who just want a chance at that job, a bit of money to get the lease on that apartment, some time to write that novel? A large black man was talking to a bum, twisted and snickering and drooling and cursing.

"Go 'round the corner man. I can't help you no more. Go 'round the corner." I looked into his eyes, this man, this volunteer, this messenger of God, this model member of the flock, and his eyes were full of love and sympathy, understanding, full of it, *full*—just not enough to go around. Lily's story was the story of all the people with false identities, all the Mr. M. Nasirullah's, the slit-mouth Colombians, the Mimis even, and I *had* love and sympathy, I *had* understanding. Just not enough to go around.

Last night I wasn't working but even when I don't work I can't sleep, my body wired into the beat, the club controlling me like some perverse and twisted remote. I stay awake until four A.M. usually, and when I sleep it's sordid and alcoholic. So last night I surfed the Internet a little, and who should I find but one of the old Brooklyn roommates from the Raoul apartment, in some band that is, apparently, *HOT!HOT!HOT!* across Europe and Japan. People from the past always turn up again in New York, circle around like fetid water in a blocked sink, a scuzz of oil, a jism of grease. I wondered, briefly, about Lily, about the ending to her story. But there are too many stories about people like her, people like me, contravening the conditions upon which we were present in the United States of America, nonimmigrants accepting unauthorized employment, upon which grounds we could be subject to deportation. At first I liked speaking up, getting my voice heard, feeling like I was making a difference, writing articles, attending meetings about these people—the injustices! Did the Republicans know it was near impossible to get a H-1B working visa due to the time restrictions and limited numbers placed upon them, even for white, educated former sailors and pill poppers? But this brief month of activism was before the situation got really bad. And when you start struggling and twisting and biting and scratching, life clawing you down into a whimpering ball, you just don't want to know anymore. You don't want to hear other people's stories. Fuck trying to help everyone else. Fuck your whining and your bitching. Fuck your hardships and your sob stories and your lined, wrinkled, sad faces. I could only take so much of it. Lily knew that too. I guess she doesn't hold it too hard that we're not friends anymore, after our emotive sharing of experiences, group hugs and all. I guess she's used to people moving on while she stays behind, trapped in Social Insecurity.

This is all I can afford her: a new name, a paragraph in this tract otherwise devoted to *me-me-me*. And now I must move on. Time is passing, and we—that is, Mimi and me—have work to do.

3

WHEN I GO INTO WORK I switch off. I feel nothing, have no opinions, no sense of shame, no emotion. Everything closed, tucked neatly out of sight. In that way you become a negated space, a void for people to fill in however they desire. Mimi, the walking, talking doll, the paint-by-numbers English chick, whatever you want, I'll name the price. I'm the cute, young, private table dancer who makes people laugh and does things men in their forties only wish their first wives had taught them . . . (incredulously) *Where do the kids get it from nowadays?* . . . (curiously) *How many people you slept with, Mimi?* . . . (nonchalantly) *Oh only two or three. I don't really believe in sex before marriage,* letting a sly knee slip between legs, a breast stroke the side of a man's face, a careless sigh escape, look deep into someone's eyes.

They say you can always tell a liar because they can look you straight in the eye. Someone should tell these pricks that. "You having a good time, Mimi? You glad we met? I'm different from the average guy, right?" But of course, *mi amor,* but of course.

How do I find this job tolerable? *I don't kiss.* It's Julia Roberts, it's Pretty Fucking Woman, and the time when one Champagne Room client did slip his tongue in my mouth, I got drunk on tequila and cried and cried and cried. My body is not my mind. But somehow my mouth is supremely intimate. I use it to tease but never to clinch the deal. You learn to let everything else wash over you. You learn to deal with loneliness. You learn how to dance like you believe it, with tricks and lies, wielded by the experts—women. Life is a lie. I defy anyone who can claim to live without lying.

The other day I thought I heard someone whisper my name behind me. Not Mimi, but my real name, the one my parents gave me. I almost didn't stop, until I recalled vaguely, *That's me*. There was no one there, of course, of course. It's almost too easy, giving up my past life to take on this new one. I leave her behind—the student, the scholar, the graduate, the good girl—and become Mimi instead. Somewhere in between are the parts I prefer to forget.

Although I wonder, sometimes, if I really have left her behind, or if every time I gaze steadily without seeing into someone's eyes as I murmur another lie, another name, the emptiness gazing back is just a confrontation with the other me.

Raoul paces in his room agitatedly, floorboards creaking beneath cracked cowboy boots, an aggression to match.

"Hey, English girl, I wanna word."

"*Later* Raoul."

Focus shifts, falls onto sheets of paper, random snippets of information, convoluted sentences, grotesque paragraphs about immigration staring at me dolefully. I was working on a new article about immigration reform, talking to an editor while reading an e-mail about obtaining something called the "I" visa—a journalist's visa for foreigners that allowed writers to stay indefinitely in the United States while working on U.S. issues for foreign newspapers. Close eyes, twist the cord of the old, shitty phone around my finger, try and forget worries, move on . . .

—the requirements for the I visa are proof of funds, letters from UK media companies on letterhead specifying purpose in the U.S.—

I turn my focus back to the telephone.

"OK, I'll have another piece done by Friday. D'you know when I'll get the check through?"

—as a non-immigrant visa, meaning a visa that allows one to reside in the United States indefinitely but does not put the visa holder on the path to a green card, it is far easier to obtain than an immigrant visa, yet can be just as valuable—

"I'd quite like the money *before* next month if possible, could you talk to Accounts and let me know what they say? OK, thanks. Bye."

I hang up, rifle through some papers, heart pumping. Raoul stands and watches.

"Sorry, writing stuff. What can I help you with?"

He stares at me through arctic eyes narrowed to razor slits. His gaze doesn't waver as he reaches into the back pocket of his jeans and expertly kicks the cat with one pointed weather-beaten cowboy boot. He produces a cigarette. Lights it.

"So, New York treating you well is it, English girl? Made friends with the Hasidics downstairs yet? They love little girls like you. If you ever run out of money they'll always throw you a couple bucks for a handjob. Remember that."

He emits a dry little laugh, ratcheting back and forth in that sahara chest of his. He turns his sculpted face to one side for a second, chiseled carelessly so the exterior seemed fine art, but a closer, harder glance, just one more second of study, and you could see the tiny flaws, the imperfections, the lines of anger and volatility set in that face like a madwoman's curse. He scratches his groin, a sigh, a bestial grunt of pleasure.

—for the (genuine) employee of a newspaper, broadcasting corporation, or magazine, the visa application procedure is relatively simple—

"Raoul, shouldn't you be getting back to your cardboard box?" I ask, irritated. Catto jumps onto my lap and purrs.

"Cat has shit on its ass," Raoul says neutrally.

"D'you want the rent or something? I haven't had my check through from the paper yet, but they owe me like a grand now, so I have more than enough."

"Shut your mouth, girl. I don't wanna see that mouth moving no more. Silence, calm."

Peace. It swamps over the chill space like the invasive warmth of a tranquilizer, peppered with the distant clash of a cymbal from the recording studio out back, and the words crowding in on me from the papers scattered on my floor, insolent black print.

"OK, we got peace. I wanna talk to you. I read one of your articles about immigrants. Seems you got a bit of talent going

on there. Though I don't think hanging out with your little illegal friends is gonna be good for you, English girl."

*—but for someone like me, and like you, Mimi, who has never
written for a UK publication, worked in the media, or held
down full-time employment in anything other than a local
pub, the visa application presents an interesting challenge—*

I close my eyes briefly and shake my head, *no, scrap that sentence, this is not meant to be about me, never about me* that
indefinable, odd feeling of clawing panic flapping away inside
me like a reptile in its death throes.

"You OK?" asks Raoul curiously, leaning into my face. The
phone rings again.

"Hello? What? Oh hey. What? WHAT!?"
Click.

Raoul sniggers and wanders over to the bed, assuming his
customary position—horizontal, hand on genitals, scratching.

"Problems, English Girl?"

*—if you get the I visa (and it's easy, if I can get it, by making
up an Italian newspaper that doesn't exist and writing myself
a letter of employment, you can) well, if you get it, you're
eligible for a five-year visa, which allows you to come and go
without question by Immigration authorities, plus a Social
Security card, so you can file taxes—*

"Yes, fucking problems. The paper won't pay me. Said they
need a Social Security number, even though I'm freelance."

"So give 'em your number."

"Raoul, I don't have one."

—if I were you I'd call your old university friends (you must know some useful people if you really did go to Cambridge, surely? Unless you're a complete moron . . .) and gather letterhead from national newspapers and magazines based in the UK—

The phone rings again, an insistent, shrill cry, like the retarded boy in the playground, rocking back and forth with his little battered *Dukes of Hazzard* car clutched dully in that damp hand, the buzz emitted from his cracked lips, a radio transmission of dog whistles *ee ee ee.* Once he had earwax, violent green pussy wax, pouring out thick, voluptuous clotted cream rivers from his ear, yet he did not waver. *Ee ee ee.*

Raoul raises an arrogant eyebrow.

"So leave. New York just ate you up, English girl. Just swallowed you whole and here's the fucking aftertaste, a belch, and some heartburn."

"That's the thing, Raoul. I can't leave. Not now. I filed."

—just hope that the immigration backlog keeps them from checking references and letters in too great a detail—

"Whadda you mean?"

"I applied for a visa. A journalist's visa. I filed my application yesterday."

—the average processing time for the I foreign media repre-
sentatives visa is six to eight weeks—

Raoul's hand extends stealthily down the front of his Calvin Kleins, reaches thoughtfully into the innermost depths of his groin area, scratches tenderly, readjusts, emerges again. He lights another cigarette and holds it aloft, like the Statue of Liberty, and in the dull gloom of a dark afternoon the little red glow from the end shines soft, insidious, devilish in the growing darkness.

"Don't see what the problem is."

—should the applicant be the holder of a current visa and
present in the United States, the form I-539, application to
extend/change non-immigrant status, must be completed be-
fore the new non-immigrant status (in this case, the I visa)
can be approved; once the form I-539 is completed and sent
off to Immigration along with the passport holder's I-94, the
visa applicant cannot leave the United States until the new
visa is approved or rejected—

"I can't leave until it comes through—I don't have the papers to get out, the little white form they give you when you come in. It's called an I-94. It's really important—you're screwed if you don't have it—and the Immigration people have got mine. I can't leave, and I can't work until the approval comes through and they send it back."

The cigarette drips ash, soft and liquid flakes of glowing amber.

"Well, I was gonna see if you wanted to hook up with me tonight. But seems like you already got fucked up the ass plenty this afternoon. Wanna beer?"

Raoul snickers, yawns, stretches, belches, cracks a bottle open, *glug-glug-glug*. I sat in the darkness awhile and I feel kind of lost. I *felt* kind of lost, sitting in my gloomy loft-room on Rutledge Street off Bedford Avenue in Brooklyn, New York, as outside the Hasids hovered uncertainly, looking for goys to turn on their light switches, turn off their ovens as the Sabbath broke. They came to look for America, so they said, and didn't find it, not exactly, so they created what they wanted instead, Little Poland in Brooklyn.

You may not apply to change your non-immigrant status if you were admitted to the United States in the following visa categories: (A.) VWPP. Visa Waiver Pilot Program (or the Guam Visa Waiver Program)

Little Poland, home to Raoul and the musicians and me, but not really our place, not really. It was never our place.

From somewhere deep in the bowels of the apartment someone started playing a guitar, a lone voice quavering across the empty dullness of Brooklyn on a Friday evening. You keep looking but all you find are opportunities as fleeting as your first love.

(D.) As a crewman

So you either retreat to what you know, locate your corner, stake it out, and make it into mini-Poland, mini-England, mini-fuckknowswhereland, a replica of what you left behind, or you become someone entirely different, new, fantastical, illusory—an American.

(E.) As an alien in transit or in transit without a visa.

A generation of parentless, nongestated hopefuls; a labor that started somewhere mid-Atlantic, a birth that happened smack in the middle of it all, the Statue of Liberty gracefully overseeing proceedings.

(K.) As a fiancé(e) or spouse of a U.S. citizen or dependent of a fiancé(e) or spouse.

Raoul started humming to himself as he took a loud swig of beer, and I couldn't help smiling ruefully, starting to get it all now.

(S.) As an informant (and accompanying family) on terrorism or organized crime.

Starting to get what was happening, starting to get New York, the way it worked, the tricks it played on you, the mocking glance, the spot-lit glare of attention, the ruthless rejection, a move on, past, beyond. Be careful what you wish for, said Fat Bunny's glance, and I was finding my voice, re-creating myself anew as this Mimi character, this writer who headlines papers and then gets bumped because she doesn't have the right visa. *Oy vey.* Five minutes of fame. And the rent to be paid next week.

"I got you a beer, English girl," says Raoul, appearing suddenly in my doorway again. He holds it out sullenly, and then breaks into song, "*Let us be lovers, we'll marry our fortunes to-gether* . . . Fucking hate this song. C'mon. Leave that shit. It ain't so bad. It's America. It's New York. Just fucking ride with it, English. I won't let anything bad happen to you."

He looks at me almost paternally, and I could read that glance, the Saviour glance. But I didn't *need* saving, I had never needed saving. Raoul looks at me and I look back at him, hold his gaze. Something passes between us. He acqui-esces, but I can sense that I'm now a challenge *those hips* and that poor and lonely in America, also weak prey.

"Drink, English girl?"

I smile, and take the beer from his hand. "It's Mimi, arse—*ass*—hole."

All you really want, sometimes, is someone to say, *It's OK to fuck up. Come home*. But for all the family I have, there's no one to say that, no one to mean it. What's easier is this orphan girl, this Mimi doll, this new identity, this girl whose movie reel plays determinedly on, and stubbornly, like a brutal editor, omits the scenes that detract too literally from the plot *those hips* though which, perhaps, may add to the scene. This girl who can do *anything*—except, perhaps, ask for help.

I go back to Buon Giorno.

Lucia, the new Italian waitress, greets me at the door. Benji is sitting hunched over in a corner mumbling about bells. Tina's behind the bar, already downing the JD, her imposing frame zeroing in on an unfortunate male seated alone. Before I can grab her attention, Lucia starts talking.

"English, how are you, English? I am not *gooood*. Not at all."

She lolls dramatically against the bar, a woman in a melodrama, bosom heaving. Her pupils dilate and retract in time to the Gipsy Kings.

"I go to Canada for a week, and they will not let me back in. These asshole Immigration people, they say to me, 'Why is it you spend so much time in this country? You must return to Italy.'"

She snorts loudly and wipes traces of white powder from her nose.

"So I say to them, *Fuck you motherfucker! Your country suck! I don't want to live in this America, I go home! You suck cock motherfucker!*"

A diplomatic reply that I'm sure endeared her to those in Customs.

"So then, they say to me that I have ten days to get out of this country, so I come back to New York, and I decide. I must get married—*to the American*."

She pauses for theatrical effect, continues.

"So now I have nine days left to find the husband. I put the advert on craigslist."

She sniffs haughtily, the lady of the manor, hacks up a large phlegmy glob that she deposits in a shredded, linty tissue retrieved from the pocket of her jeans, and disappears to the ladies' room, wobbling like a custard.

New York City, a dream and a nightmare. You start contemplating the incomprehensible, incorporating it into everyday living. Oscillating between the lives of the people I work with and my own life here, strangely illusory and insubstantial, everything starts to feel fictional. What is real? The curled-up degree certificate in the bottom of my suitcase? The five years spent traveling alone around the world? The rejection letters from company after company? The bank statement so depressingly void of digits before the decimal point? The dreams that keep me on this peculiar path, stop me from jacking it all in, book a ticket somewhere new, put a middle finger up to the city that wouldn't accept me? Or the fears that keep me from going back to London, insubstantial fears, fears of being nobody among my glittering contemporaries, fears of being nothing there, not even (dare I say it?) illegal? Or the knowledge that I'd been in the U.S. for eight weeks and seemed no closer to finding a base and filling in the empty spaces that were so glaringly apparent in my life from years of transience—was that real? Or could I just gloss over it? It's irrelevant! I'll laugh about it in a year's time! It's all part of growing up, of adventure, of life experience.

Tina nods to me chirpily, her mouth twisted into a grin.

"*Gimme a Woah!* English, how's it going? You ain't working today are you? Hey, did I tell you about that fucked-up threesome I had that time with the bartender from O'Grady's with one arm . . ."

"Tina, I need help."

She stops, frowns, her eyebrows knitting heavily together.

"What kind?"

"Social Security number."

"What's it for?"

"It's for me. I need to get a new job. I can't keep working

off tips, and freelancing doesn't pay. I need a real job, a wage, not working sixty-hour weeks for sod all. You know how it is. Most people don't check the visa, they just want the SS number, so it'll tide me over."

"Thought you had a visa? Just get a journalist's visa, easiest kind to get, that's what I did back in Australia. Made up a fucking newspaper, wrote a few letters on letterhead—*bang*, ten-year entry."

"I'm applying for that. I just need a job now until it comes through. Soon. And the only way I can get a decent-paying job is that damned number."

Tina pauses, nods. "Hey, Julio," she yells to a waiter. He turns and walks over. "English here needs your help."

He flashes me a disarming smile. "Why don't we go outside for a cigarette?" He opens the door, and we sit on a doorstep, just out of sight of the restaurant.

"Whadda you want?"

"Social Security card."

"No problem. We'll text you the number tomorrow. The card will take, maybe a week. It'll cost you fifteen bucks, pay on delivery. All good? Cool."

He hurls his half-smoked cigarette into the street, where it rolls, stops, smolders. Already the snow had gone, spring was creeping in. New York was changing, starting to wake up. And having hovered, frozen in stasis, the Mimi side of things was beginning to mature as the ice thawed, the buds opened. And it was painless, that's the strangest, most unusual thing about it. This Mimi-puberty wasn't like the first, dredged in Sylvia Plath poetry and black clothing and stylish anorexia and tears and marijuana and acoustic guitars and dry humping spotty boys with Oasis hair and corduroy pants. This was utterly painless, and even the fear of doing something illegal, something that could have me thrown out of the country, something that was completely, unmistakably *wrong,* was complemented by that sharp pure smack of living, that pleasurable sting of existence, the realization that this, definitely, was something more.

My new employment, secured with the fake SS number, is directly opposite the gaping wound where the World Trade Center used to be. The basic premise was that I would be responsible for interviewing potential carers, nannies, nursing aides, butlers, chefs, housekeepers, and other staff for the crème de la crème of New York society. Brenda, my boss, explains my duties in great detail.

"So then you, like, pick up the *phone* when it *rings,* and there will be, like, a *person* on the other end, and you have to say 'Hello, Star Skivvies. How may I help you?' and they will *reply* . . ."

The office is beige and pink. They play supermarket music continually at a tone set to resemble Chinese water torture. Brenda wears brown tweed and shoulderpads. I spend an hour playing solitaire on the computer. The phone rings.

"Hello, Star Skivvies. How may I help you?"

A quavering voice trembles across the line.

"It's Po-lly. Who're *you?* I don't know your voice. Who are you?"

I put the call on hold and tell Brenda that it is Polly. She mouths (using accompanying hand gestures) that I should tell Polly, one of their clients, a Texan septuagenarian millionairess living in New York, that her nurse, Ramona, had gone to the hospital to have a cyst removed from her inner thigh and that Nurse Gloria would be caring for her today. Charades over, Brenda resumes instant messaging with Leroy in the PR Department, on the next desk. I·go back to the call.

"Hi, Polly, Ramona can't make it today . . ."

"I know, but I don't want a *noo* nurse, I jes' want my Ramona or *nobody*, young lady . . ."

There is a scuffle in the background. A croaky male voice yells, "Is she young? Good lookin'? Ready fer anythin'?"

Polly's voice tremulously reemerges.

"*Shurrup*, Bill. That's ma husband. Tell me, young lady, this Gloria, is she . . . *black?*"

"Erm . . . no?"

"Wa-all, I guess I kin have a noo nurse jes' fer *one* day. I'm jes' worried about the time it takes me to open the door. It takes me a real long time to open the door. What if I spend all that time gettin' to the door, and she ain't *there* no more?"

I check the time. 10:20 A.M. Gloria is scheduled to arrive at 11:00 A.M.

"Polly, tell you what, how about you set off for the door *now*, and by the time you get there, she'll probably be standing on the doorstep waiting for you."

"Oh. I guess. Oh. I'll get up now. Oh it hurts. Oh the *pain* . . ."

I hang up.

Star Skivvies prides itself on its staff-selection process, which is, according to the website, "likened to Fort Knox" in its ability to filter out "smokers," "those with fake documentation," "illegals," and other "undesirables." How they managed to miss the chain-smoking illegal on the front desk answering the phone for ten bucks an hour with a fake SS number and no work visa is anyone's guess.

Back in Brooklyn. "How the hell you manage to get that job?" Raoul inquires as he tenderly cradles his scrotum and holds aloft a Bud Light glistening with dew, standing in the doorway of my room wearing a pair of graying boxer shorts that are disturbingly full. His attitude had changed. He was now playing the role of concerned parent, plying me with beer and food when I stepped into the apartment, telling me about the JAP he was fucking, carefully watching my inscrutable face for signs of interest. He was not used to women ignoring his charms. He was coiled, ready to snap, but he was admirably controlling his temper and his sexual frustration. I didn't trust Raoul. I look at him sideways. He assumes a vacant expression.

"Craigslist."

He grunts, amused, hands me a beer.

"So what's the plan now? Stay there until the visa comes through?"

"Well, I guess. They pay me in cash, which is nice. But I'm still trying to write more articles for other newspapers. I was going to do a piece on illegal sex workers, sex trafficking—that kind of stuff. Going over to a stripclub at the weekend to speak to some of the girls. To be honest, I think I'd rather be a fucking stripper than work with Brenda."

Raoul looks at me and laughs.

"You ain't got the titties for that one, girl. Good job as

well. You don't wanna be one of them fucking hos. You wanna watch *Hiroshima mon amour* with me afore I get back in the box?"

We sit on the sofa wrapped in a duvet. I feel defiant. I didn't, have never, liked being told what I can't do. *You'll never get to Cambridge,* they said back home, because people didn't, not from my town, not to read an arty-farty subject like English Literature. I don't like being told what I can't do. I catch Raoul looking at me hungrily more than once, *I don't like people thinking they know me, my actions,* but I stare resolutely at the movie, ignore a tentative hand on my knee, until I fall asleep and wake up in the morning, alone.

Monday morning in the office. Brenda reveals to me a new gift—in the form of office attire, complete with shoulderpads.

"I thought that you could do with some more suitable clothes. Maybe baggy combats aren't the best wear for some of our more priority clients? We're, like, the same size, right?"

Brenda brandishes a size 16 jacket.

Swamped in tweed, bolstered by shoulderpads, and inhaling the pungent stench of ozone and menopause, I commence my sentence. The phone rings.

"Hello, Star Skivvies. How may I help you?"

It is Polly, the septuagenarian Texan millionairess.

"Who's that? Who is it? Is that *Brenda?*"

"No, it's Mimi. How are you, Polly?"

Bill, Polly's dearly beloved, passed away on Friday, presumably after overexposure to their noo "colored" nurse, Dotzy, from St. Lucia.

"I've lost his teeth. They're *gone*. That noo nurse *stole* 'em. Tell her to give 'em back. I need Bill's teeth fer the funeral. I can't *bury* him without his *teeth* . . ."

She starts to weep hysterically. I switch to speakerphone. Brenda snickers cruelly before turning back to *People* magazine and a bumper packet of Twinkies, keeping one eye out for any new instant messages from Leroy in PR. I transfer Polly to the harassed office assistant, Sally-Jane. Sally-Jane is Brenda's favorite target. She bears the brunt of the brutal and cutting instant messages that Brenda had honed to perfection after years of mastering the skilled art of office sadism.

```
SJ, R U S2pid? Do u want 2 keep this job?
```

Sally-Jane flutters anxiously.

```
Have u put on w8?
```

SJ palpitates visibly and retires to the photocopier. I had earlier informed Brenda that I possessed a debilitating and highly unpleasant bowel disorder that necessitates frequent hourly trips to the bathroom, thus ensuring my cigarette breaks go uninterrupted. Noting that I have twelve callers on hold, I decide it is prudent to exercise one of such breaks, and vanish to my usual spot outside Ground Zero.

Returning to The Office, I am greeted by a sheaf of letters that have, yet again, failed to live up to the high standards set by Brenda and must be retyped for the sixth time. I surreptitiously click on the Internet while Brenda works industriously on her eleventh Twinkie of the day, and I start to write an e-mail. Instantly my IM flashes.

```
    R U on the internet?
```

I close the window and return to correcting letterheads. Check the time. Reach, quietly, for my cellphone. The IM icon flashes.

```
    R U making personal calls?
```

The phone rings.
"Hello, Star Skivvies. How may I help you?"

I arrive home that night to find that we had run out of toilet paper, we could no longer reach the bathroom because of the amount of trash piled in front of it, and the cat had developed unsightly dags all around its derriere. The musicians were nowhere to be seen. "Japan," says Raoul vaguely from his horizontal position on my bed, presumably favoring it to his own. "On tour. We're looking after the apartment." We, this ubiquitous *we*. It makes me uncomfortable, though why I couldn't tell you. I wasn't fucking him and had no intention of it, though I could, and probably would have, under less trying circumstances. I used to believe, once upon a time, that you should save yourself for the special ones, the ones you love, the ones you care about. Then when I left the old me behind, started to unleash this Mimi-monster lying sleeping within me, I stopped.

I venture deeper into the apartment. A thick, fierce stench

wafts up from some indefinable location, disseminated swiftly through the loft by the industrial heater blasting like a giant blow-dryer. I follow the aroma of poop to what is not, as I had thought in a brief moment of terror, a deceased roommate, but a plastic box hidden behind a molding sofa, half a bicycle, and a drum kit. Upon removal of the lid, I am greeted by a veritable Pompeii of fossilized kitty crap, resembling miniature Terra-Cotta Warriors. I reach for a nearby garden trowel, and through a process of trial and error, manage to deduce that rather than throw the entire box away—litter, crap, and all—it is possible to sift gently through the offending articles, remove them, and *recycle* the actual litter, so that the apartment *smells* only of cat pee, as opposed to shit. The ingenuity of this astounds me.

Next morning. The Office is eerily quiet. Even Sally-Jane desists from typing away in her usual manic mode, and glances at me nervously as I slink in five minutes late and head to my desk. Brenda appears. She wears the look of one deeply, deeply bereft.

"Mimi, could you please step into the office?"

I can smell, beneath the menopausal woman and ozone stench, that unmistakable aroma of imminent unemployment. What I fail to detect is USCIS on hold to Brenda as I walk into her office.

Routine, routine. We all need routine. I established mine as soon as I could, in the only way I could. When I lost my job and my money and my hope and my Social Insecurity was exposed for all to see, I found routine in madness, found what else I could sell, and sold it. Routine ordered a life filled with transience and replaced the temporary and the unknown with the predictable and known. Routine—ah yes, we all need routine.

4

WITHOUT BLOOD THERE IS NO ATONEMENT, it said
on the door to the dressing room toilet cubicle, next to a sticker
of the Virgin Mary, and a Sharpied KUNT scrawled inexplicably
across the tiles. It always reminds me of school, the toilet cubicle in the dressing room. Reminds me, painfully, of things I
would prefer to forget—first times and awkward transitions
from adolescence into childhood. My first time was as loath-
some, distressing, sleazy, and painful as I had anticipated. But
there was no blood at least. When we locked ourselves in the
girls' bathroom to compare teenage notes, I remember the
universal gasp when this fact came out. *There was no blood.*
My eye slid back to the curious, looping, spiky graffiti at eye
level to the toilet, where some haunted religious soul had
leaned carefully forward (being careful not to drip), and etched
it onto the door, and then pulled up her G-string and gone
back out to dance.

without blood there is no atonement

It was curiously appropriate, now I think about it. My first
time, you see, instilled in me the gift that would later serve as
my survival instinct in later years, in stripclub years, stripclub

years like dog years. That first time as her—degrading, humiliating, unwanted, nauseating—helped me out a little later as Mimi, although I can't help but think that Mimi would have . . . oh never mind. There was the other first time, Mimi was there for that. That other first time. *You* know. When you got paid for it.

"What's your name, girl?"

I look up dully, eyes sweeping over filthy concrete, resting on the yellow NQRW 7th Avenue sign, focusing, unfocusing, eventually settling on the speaker. A pretty, wide-eyed, tiny Asian girl with hair down to her butt is regarding me with curiosity. I shrug, look away. The girl laughs, a merry laugh, a laugh that has had a few drinks, but not enough to fall into oblivion. Enough to talk to strangers.

"Don't be like that. I was just asking your name. I seen you working in Crobar, right? Bad day?"

I shrug again, cave in. "Crobar? I don't work there. I just lost my job."

The girl whistles low, giggles. The platform is empty save for us two, and an old white guy picking bugs off his shoes and splatting them between his fingers.

"So you're looking for a *job*."

"I'm looking for a job."

She stops and gazes at me from the corner of her eyes, as if the angle gives her a unique optical glimpse into my soul. It was as if she was scrutinizing me, hard, looking for signs and scars of living that would lead her to her destination, some clue of who I was, what I was.

"Hey, I remember how I know you. You were in Foxy's,

hanging 'round, trying to get a job as a waitress and asking questions."

I look away angry, and she laughs again.

"Hey, no worries. Thought I knew you from someplace. I know Dolores wasn't real friendly but a girl just left, so they're looking for someone right now to do the day shift. You should come back tomorrow, speak to Dolores again."

"You a stripper?"

"Nooooo, hell, no! My boyfriend would kill me. No, I'm just a waitress, so we'll be working together. But waitressing's OK. Stupid outfits, but hell, it's cash. I work at Hooters too. Just come in tomorrow early on before some other hoochy bitch gets the job. My name's Lily."

"Thanks," I say.

"Oh, and one more thing."

She pauses and smiles slightly at some joke I don't get.

"It's 'dancer,' not 'stripper.' We don't use no words like that in the club. It's, like, rude to the girls. *Dancer.* Remember that."

Stripper, dancer, ecdysiast. A train draws up and Lily gets on. She pulls a book out of her bag, *LSATs Made Easy.* And then the train leaves, and it's just me and the bum, picking bugs off his boots, squashing them methodically on the concrete platform.

"Mimi." I feel a tug on my arm. "That's Dolores, sitting in the cash booth on the phone. Just wait until she hangs up and ask about the job. Good luck."

Lily saunters off, a body that burned onto your corneas like a branding iron, drinks tray twirling. From behind the bar, aureola glare, seeping across breasts streaked with jagged blue veins, a yellowing canvas glossy with baby oil. It was like being stuck in a virgin's wet dream. It was like being stuck in a strip-club in Midtown Manhattan at four P.M. on a Monday afternoon. *Oh.*

"You after a jawb?"

Dolores is addressing me with her left eyebrow. I can see this because the skin hanging over her eyes has been spectacularly lifted, sliced, and pinned, ensuring even a commonplace eyebrow raise turned into a spectacular battle between gravity, nature, and surgery. Her jowls, it appears, have yet to surrender to the slash of cold steel.

"What's your name?"

"Mimi."

"You twenny-one?"

"Yeah, I'm actua—"

"I'll see you tomorrow, Mimi. And for fuck's sake, wear some fucking makeup. The guys ain't here to listen to your goddamn accent and talk about da *New Yorker.*"

43°59'N 7°9'E

Cooking in the galley, a hot day, hottest summer in France for years. It was still midseason, I had not yet met the Captain of *La Bella,* nor did I know that in three short months I was destined to sail across the Atlantic with a crew of four men. Now it was summer, busiest time of the year, hottest time of the year. People had been dying, dropping like flies in the heat—the old, the infirm, mainly—though I could see that we were not all immune. It was too hot. I seared tuna and watched the heat scar into the pink, rosy flesh. The boat rocked gently even though we were in port. We had a week before guests would arrive and we would have to be on call 24/7, serving drinks, food, anything they required. Now it was just preparation.

He came up behind me and I didn't hear, the sizzle of the fish and the prickle of hot fat on my arm a trickle of sweat down a damp forehead *tired* been out the night before and he wanted cooked food for God's sake miserable old *cunt* it was one hundred degrees outside and I wanted a beer wanted to get *out* of this job I'd only been in for two weeks but I needed the money and he slipped an arm around my waist a mouth— an *old*, wrinkled mouth, curiously dry—as it rasped across my skin old man mouth seeking mine. I went still. Froze. Did nothing. The tuna sizzled and the flesh puckered and scabbed into a black, chalky burn. Hot, hot, hot but I went cold. It was silent. *Please don't*, I whispered.

I'm sorry, he said later, *I don't know what came over me. I couldn't stop myself. I . . .*

It's OK, I said, and avoided his eye, and the deckhand, listening, slunk away into the cabins and pretended not to hear. *Am I too old for you?* And then anger, *I've heard you coming back to the boat with other men, I've seen you in the bars drunk, why not me? Why don't you have a boyfriend? Girls shouldn't sleep around like whores.*

I don't do boyfriends, I said.

He fired me ten days later. It was a relief. To avoid him I'd taken to sleeping in the deckhand's cabin. The deckhand didn't like it any more than I did. I left them with a fridge full of food doctored with laxatives, Visine, and anything else I had found in the medicine box. And then I took three tabs of ecstasy and partied in Juan-les-Pins until dawn and walked home through the market in Antibes and the stallholders laughed when they saw me at six A.M. still giddy with drugs and I inhaled the fresh, wet, earthy smell of basil, tomatoes mingled with rich cheeses, the cool, delicious morning sun, the salty breeze. They gave me bread and coffee and chattered away in French as I ate. I had nowhere to sleep that night so I went out again, and my bags were still lying neglected on Quay 19 in Antibes harbor. The next night I shared a bed with an Australian I knew vaguely from The Blue Lady. His girlfriend was a stewardess on a yacht charter in Greece, so there was a space to be filled.

I thought you said you don't do . . . ?

Other people's don't count.

Ah.

The arrangement suited us both.

Dolores: "It's come to my attention that undercover police officers are posing as guests in order to try and close us down. If a guest asks you for a fuck, a blowjob, a handjob, or to masturbate in front of him, the correct answer isn't, 'Maybe if you come to the Champagne Room we can talk about it' or even 'Let's discuss this later.' The correct answer is, 'I'm not that kinda girl, and this is not that kinda place.' Got it?"

The "dancers," lounging in various stages of undress, all nod in agreement, apart from the Russians, who don't understand, and instead groom their square inch of pubic hair for lack of a more stimulating entertainment. I couldn't help wondering what kind of place this was if it didn't serve fucks, blowjobs, or handjobs.

"They don't do that?" I whisper to Lily. Her dark eyes widen and her waist-length hair crackles. "Noooo! It's just *dancing.*

They have to keep their G-strings on even in the Champagne Room."

"So why the fuck do guys come in this shithole?"

"Just watch," she says.

So I watch. Watch long and hard. I had become a virtuoso of watching since arriving in America. I sat in cafes ordering coffee I couldn't afford, wandered through parks, always watching, observing, noticing the tiny details. The immigrants who came and forgot where they were from, so busy being American. The immigrants who could never forget where they were from, so busy trying to be American. The ones who never even tried, recognizing the futility of such a practice, instead just doggedly surviving. I see them all, the invisible people, the people without good jobs and careers and without hope, because I'm one of them. *It's just a temporary situation, though. Just temporary.*

In Brooklyn, Raoul sits and watches me without speaking, and his silent observance teaches me how to watch, like a predator, like you're waiting for something you know will happen, like you believe it will happen, even when you secretly fear it won't.

That first day in Foxy's is disorienting, and I'm scared they might find out about my having no visa, even though Lily said it was OK, so I watch. The girls all harbor that manufactured look of boredom and distaste, and their smiles are like the smiles of a small baby about to burp—reflexive, fleeting, full of air, rumpled gas, empty. There's one, the one from the first day, with the mouth like a slit throat and a belly creased like bed linen, thighs dimpled with purple bruises, eyes smacked back far into a head that could be gray, could be, if it weren't sunflower yellow. The vowels tumble out of her like a Puerto Rican orgy, it was that slit-throat mouth that made her money, not the tarnished bloated breasts hard with silicone lumps, insolent nipples. Tired, tired, tired. She's tired, but the smile never drops, it's carried around like stigmata, and she occasionally, onstage, clutches her belly unconsciously then looks around, confused, like she dropped her last pregnancy on the floor behind her. The young feline Russian with no tits and no ass and no personality and the hungry eyes of money made it for some guys, she made it for some guys. Some guys like that look, the "I haven't had my period yet, Daddy" look. And then some wanted the impossible undulations of the Brazilians and the Colombians who, when they weren't fondling some guy's knee, were on their rhinestone-encrusted pink phones calling *hijos* and *abuelas,* chewing take-out chicken parmigiana from greasy paper boxes when it got slow, discussing their boob jobs, the business. I watch all this, I absorb.

The girls frequently dart in and out of a tiny dressing room occupied by an orca of a woman dispensing tampons and safety pins, pretzels and hair rollers from the vast recesses of her rotted womb. "I'm Maw," she tells me, after we stare at each other a good long while. She looks at my satin pants, my curly, shoulder-length blond hair, my stupid blue eyes, my lack of eyeliner, lashes, lust, and dismisses me. The satin pants. The tiny hotpants. I notice we got more looks than dancers ("'Dancers' are how they like to be called," says Dolores harshly), us waitresses, us girls who don't take our clothes off. It's a mystery why in this furtive breeding ground for sin, the permissiveness allowed us wasn't leaped upon and worried like a frenzied dog. Why do some girls take their clothes off and others earn dollar tips wearing satin hotpants? Money. Sure, money. But why do some girls have their boundaries, others don't? Sex. Sex. Sex. Watching, listening.

"I used to be a dancer but my boyfriend gave me an ultimatum: 'Marry me, get your green card, and give it up; stay and be a fuckin' whore,'" says the bartender, overstayed on a student visa, never went home. "I'd *never* dance again. Once you start, you cross a line. You can't go back. You change. Plus my boyfriend would kill me," she continues. "I love my boyfriend. I could never touch another man." *Thought you said you didn't touch them?* She gives me a look. That look says, *Watch.*

I watch more. I watch Ole Hank, one of the Champagne Room managers, the guys in charge of the floor while Dolores sits queenly in her postsurgery pinnednippedtucked splendor. ("She used to be three hundred pounds until she got her stomach stapled. She don't look good now, but hell, you shoulda seen her *before*.") I watch the huge bouncers, Pedro, Simi, the Brazilian toilet attendant who snickers and grins stupidly, like a fool, because he *is* a fool, a stupid, retarded fool who deserved no better employment than handing out candy and rubbers to the johns, but he's a sweet guy. I watch the other waitresses, who are all hot, hotter than me, mostly surgically enhanced. ("Kissed. Surgically kissed, says Lily, primly, on her break, and looks between *LSATs Made Easy* and *People* magazine, uncertain of which to delve into first.) I become a voyeur, a Peeping Tom, a silent witness, as much a part of the fixtures as the grimy handprints on the mirrors upon which we lean when Ole Hank isn't watching. I watch and I look, and as I look and watch I notice that the dancers, strippers, girls, whatever the hell they are, those assorted pick-'n-mix candy dolls of lurid plastic, they too are watching. They watch the door, they watch the men, they watch the money, smell the money, stalk it, suckle on it, and in the absence of money, they sit down and bitch about the new girl's fat ass or the old girl's coke habit. And the dancing. *Well*, the *dancing*. Girls twist around men like sinews as dresses fall and sighs escape. Insolent breasts, nipples, brittle and sharp, about to snap off in the icy blast of the AC, and the men's mouths snap like turtles reaching, reaching, but there's a knee suddenly in the way, pressed hard, urgent, and the swelling it encounters distracts from the need for the mouth, and the knee rubs rhythmically up and down, up and down, eyes flick idly to the side checking for Ole Hank who is the arbiter of grinding (GRINDING: the act of stimulating a man's genitalia through rhythmic pressure of the knee or buttocks; *verb:* to grind; *progressive:* grinding; *past:* ground), and I could have *sworn* a meeting of lips, their heads are so close, and the hands creep up, a little further up, gently up. "But there's no touching, you see?" whispers Lily. The girls touch, but the guys don't, else Hank is on 'em and Pedro and Simi throw them out. *But what about the Champagne Room? What's the deal?* The deal is (drum roll, *please*), the deal is, *the connection between palm and cheek*—no, sorry, *the connection between hand and cock.* "You serious?" I ask. "I dunno," she shrugs. "I don't go in there. I guess you negotiate with the guy before you go in. No sex though. Just, like, second base, maybe a handjob, something like that. My boyfriend would *kill* me if I did that."

I watch and watch. I absorb it all, the skank, the sleaze, the excitement, the boredom, the stink of money. Is it all so shocking, really, this titillation, this flash of a boob, titties-and-ass, bored girls writhing over sex-starved bankers? In a world where A can explain to B that monogamy doesn't exist, except in his girlfriend's head, which is why he can happily fuck C up the ass ("... and that girl's a *real* goer—first time we had sex, she grabbed my dick, pulled it outta her pussy, jammed it right up her fuckin' *asshole*"), is it so shocking? Gently, gently, her fuckin' asshole expanded like a warm mouth and swallowed him up, and he was lost, forever, to the old ways of "being faithful" and "nights in with the woman," because he was initiated into the new order now, the twenty-first century, New York City, where everyone's fucking everyone, a hyper-sexualized semitic city of lights, a pornographic light show, in the midst of which the stripclub seems actually, *really,* quite tame.

I go quietly home at eight o'clock with a hundred bucks in tips. No one really notices me that day. It wasn't that hard. It wasn't that different. After the initial wince of disgust, I was easing into it. It wasn't that bad, really. I could imagine being part of it, more so now, than I could imagine being an editor on a magazine, or a lawyer, or something that gave me my 401(k). My respectability, my health insurance, my sanity. Nice Cambridge girl, will say the headlines, turned STRIPPER! But to be honest, you sell what you have, what you know, and however it's packaged, you had that crack, that flaw, that fucked-up genetic blip in you from something, from somewhere. You didn't just turn up in this place *by accident*. No way.

After a week it's normal. I can outstare even the Colombian's tits. It's become routine—sighs, gasps, loneliness. It's something I feel like I've known my whole life. I guess I have, in a different guise, in a more acceptable guise, a more secretive guise, a more normal.

"Hanging out with you is like hanging out in a concentration camp," I tell Raoul, as he lies silently on my bed emitting indolent puffs of smoke into the air.

"Have you ever been in a concentration camp?" he snarls back.

"Yes. I went to Belsen on a school trip."

"What's it like?"

"Like hanging out with you."

"When you gonna get a real job?" he snaps, suddenly humorless.

"When my visa comes through and I have real papers," I reply calmly.

"I don't like you working in that place, English girl. It ain't good for you seeing that shit. You're gonna end up like those whores."

I shrug, roll over, lick his stomach, feel him grow hard beneath me. My tongue traces down to the top of his pants, a small damp patch spreads through the fabric. I roll over and reach for a magazine. Raoul looks annoyed. He's annoyed because I walk away before he can walk away from me. I keep doing it. It's one of my talents, leaving, a talent he thought, wrongly, that he had mastered. It torments him, niggles at him, gnaws at his hard, pebbly heart. Sex was clinical, adequate, rough. It would do, a distraction. I never sought out distractions, they came to me, like the Cuban musician who had accompanied me home last week. Raoul had been furious when he found us in the morning drinking coffee, me wrapped in the Cuban's leather jacket. I had laughed at his anger, humiliated him, and he hated me for it, even as it made him want me more. The more I reveal my disdain, my independence, my complete absence of need, desire, want, dependency, the more furious he becomes. I enjoy tormenting him, I'm good at it, I've had enough practice. And he deserves it.

Raoul sits up, reaches over, grabs my breast roughly in one hand and with the other pushes me down onto my back and tries to kiss me. I wriggle out of his grasp and glower at him. He slaps me hard. I cry out. My mouth starts to bleed from where I bit the inside of my cheek. I smile at him, coldly, with hate.

"You're not my boyfriend, Raoul," I murmur quietly, and in response he says something very strange, very odd, rude even, not a little out of place. He says my real name.

I walked through Central Park one morning, before I went into work at twelve. There was a tramp—a "bum," you Americans would say—lying on a park bench. He was cooking in the heat of a May afternoon, stewing in ammoniac shit and fecal sweat, in excretions and deletions and pure, apoplectic filth. But what struck me most was the wrinkled dick sticking out of his pants like a dehydrated mollusk, the crusted, oozing lesions it hosted.

Day eight. Around six P.M., when businessmen leak in from canned fluorescent lights and masturbatory deals to get their dicks ground and their egos petted. I knew the score by now. *Hank was the floor manager; you went to Hank with any problems. That girl you didn't talk to; the other dancers were OK. Don't talk to the House Mom when she's doing the makeup.*

Always make sure you have a pedicure in case Kim, the other manager, catches you. Don't mention plastic surgery to Dolores. Act dumb. Flirt. Flirt. Flirt. I knew the score. I know the score. I'm walking through the club, and I've replaced the dowdy flats from two weeks ago with six-inch wooden platform heels and the blond hair is blonder, straightened, and the face doesn't look like a face I've ever seen in a mirror before, and this girl fit in OK, fit in like a Paula would fit in, this girl called "Mimi" with no last name and no Social Security number and no one to ask.

This time some young guys come in from Boston—bachelor party, bankers. And this girl is standing by the Funny Money machine—the machine right by the cash desk where Dolores sits unmoving, like a boiled crustacean. There are no ATMs in the club, just these machines that swallow your card and vomit out pink pussy Cash laced with naked ladies at a 10 percent surcharge, which can be redeemed by us for real money, minus 20 percent for the house.

So she's standing there, right by the Funny Money machine, this girl, this waitress, I forget her name now—her real name, anyway—but I could have told you the one she goes by. And the guy rolls up and she ignores him—she's a good waitress, not one of those girls who go in the Champagne Room and fuck up the dancers' trade and whom they hate, because if you want to be a dancer, *be* a fucking dancer, pay your rent money to the house, and earn it back onstage; don't be a fucking waitress, a weasel server stealing clients, pretending to be pure. But he's offering her a drink, and she's taking it—hell, *I'd* take it too, standing on your feet all day for dollar tips *sucks,* and they encourage us to drink because then the guys are going to spend twice as much, *capiche?* I watch because I'm still in watching mode, and there aren't that many of us, waitresses I mean, who *do* sit down, despite its being preferential to working your ass off with a fucking drinks tray. Lily sat with a guy the other day for a half hour, Russian guy, mob they said. He gave her a hundred bucks for talking to him. So I watch, and what's going on is this guy starts talking real loud about wanting to go in the room, and then it's like this little light goes off in the girl's head, and she's purring. Yes, the bitch is purring, and from then on it's plain sailing. Knee between thighs, looking demure, sip of Corona, makes the guys laugh. She has personality this one, and it's refreshing to laugh with a waitress instead of a stripper. Strippers are easy, but everyone knows to score a waitress in the Champagne Room is the triple word score, the double twenty, the full fucking house. Not long now, she's reeling him in, a nod to Hank and he slides over unobtrusive as chlamydia, and before you know it, those two are in the private room.

I go away for a while this afternoon, so I can't tell you all that occurs, and after all, it's between the dancer and the client. But when I come back, she's there too, and it all makes sense. I could tell you her name, see, her real name. Or I could tell you the name she goes by. But you probably know by now. You probably know.

There's no sex in the Champagne Room. "There's no touching, you see?" says Lily when she sees me afterward. In the room I had seen a dancer, a real dancer, and her eyes looked through his and I could see distinctly the hand burrowed into the warren of his flies, rehydrating whatever was within, and you couldn't tell from her eyes what she thought, but in my corner of the room I heard and felt the wet gloss of shame and the guttural wrench of instinct and training, pleasure and sickness, the little death of release, relief—the wet, slick orgasm of money, the security it brings.

"You know, you should think about auditioning, Mimi."

Hank, ectothermic, never blinks.

"Auditioning?" I say, slugging back a Corona, pretending it had never occurred to me before.

"Yeah, as a dancer. I can tell you'd make money. You'd make some good money for us." His smile is sly, fond, his hand reaches instinctively for his bow tie, the arms thin in the drooping black-and-white checkered jacket.

"Hey, you gonna audition?" asks a redhead built on longitude and nicotine and handjob expertise. "I can hook you up with a bachelor party Saturday if you want. Good practice. I can't do it, gotta go see my boyfriend DJ in a club in Chelsea. You up for it? Easy money."

"*There's no touching* you see?" says Lily unconvincingly. "If I didn't have a boyfriend, I'd do it. Easy money. You don't have a boyfriend, do you?"

"No," I say. "I don't."

5

WE ARE, IF ONE ADHERES to traditional, Middle American, conservative (and probably liberal) standards, deviants of the first order by the time we grasp that stinking brass pole, perspiring gently with baby oil and gray smudges of dead skin sliced off greased-up thighs. We're there because we have indulged in fucking, have been fucked indiscriminately, have had our legs opened by a rough hand, probing fingers, have gently guided a thousand and one pricks into the dripping crevasse within. We have fucked when drunk, on drugs, when sober. We have fucked without guilt, without enjoyment, with pain and pleasure and the accompanying regrets. We have had our hair pulled until tears welled out of eyes so sodden with ecstasy and coke that they can barely focus, rag doll bodies pulled up, pushed down, fucked hard, slapped harder. The bruise of men's kisses has stained our breasts like crushed berries, fading gently into the sickly olive of a memory. Fucking is something that has guided us gently to that stage, so that the pornographers we are in the bedroom have found their rabid release in ghastly makeup, a calculated touch, lascivious glares. And somehow it impeded our growth as human beings, started to act on us in reverse, so that the longer we stayed in the business, the faster we wanted to resort back to that mewling, puking babe crying in a mother's arms—a mother who would just as soon pluck her nipple from our boneless gums, dash our brains against a rock.

Of course, there are also those who do it just for money. Or kicks. Or because they like it. Or because they can't face the alternative, and for them the alternative is probably a stint on the checkout at K-Mart in Mississippi, or Moscow, or Kazakhstan. But it sounds better the way I say it, don't you think? It sounds better when the darkness you see in me now at the end of it all is corroborated somewhere, deep down in the past, in actions long gone but deeply engraved, actions that make what follows somehow understandable, comprehensible, *OK*. Because if we were fucked before we ever got on that stage, what happens after that can be seen as merely inevitable.

The wax hurt. The wax fucking hurt.

"Hold still Mammy," instructs Olga as she splays me open like a spatchcock chicken. "Be *brave* Mammy." She dips a wooden spatula into a bubbling pot of brown goo enticingly sprinkled with other people's curly dark hairs, and liberally spreads it over my pubic region. "No cry Mammy. Hold skin tight Mammy." She picks up a clean cotton cloth and smooths it over the brown goo, pressing on it hard. She peels up the furthest corner with the greatest of care . . . and rips it off. There is blood. There is pain. There is cursing—from me. "You make much *noise* Mammy. No be baby Mammy." Olga soothes me in a smothering voice, grasping me tightly to her immense bosom and rocking me like a child, but the eyes are cold, all money. "Be brave Mammy. Be *brave*."

Afterward I'm ushered into a booth and left to undress. I

step into a TARDIS-like compartment, a blast of orange mist, a tongue that tastes of Belsen. I step out of the gas chamber and dry off the excess with a towel, which sheds white lint over my (now satsuma) body. "Ah better!" Olga proclaims as I reenter the salon. She plucks absently at the outline of her nipple underneath the white coat. "Very pretty Mammy! You want spa mani-pedi as well? Special price!"

There's a special price on mani-pedi, a special price on hair-free, a special price on shaving and moisturizing and primping and scraping and plucking and faking, faking, faking. Plastic talons and chemical melanoma, but the batteries are running low, and you can't fake it when the juices ain't running. I'm scared, there, I'll admit. Scared like toothache, irritating, but not palpable, like cancer, like tumors, like death. Before we ever stepped onstage we were cracked, flawed, fucked up, fucked hard, but we weren't malignant.

"Where you going?" demands Raoul, and I stare at him hard and he snorts and his right fist curls up, and I don't look away until he nods assent, and I say to him, "That was the last time, Raoul. You're not my boyfriend." And then his head dips, inclines, and he gives the vaguest nod, and when I leave he's sitting at the kitchen table with his head in his hands, and when I walk down the street I know he's calling the JAP version of me, and all I can think is *Thank God that's over with*. In view of this, in view of the Mimi-bitch already working through the roommates and breaking hearts and making sure there are no saviours for this fable, it's no surprise where I'm going, what I'm doing. I make my way to Penn Station for six P.M. to meet a man called Igor, a white limousine, and seven strippers.

. . .

"Hey, girls, wanna do a lesbian flawr show with me?"

Narissa pops her gum and for a second the pink tumescence flounders, deflates, and her tongue slips out like a lizard's, roots around, snaps it off snagged skin, retrieves it, chews. She helps herself to a bottle of champagne from the limo's cooler. Lucy giggles, laughs like candy, all quivering and glossy and sweet, butterscotch brown skin and tightly coiled snakes of hair beneath a cheap black wig and an accent from the South, simmered down to a rich treacle. Igor, head-to-toe Armani, a white man with a black voice, reeking of Viagra and heartburn, grins. Julia, a twenty-two-year-old model *slash* single mother *slash* dominatrix *slash* club promoter *slash* anorexic bitch, looks vaguely excited, her exquisitely cut face branching into a cheap sneer, which just passes as a smile.

"Floor show? I will! Oh whattha *fuck*, how many calories does this champagne have? I have to like, *lose* five pounds by Monday or my agent's gonna *fire* me. Fucking *asshole*. Like I *have* five pounds to lose. *Mimi*, feel my tit, Mimi. Is that a fucking *tit* which can take the *loss* of five more frikkin' *pounds?*"

Julia sticks her tits out. Actually, she sticks out a rack of lamb with two doll's house–sized pepper pots protruding from it awkwardly. She holds the pose and shows no sign of desisting until I gingerly poke a nipple with my pinky.

"I had *great* tits until I had my frikkin' *son*. Breast-feeding just *ate* 'em up. They just *disappeared*. Fucking pregnancy."

She grabs the bottle of Veuve and swallows loudly, displaying an obvious talent for *something* if one takes the vivid convulsion of her glottis as any indication. A vein pulses slightly in her scrawny alabaster neck. Igor assumes an expression of vague concern.

"Baby, I wanna make you promise me you're gonna grab some food in the party. I don't want you passing out on the fucking flawr like last time, you hear me?"

Julia swallows loudly, belches, cackles. The vein throbs some more. Igor glances at me. His voice is dark chocolate; but the cheap kind. The kind on sale because it's gone white with age.

"*Damn* Mimi, you looked twelve years old in the picture they sent me. Loved the Snoopy T-shirt baby! So you dance at Foxy's?"

Champagne. Champagne—the drink of champions. Or is that milk? It fizzes in my nose, and my vision momentarily crackles into a buzz of static, and my voice, when it comes, sounds a little fucked, a little high-pitched, even to me.

"Erm, *kind of.* I was a waitress. Well, I *am* a waitress. But I'm thinking about dancing. I have an audition next week. I've danced before though. Like, in England. I have experience."

Igor smiles, unconvinced. Narissa starts talking again. This becomes a theme for the night. Narissa talking. *Narissa is talking everyone! Take note.* The girl can talk, or at least approximate it. Her mouth moves, we listen, but all the while I'm thinking, if she shut her mouth, they'd be hell to pay the other end, what with the stream of excrement flowing so damned strong and needing some outlet.

"So, whadda they want Igor? Same as last time? Flawr show? Pussy lickin'? Anyone bring any dildos? Those fuckers had better tip well. Gotta pay my tuition fees for next semester."

"Oh, where you going to college?"

Lucy's face is wide and open and sweet. You know the face. Rape victim before the betrayal, Act 1, scene 1: Hint of world weariness but with fortitude and the Good Book struggles through, possibly reinforced by a meadow scene of yellow flowers, eager butterflies, small child.

"In Brooklyn. Trainin' to be an accountant. You?"

"Oh, I just got here. From Georgia. I start NYU in the fall. Law school."

Everyone gazes at her briefly, a silence punctuated by the rapid succession of burps emitted from Julia's mouth. And then conversation moves swiftly on. Having a degree pre-stripping made you a bit of a loser, I suspect. Fictional degrees are de rigueur. Because if you have a degree, you certainly shouldn't be here, and if you're doing this for fun, you're a fucking jerkoff hoochy-ass bitch who needs to get a life. So I don't say anything. Just grab that bottle right back from Julia and drink, and she looks on in approval as everyone compares acrylic claws, a topic that is safer than the inimitable allure of the fictional promised land at the end of our stripping careers— paid-up home, 401(k), rich (dead) husband, and a face-lift.

The limo sweeps sleekly over the highway.

The marina in New Jersey. A volley of whistles and cheers bounce off a granite sky, making us wobble uncertainly as we walk along the jiggling gangplank to an audience of white-outfitted bemused crew. They hustle us swiftly into our dressing room—a tiny bathroom consisting of three stalls and a long mirror. Three girls stride in after us, tall, black, and oozing boob, shining with the excess of confidence that comes from avid coke consumption and free Veuve Clicquot in a white limo. A small, dumpy Hispanic girl sits quietly in the corner, slips off her T-shirt, looks timidly around.

"Can someone help me put cream on my back?" she asks, barely audible, in a victim voice that has already received the worst of life, probably from a blood relative, and really doesn't expect any better. Together the girls turn to her with bright open smiles, and then stop. Her back is scaly with a fiesta of ringworm, topped off with peeling skin from too much Jersey shore. It had been an early summer, and for her, an unforgiving one. Silence. Lucy steps forward and smiles sweetly, gently.

"Sure hon. I'll do it."

She squeezes cream onto her smooth palm and places it warmly, softly, with loving care, on the little dumpy girl's raw back. The other girls turn back to the mirror, and start shoveling glitter, powder, creams, and lotions onto faces that looked barely legal, and I silently congratulate myself on having fitted in somehow, in a way in which this girl, this little fat butterball of repulsion and abuse and a hangdog air of cringing expectation, this little fat butterball oozing serum from scratched and putrid flesh, has not.

It's a dog-eat-dog world, stripping.

Slap on, slapped up, the girls walk up the stairs to the main salon, where music pulses and the roar of the semidrunk cascades down steps. Tripping in heels with the gentle swell of the boat, gulping, scared, scared shitless, scared of everything, scared of the orange tone of my flesh, scared I can't dance, scared because this is something I'm not used to, broad daylight, still only 7:30 P.M. and night hasn't cast its shroud over New York, and Narissa is still talking, and Lucy's laughing easily, and Julia's still sniffing and blinking from the coke smacking her brain cells, jabbing them before following with a fine upper cut, boxing out the sense she never knew she had, and the little dumpy girl hides in the bathroom, and the other three tall, beautiful, confident black girls, vaginas on legs, nothing but vaginas on legs, sashay easily up those damned stairs, into the room, pick their men, swing a long, slender leg over an expectant quivering thigh, let crotch slap against crotch in a straddle like a toothless grin, and Narissa teeters into the middle of the room, and fifty Colombian men all pause for a split second, a sliver of time barely significant like the touch of that finger on an inner thigh, until she yells, "Where da *fuck* is da bachelor?" and having located him, rips her dress over her head, jumps onto his lap, followed shortly by Julia, also derobed and sporting fuck-me boots and she's now grabbing Narissa's little red G-string (*my* red G-string), and despite the fact there's only two of them and fifty guys, it's like an ocean of titties and bare ass and neatly waxed pussies and long limbs flailing and pink tongues flaring out in a fire stream, lizards catching flies . . . But Lucy's the wise one, because she demurely grabs a Red Bull, sidles up to the best-dressed guy in the group, and bats those big, brown Southern eyes . . . *and I'm damned if I see that dress come off at all.* And Igor's looking over, raised eyebrows, I can see what the jerkoff's thinking (*Snoopy* T-shirt?) so I grab the nearest drink from a willing hand and wait for that backhand slap of vodka to beat out the inhibitions. I turn toward the slap this time. Down it, slip outside, cigarette, steady, *steady*. Fucking *hands* shaking. I can do this. Statue of Liberty there. *Wanna drink, rubia?* The men leer at me. Yeah, I'll take a drink. Another. The girls come out, hand me some more. I catch Lucy's eye, and she smiles sadly. Music. Fuck, this isn't so bad. This is *fine* once you get the drinks in, you can't even feel the hands pressing between the flimsy wedges of fabric, between your conscience, your need to pay the rent. *Call Dad.* Can't call Dad though. He can't even pay the fucking bills. *You on your own now baby,* Lucy whispers, winks. I grab a proffered twenty-dollar bill, the dress is off . . .

The music's louder, the sky's darker, there's money in my G-string, and I'm drunk, and Narissa and Julia are still rolling around on the floor as dollar bills float leaves gently around the flawr show, and then a skinny arm protrudes from the writhing limbs and whips my G-string down, slo-mo as my legs give way and my eye's caught on a corner of the ceiling with sagging balloons taped to it, focus shifts to a carpet, midnight blue, small yellow diamonds, someone's sneakers, yelling, an indistinct crackle of noise like static, if I readjust someone's leg, and another, but there's a hand attached to the body I can't quite lift my head up to see, because my head's pinned down by a skinny model knee on my chest, a foot on my hair, and the hand is somewhere it really shouldn't be (that's what the bouncers in the club are there for, surely?), but it's not the club.

"GET YOUR FUCKIN' FINGER OUTA MY ASS JERKOFF!" screeches Narissa as an errant digit from an onlooker eager to participate in the action threatens to disturb the delicate equilibrium of snatch licking taking place on the carpet. Julia emerges from between her legs with a tongue still glistening and finds an excellent opportunity for negotiation. "More money," she announces in a curious monotone, and the whoops and the laughter pause as they scrabble in jackets for more cash, and it rains down again, bigger denominations, and then there's a model between my legs, and a murmur from somewhere, "If you wanna be on top let me know, I think we have about two grand here, we can get more," and between *her* legs is the face of an English girl, whose familiarity with the female anatomy is becoming increasingly intimate with every gyration of those skinny model hips, the money keeps coming, the money keeps coming, the music's louder and outside the skies begin to darken, not that I can see, from my horizontal vantage point lying naked with skinny model ass plumped on my face in the middle of a salon on a 200-foot yacht cruising around the Statue of Liberty, but it certainly *feels* darker in here. It certainly feels darker. And the moans and the groans and the frenzied pumping and squirming of body parts is all something I know well, know so well, it's so sadly, sickly familiar that I realize, all at once, that I ended up here because, like the rest of them, I was gagging for that slap, begging for what girls should never do, never have to put up with, never have to witness, experience, or feel. Not the nice ones anyhow. Not ones like me.

43°59'N 7°9'E

When the Australian's girlfriend came back, I moved out and found somewhere else to sleep. That was how I met Jon-jon-the-jaapie.

My eyes were rolling and I could feel it, and I couldn't remember where I'd been, but I knew where I was, and when Jon-jon opened the door he knew where I'd been because my eyes told him. So without a word he led me in, laid me down, stripped my clothes off, and there were no kisses, not that I remember, not that I could feel, but what I could feel was the drug permeating my body and my body following instinct not instruction. Instinct dictated what I did, because my head was incapable of it. I remember it didn't hurt but from somewhere I felt like it should, and nothing happened after he wrestled with me for a little while, so he stopped. He went into the next room, woke up the other guy, one I hadn't seen before. He came in and he was butt naked and he put his hands on me, and I said no, and they were fine with that. Jon-jon kissed me a little and petted me, and the second one sat down and watched, all the while smoking a cigarette, which dangled loosely from thick lips, and from its red glow I could see that my body still looked young even as it felt so old, cold and trembling from the inevitable comedown. Jon-jon lay back down again, and this time I think it did hurt. In the morning the apartment was empty, and I let myself out, and the streets were quiet because it was 7:00 A.M. and France had not yet woken up. In the morning the apartment was empty, and I let myself out, and sure I felt the sting of that slap but if you dwelt on it too long, if you thought about it too much, you'd go crazy. So you turn your head to the sky, let the sun caress tired skin, lidded eyes. Open them. Walk on home in the sunlight, hope that the other two in the room you were staying in had gone out so you could sleep, thank God you can move onto the new boat Monday, and forget.

When you're facing utter degradation, even actively courting it for the money, you remember the times before, when you did it for curiosity, for kicks, because you were fucked on ecstasy, had drunk too much tequila, because you were on that slippery slope to destruction, because you just stopped wanting to be good, or somehow believed you were never good to begin with. And it's different, doing it for money, tirelessly plucking those fingers from worming their way into your anus, your vagina. It's different because the other girls have your back, know where you're coming from, detach from their bodies so you do the same, so you can have your tongue lashing away like a lawn trimmer over a numb clitoris, and a half hour later be standing, cool, unshaken, on the aft deck of the boat, sharing a cigarette and counting the proceeds, and knowing that whatever dark memories are stirred up by this curiously frigid act of flawr show sex in a bachelor party on a motor yacht cruising the Hudson, they have those memories too. And looking into Julia's eyes, her beautiful eyes and beautiful face, you can't help but know that whatever you've done, she's done it as well, a hell of a lot harder.

"Hey, you wanna see a trick?" calls out the prettiest of the tall black girls, in a tight-fitting corset barely containing breasts exploding volcanolike from its depths. "Watch." Men gather round in the gloom, clutching drinks and paper plates of soggy quiche and sweating lettuce. She bends over the buffet table, carefully pushing the cocktail sausages out of the way. She unfurls a paper napkin, and places it carefully on her behind, her butt curving deliciously into the topography of her lower back. She turns back to the buffet table, chin in hands, and winks cheekily. Suddenly a rip-roaring fart echoes in the light breeze, and the napkin lifts up, startled, before gently floating to the ground. There is a gasp of mutual admiration, then cheers and applause.

"Why you do this?" one says to me, and I look into his face and laugh, turn to Julia who's snorting a line of coke from the back of her hand, kiss her long and hard and tasteless on the mouth. Then we both laugh, and Julia asks me if I would like to be her standby partner for the sex show, which she does occasionally, when the modeling work isn't paying too well, now she's getting too old for bookings at the ripe old age of twenty-fucking-two.

"It's disgusting, this job," says the guy again, his English straying into the familiar Uruguayan lilt I know from having lived in Argentina. He looks at me, and I feel a twinge of something. Annoyance. "How do you do this and sleep at night?"

"I don't kiss, jerkoff," I say, and kiss him for the hell of it, and a breeze teases my thighs and between my legs, caressing where I'd been licked and scratched and poked . . . and I never managed to locate that G-string, some cocksucker was probably beating off to it right there and then. Another guy pulls my hand, leads me back into the darkened salon. *"Baila?"* he says, and we talk Spanish for a while as I dance, and he tells me they all work in a factory, he sold coke too, and the party was for the boss's son who is getting married, it was a tradition in Colombia, to throw a party for the workers, or some shit, and my mind was drifting off, my dress was drifting off, another dance, and it's only then that I realize his hand is between my legs, his fingers are prising me open, it hurt. "No," I whisper, and my eyes are wide, I can feel the whites showing, and in his black, black face I see the whites of his eyes, the room's empty save for those whites, those fucking orbits glittering in a dark universe *"Basta, pelotudo,"* I muttered, and I slap him, and he laughs a creepy laugh, like an old dog hacking its lungs up, and gives an awful shudder. It's time to leave.

In the dressing room we count the money, everyone pointedly ignoring the stall with an empty condom and a fizz of jism floating in the toilet from where some guy got lucky, some girl got dumb. Nine hundred bucks each for three hours work. In the limo we tease Igor, and laugh at Narissa, and watch Julia be sick because she ate a sandwich and she's worried about the calories, and he lets us out at Penn Station. I walk a few blocks with Lucy, the Southern girl, and we talk, exchange numbers, meld into the crowd, just two girls walking down Broadway together. Insignificant. You look at the people walking past, and they notice nothing. You're still the same person, and it's comforting, that anonymous reassurance. I feel happy because I made money. I don't feel anything else—shame or misery or disgust, the things you might think I'd be feeling at this point. In truth I don't. I block it out, because I need the money, and there's no safety net in life, save for that soft mattress of good, solid cash. In truth I feel nothing, because I've felt it all before, and it's useless—regret. I've felt it all before, in another time and another place, the same damned thing.

I call Lily to let her know I'd gotten home safe. I don't tell Raoul where I've been. He's not my boyfriend. I call my brother too, over on the West Coast with his wife and their kid. I make out it was easy, and it *was,* but not the kind of easy he thinks.

I stripped with detachment; I stripped always as Mimi. Like the rest of the girls, the faded sepia memory of the "first time" ever present as a peeling backdrop to our rotting stage show. I had fucked, been fucked, knew fucking—perhaps the only prerequisite, really, for the job. If I hadn't had Mimi I don't know if I could have done it, in all honesty. I need her, you see, and that need scares me. That she has become an indelible part of my existence scares me. I need her to corroborate who I am, the ghost behind the words, the words delineating only her, ignoring the parts where I was present. I could distinguish between the man who saw me as a whore, a bitch, a stripper, a sexualized creature distinct from the mother who gave birth to him, the wife who will bear his children, and the man who saw me as a mother, a wife, a friend, a lover. But could they, now, see the difference between me and Mimi?

Sex is different from love, people say. An obvious distinction, but one whose fallacies kept us sane. I think we all—men and women—have our dark sides, our mistakes, our lustful, out-of-control moments that lead to minor indiscretions, a kiss in the darkness, some fumbling, a gasp, a cry, regret. Sex workers, people like Mimi, like myself, were more honest about those indiscretions, and what they allowed us to achieve— ready cash. Instead of burrowing our sadness, it's written all over us in an ironic appropriation of our own shame, turning it into a shield that makes us strong enough to walk onto a boatful of fifty men and strip naked for them without crying over the loss of our innocence. It means that we can lick and kiss and curl our tongues into a stranger's most intimate crevices and shrug it off when we pick up our paycheck. It meant that we can erase our own existences under a silly faux name, a fictitious, fantastical existence, take the money offered us to compose a history to go along with the make-believe, package it up all pretty, sell it. We can even, in certain cases, go a little further, take the extra two hundred, lock ourselves into a toilet stall with a man whom we do not know, who panting and grunting and breathing thickly, removes a Trojan from its wrapper with trembling hands, pulls it rapidly over his cock, spits, rubs the shaft, slaps our face against the wall with a sharp thud so we gasp in pain as he thrusts urgently, deeply, roughly.

She calls me the next day. Lucy, the Southern girl, butterscotch and soft thighs and a neatly manicured pussy of one rectangular strip, shampooed daily, conditioned once a week. I invite her over to Brooklyn because she needs a place to stay, and I figured the band is so used to itinerants sleeping on moldy couches that they wouldn't notice a small girl curled up in the corner of the painting studio.

"So you have fun the other night? Igor's great, ain't he? Fucking love love *love* that dude. I e-mailed him from Georgia and he hooked me up straight."

The little dumpy black girl with the flaking back on the boat was all about abuse and cowering from the slaps. She wore those wounds like they were a scarlet letter, with reverent misery. Lucy, in contrast, was all sweet-smelling harvest hay and wet, sticky, rolling in the barn, and soft flesh that enveloped you like a murmur. Clean, safe.

"That white guy I was talking to. He gave me, like, a thousand bucks to stay with him all night. Didn't even take my dress off."

"You got lucky," I snort.

"Oh, I saw that floor show. Girl! Now *that* was funny. So, where you dancing? I gotta get a job afore school starts, I'm totally broke. My Daddy's paying my rent when school starts up but he ain't giving me shit now."

I crack open a beer and hand it to her.

"Oh no. I never drink. We weren't allowed to in Atlanta, so I just got used to it. You work at Foxy's?"

Another lie? I consider it. But there's too many lies around.

"Uh, yeah. As a sodding *waitress*. Can't you tell?"

Laughter, clean, pure laughter, siphoning through you like a hosedown of the soul. You think you're clean and good, and then you feel things you forgot long ago, and you realize you were never what you thought you were after all. You're still waiting for the burial, or the resurrection.

"*We-ell*, Igor and me was looking at your picture afore you showed up, and lemme tell you, you don't look like a stripper in that picture. But *girl*, now you pulling it off pretty damn well bitch!"

She collapses onto my bed and giggles again, high and irrelevant, sordid and cheap, a little wrong. I feel edgy now. Uncomfortable.

"So how come you have nowhere to stay?" I ask.

"I met this dude on the Internet, Eric. He's, like, an investment banker. So he put me up for a few days in this hotel downtown in the West Village until I could find my feet, get hooked up with an apartment and shit. So we went on a date the first night, but to be honest, he's not really my type. We had like a good time and all, ate some crab, then he ate me out for dessert, but I don't really like to be, like indebted to people, you know? Girl, you gotta Tampax I can use?"

She bustles out to use the bathroom. I believed the myths before I started working: *It's all about empowerment! Embracing our vaginas and exerting power over men!* The myth that replaced the other myth, the older one, the more accurate one: Strippers and porn stars and all those people in the business are stupid, abused, fucked-up whores with Daddy issues. Maybe they just wised up and saw where the money was. Maybe the whole world is all about sex now—sex and money—and these girls are the only ones not pretending. Maybe we're just as screwed up as we appear to be.

"So how did you get into stripping?" I ask when Lucy returns.

"I wanted to be a model when I was at college in Atlanta. So I got some pictures done and sent 'em to this agent. Big, fat white dude, Lenny. He grossed me out. You know when you get a bad feeling from people? I didn't like the way he looked at me. He kept telling me he'd get me bookings, that I was beautiful, all this kind of crap, but he didn't do *shit*. Then one day he asks me if I want to make money on the side 'cause I ain't doing so well with the modeling. So I was broke, and I didn't wanna ask my Daddy 'cause there's six kids in the family, you know? And he has enough to deal with, what with my brother being disabled and all, and he's so proud of me going to college I knew he'd give it to me when he couldn't afford it. Though he'd shoot me if he found out I did this shit. So anyway, I said yes. Turns out Lenny meant *escorting*. So he'd call me, gimme the name of a hotel, and I'd turn up and sometimes the guy would be OK, and most times the guy would be freaking *gross*. And it's not like you could choose. It ain't like in the freaking movies where the guys pay some bitch for the conversation, take them out for a four-course meal and the opera. I did it for a while, but he was taking a big cut of the money, and it didn't feel safe, so I left. He was real mad, kept calling me and saying he'd tell my family and shit if I didn't work for him no more. I just ignored him. Didn't say nothing. Didn't reply to the calls. Eventually he shut the fuck up. But then I ran outta money so I called him again and he hooked me up with a job in a whack shack. You know those places? Where a guy comes in and jerks off while you dance? It's kinda gross but the money's all right and they can't touch you, so it's OK. I kind of figured I could make more though, 'cause I was one of the better-looking girls, you know? So I left there and started working at Leopard's—you know, the stripclub?—in Atlanta. I *loved* Leopard's. Classy place. Nice clientele. Clean, no grinding, no touching—nothing like that. Guys would come in, take us into the private room for three to four hours, businessmen from New York, an' I always got chosen 'cause I was intelligent and could actually hold a goddamn conversation, not like some of these bitches, all blond hair (no offense, girl) and fake titties. I got real tits and I talk to the guys about politics and current affairs and all that shit, I ain't some dumb fucking bitch getting a guy into the private room by promising God knows what. Guys love the fact I got ambition and I'm getting the hell outta this business. That's how I like to dance. You talk to them and you make them wanna date you; you don't offer them a goddamn handjob for five freaking bucks. I remember one time these guys came in from school and just kept staring at me, trying to figure out how they knew me. It was so freaking funny, I used to take math with them and they didn't even recognize me onstage. *Love* that shit. I gave it up for the last few months of college, but when I got a place at NYU I figured I might as well come up here for the summer, make some cash afore I get my student loans. Plus I broke up with my boyfriend 'cause his parents didn't like him dating a black girl, and it kinda broke my heart, so I needed to get away from Atlanta. I can't *wait* to start at NYU, get a good job as a litigator, make some money, get away from this shit. I wanna go into litigation. So, it's OK if I stay for a week? I'll be real quiet. Maybe I can get a job in your club. And I'll help you with the audition."

We have fucked without guilt, without enjoyment, with pain and pleasure and the accompanying regrets.

She smiles at me blankly.

6

WHEN MIMI ABANDONS ME, her absence is like the absence of a lover, a Siamese twin, my heart limping on erratically without her presence to goad my pulse into a rhythm. In those briefer moments when *I* turn my back on *her*, my heart cleaves and hurls flip-flop as if I'd lost myself. I miss her, when she's gone.

I overheard another girl talking on the subway the other day, a civilian—you know, not a stripper. "So in front of the whole lecture theater the professor made her take her lab jacket off because it wasn't pressed, and all she had on underneath was a *bra*. All the girls in the class were *crying*." Oh, the shame! Hurt pride! Wounded, humiliated indignity! Shame, shame, *shame*. I feel for your exposure, all you virgin milkmaids of the world. I *feel* for it, really I do. But when it comes to pride you have to admit that I lost it better than you—much more, harder, faster, dirtier, in a more spectacular fashion than you can ever comprehend. My point is that stripping is an art, like anything, an art that one can learn. But the ability to be shameless, the ability to turn our shame into our pride—*that,* you've acquired well before you got onstage, with the knocks, the blows, the uppercuts, the scratches, and hair pullings. You either have it or you don't.

The rest of it—the coy glances, the immunity to sickly, stagnant breath, hard dicks, urgent hands, and sticky shame, the money hunger, the greed, the language, the predatory instinct—you have to learn. I had to learn.

Ole Hank was hustling the bitches like his life depended on it. The doors opened at twelve and the lustful wandered in, the bitches got primped up and the new waitress stood uneasily in the corner.

"How are you finding it?" I ask.

She looks at me with enormous eyes, like fucking Bambi or something.

"It don't pay so good. They said if we want more money we gotta go into the Champagne Room with a client. D'you do that?"

I shrug. "Have done."

"How d'you *get* guys in the Champagne Room?"

"You play on their minds and their cocks."

"Oh."

Pause.

"Whadda you *do* in there?"

"You dance."

Pause.

"You don't have to take your clothes off though, right?"

"No, you *do* have to take your clothes off, unless the guy knows beforehand he's paying four hundred bucks for a dry grind."

Pause.

Huge, liquid eyes. Whispers, "I feel kinda self-conscious about my body."

So don't do it baby. You gotta choice.

Two hours later Bambi's flirting like a fucking pro as Mimi eyes her from the corner, where she's holding a conversation with Mr. Cum-In-His-Pants, so named because he cums in his fucking pants all the time.

"What's your real name, Mimi?"

"Michelle."

"You're such a sweet girl. I can tell you're genuine because you look straight at me with those huge eyes of yours. You look kinda like Heather Graham."

One hand on your cock, the other on your credit card. Take it for what it is baby and stop deceiving yourself. It ain't nothing genuine, but the money's real enough. Mark the DJ wanders up, and he and Mr. Cum-In-His-Pants talk about their kidney stones. Did you know you have to *piss* those fuckers out? Well, neither did I, but fortunately for Mimi, this means Mr. Cum-In-His-Pants's thingy ain't working too darned good at the moment. Champagne Room? *But of course, sweetheart. Anything for you.* Hank's hustling the bitches like his life depended on it. Extra brownie points for Mimi, the quickest learner in all of Foxy's. Four weeks as a waitress and she's a fucking pro, in the non-pro sense of the word, if you get my meaning. I mean, she could be a dancer, cause she ain't serving drinks no more during those eight hour shifts. Hank hustles the bitches like his life depends on it, and enters the Champagne Room to call a time-out five minutes early when it looks like Mr. Cum-In-His-Pants's thingy may have made a miraculous recovery. Thanks Hank baby, I owe you one.

Mimi stumbles out and straight to the bar, where tequilas are lined up for the five o'clock watershed, courtesy of Mr.

High-Ranking UN Official from the good ole United Kingdom. Mr. UN is playing a dangerous game fucking with Mimi, but of course Mr. UN don't know this, and instead makes Mimi's life pretty fucking miserable, the middle-aged cunt. Forty-five, never been married, never said I love you, never known what it's like to wake up, curled around someone you care about. A heart too hard to ever be broken. You don't find the ones you fall in love with *here*. I drink two margaritas. It's enough. I turn around, and the lights are swirling pretty bad now to match my head, and Mr. Pedophile is standing next to me.

"Can you be a little girl? Can you be a little girl for me?"

"Honey, I'm twenty-six. Buy a fucking Cabbage Patch Kid if that's what you want."

The response don't go down too well with Mr. Pedophile, but Kim the manager gets the joke, and we laugh and laugh and laugh, and suddenly it's eight P.M., I'm standing outside the club, and the elastic around my ankle snaps, dollar bills floating down Broadway, dancing and twirling in the faint breeze of passing traffic. A guy stoops down and gathers them up for me. Mr. UN.

"Good *God*, girl. What the hell are you doing? You're drunk. Come with me."

He points to a nearby wine bar.

"Have you eaten?"

I shake my head no. You never see clients outside the club, but this place is close enough to feel safe. I know the bouncer.

Diet Coke, expensive Italian meats, dusky olive oil, crisp, fresh bread. Mr. UN regards me thoughtfully.

"*Bloody hell*. You look like you're about *twelve*."

Mr. Fucking UN, lives for his work, never made love, always fucked like a goddamned terrier. Trying to reach out, trying to be nice. But there's a reason why guys are forty-five and alone, and I saw that reason in the club. I down the last slurps of my Diet Coke, grab a piece of ciabatta to go, make my excuses, leave. I stand up, trip over the chair, fall down on my butt. A ripple of disgust? Dismay? Amusement? Anticipation? Hey, look guys, look at the high-ranking UN official with the twelve-year-old slut stripper, ain't it *cute?* Call the goddamn *New York Post!* Heads are shaking, Mimi steps straight into a cab downtown. Thirty minutes later, I'm sitting blankly watching a TV program I couldn't tell you the name of if I tried, and it's very strange, I'm just crying and crying and crying. Must be the tequilas, must be exhaustion. The walking, talking Mimi doll's batteries are running low, low, *low.*

Later, I sit in the kitchen with Raoul drinking tea, smoking cigarettes, and we both cry, and neither of us quite knows why.

I walk past the Men Who Hiss At You on the street on the walk to the subway the next morning. They smile sweetly at me. One of them calls out, "God bless you, baby."

God Bless You. Do I fucking look like I need *God* on top of all this shit?

I set the audition for the next week. It seems simple enough. Dance three songs onstage with two other dancers. First song, dress on. Second song, dress half off. Third song, dress off, down to G-string. End of third song, retrieve dress, wait for replacement, leave stage. This would be accomplished with finesse, with lackadaisical, flippant skill, with shamelessness.

I would adopt the bored, hard, devastating glare of one immune to indignation, of one whose pride was utterly incor-
ruptible, on account of already being utterly corrupted. It was
not the nudity, it was not the pornographic assault of a man's
stare, it was not a feeling of, maybe, sexual inadequacy that
plagued me. What divided me from the dancers now was the
stage. It was the fact I could not walk in heels. I could not apply makeup. I could not twirl around a pole. I looked like a
twelve-year-old girl, not a stripper.

Mafia Joe (who claims to have mafia connections) turns to
me with a smug grin on his lined, corporate face, one hand
planted firmly on Becky's ass, the other stroking a silicone tit.

"You auditionin', Mimi? You gotta stick to the drinks tray,
baby. You ain't the strippin' type. Not like Becky here. Tell you
what, lemme take you out for a drink after your shift and we
can talk about it. I don't have time now, gotta bottle booked."
He harrumphs, Becky's talons slide lingeringly on his knee,
and she glides away to check her butt for skid marks, gargle
with Listerine, have a quick cigarette, and bitch about Mafia
Joe, tight-assed bastard, never leaves a bloody tip and expects
to suckle on your titties like a newborn calf.

"Ah. You're taking *Becky* into the Champagne Room?" I
breathe innocently.

"Yup."

"That's great. That's *great*. She's been a little paranoid ever
since the sex-change op. I keep telling her she's all woman, but
the emotional repercussions are always hard to deal with."

Mafia Joe (who claims to have mafia connections) freezes.
Becky doesn't do so well today.

Poor Becky.

Lily takes me aside and presses her saline tits into my face. She's proud of those little puppies. But only her boyfriend gets to see them, oh yes. Only her boyfriend.

"Your friend auditioned today. Black girl."

"Lucy?"

"Yeah. She was hot. They said no though. They don't like having too many black girls. It's good that you're a blonde."

"Yeah."

"But it ain't enough. You're gonna need a lot of help if you wanna get hired as a dancer." She cracks her hot pink gum and presses those puppies, those curiously hard puppies, deeper into my face. "I heard what you said to Mafia Joe. You're funny. You're clever. But the other girls don't like that. Here's what you gotta do . . ."

Behind us Bambi whistles through her teeth at a Scandinavian tourist grinning crooked and sexless. You can tell he's squirming in his seat thinking about plunging his dick deep into her with a few slaps on her ample ass, a cry, a convulsive squirt of pleasure. For a quiet bitch scared to get her tits out last week, Bambi's a fucking hustler all right.

the ability to turn our shame into our pride

That bitch is a hustler.

"Oh my. That man is *damn* fine. I'm gonna be havin' me a piece o' *that* after my shift ends."

"He payin' for you to go to the Champagne Room?"

Bambi sniffs and flicks an acrylic ringlet from her eye, dislodging her wig slightly so that her pinned, slapped afro peeps out jauntily from beneath.

"No. We talked about it and he decided we should jus' hook up *after* work."

There is a ripple of disapproval through the ranks.

That damn bitch is givin' it out for free now. What hope is there for the rest of us, y'all?

Bambi sniffs indignantly.

"Shut the fuck up. I'm auditionin' next week with Mimi 'cause I'm sick of y'alls bullshit. There's money out there and youse just too damn shamed to go get it."

"I thought you were afraid of the Champagne Room," says Basia flatly, a flat voice to match her flat chest, flat personality, flat, ovulating, eggy breath.

Aishwarya, a Champagne Room regular who, it is rumored, has enormous nipples like dinner plates, which are the only thing that prevents her from quitting her job as a waitress and becoming a dancer, giggles.

"Is money baby. No one shy when money at stake."

West Fourth. Used to be Times Square, but Times Square got Giulianied. Gift-wrapped. Sugar-coated, candy-frosted with a thick layer of acid-inducing buttercream. Made up for White Trash America. The rules came in. No stripclubs within five hundred feet of schools, churches, day care centers, homes— unless 60 percent of the space was devoted to "non-adult activities" like watching sports, eating sushi, and playing pool. In America ogling titties is what makes you an adult, and you can have only 40 percent of your time and space for that. So, West Fourth. In the twenty-first century, West Fourth Street is where you go to buy your crotchless panties, your battery-operated devices, your see-thru plastic heels, your acrylic hair. We're in a store, attended by a titless goth child of the Marilyn Manson variety. "Love those heels," she drawls in Middle American. "I'd wear them to go to a club." She points to stripper heels that resemble a weapon from Hammer horror films, sharp, pointed, silver, deathly. Lily, Lucy, and Bambi inhale in awe. I have to tell you, I have my doubts about the new company I'm starting to keep. I really have my doubts.

"Mimi, you gotta get them. Girl, they *hot*."

Hot is a subjective term. *Hot* applies to breasts bulging like bursting carbuncles; hair so long you could wipe your ass with it. *Hot* refers to an iris papered over with plastic indigo coloring, rimmed with thick black kohl liner to whiten the yellow of bloodshot, coked-up eyes. Hot is plastic-fantastic, hair-free holes, feminine excretions exuding a Victoria's Secret stench. *Hot* is subjective, but subjectively, objectively, I am *not* hot. I take the shoes. The girls are enjoying this. They sense the waves of doubt exuding from my boyish pores and assuage me with G-strings, Lycra dresses, cosmetics, hair-removal products. I had the soul of a stripper but lacked the science. Later, much later, months afterward, I will sit in a different club in front of a female journalist, a microphone peeping surreptitiously from her bag. "Can *anyone* do this job, or do you think you have to be a particular type of person?" she'll ask. "Do you think it changes you, your perception of men?" And I will pause, as if I'd never heard these questions before, these clichéd questions I am asked a hundred times a week, these clichéd answers, unvarying, uninventive, unused, and blithely replaced by what they want to hear. "No, it doesn't change us," I'll say, and then stop, wondering whether to go further. *Because by the time we get on that stage we are already beyond redemption.* She'll call me up later, the journalist, tell me she thought about my response. "I wonder sometimes, if I could do it. Dancing," she'll say. "Because I've had that, you know, flawed past kind of thing. I've slept with a lot of guys, done some kinky shit. I think it'd be kind of . . . *sexy.*" My smile will be twisted. *Just because you like anal doesn't mean you're a stripper.* But I'll do the verbal equivalent of noncommittal mumblings, assent, soothing, letting her take what she wants from the situation without taking anything from me—and all the while she fails to realize that *this* is what makes you good at the job. Not the other thing.

On the subway Bambi grasps the shining pole in the middle of the compartment, lifts herself effortlessly off the ground, twirls around. "How'd you learn that?" Lily squeaks, crossing her arms over those puppies, those devastating puppies, those little babies For His Eyes Only. And Bambi just laughs. "A long train ride back to Harlem baby, two kids to feed and the survival instinct. Hooters ain't doing it for me, you know?" She looks at me. "You'd better start playing that *Rocky* soundtrack and wearing those heels. 'Cause you ain't walking like no stripper white girl. And you know it."

How do you get the skills? You watch. You watch and watch, like I did, like you're watching the program of the century, the grand finale to the meaning of life, the answer to every question you ever vaguely wanted to ask God, to find written in the Koran, to emerge from the murky depths of a meditation. You go home. You make friends with a stripper who moves into your apartment next to the kitty litter box and tells you exactly how much pressure to put where with what body part and when. You hang out with the biggest hustling Harlem bitch who walked the earth, and you observe how she narrows her eyes, glances at that pride, and throws it beneath the squealing brakes of the NQRW even as she puts a slender leg onstage, waves away the offer of assistance, and glances at me contemptuously, knowingly. You ask advice from Lily, whose pride, so tied up with those puppies, the LSATs, and that boyfriend, prevents her from stepping onstage, but who knows the industry, knows the men, knows, knows, knows what it is to be a woman—and knows, even more than I do, what it is to have secrets.

43°59'N 7°9'E

When the Australian's girlfriend came back I was with Jon-jon, but when Jon-jon went to sea I was back in the crewhouse, until Johnny Monaco stepped in. I knew him from The Blue Lady, smoking joints, drinking pints, selling tabs of ecstasy on the sly. He worked as a mate on a boat that sat in port all summer, allowing him ample access to extracurricular activities. We became friends, and then a bit more, because I was still waiting for a new job, and you need to have something to occupy your time. So I was with him, but he was with his girlfriend. He had managed to convince her to let me move into their apartment for a few days until I found a new job on a boat. She regarded me with suspicion. Rightly so. We would kiss and pet and fondle like schoolchildren whenever she was out of sight. One night, five days after moving in, we all went out, dropped E's, drank too much. It ended up, inevitably, with a shattering plunge into a foursome. But is it a foursome when two of the four are not interested in anyone else?

We lay on her bed, entwined in a long, drugged-up, laby-rinthine kiss that drew us further and further into a giggling vortex, head spinning, senses exploding. The girlfriend was on the sofa with the other man, the first mate on a luxury yacht. After a half hour or so she stood up naked, ran over to us, whispered anxiously in his ear, and the other man walked over and plucked me from the arms of my illicit lover, splayed me gently on the couch, and ignored my fretful, confused strug-gles. His knees pinned my thighs down and as I split in two I heard, distantly, the sound of her sobbing, and then I realized it wasn't sobbing, it was a cry of pleasure, and in the dark I saw the writhing of limbs white and perfect in the moonlight, and the only tears were coming from me as I braced against the sofa, too dead to be painful, too far gone to be inconvenient. *Sorry,* he whispered the next morning. *Have fun?*

Sex and guilt, this almost insanely perfect dialectic, are what feed me, clothe me, pay my rent, sustain my dreams of writing and living in America, what wake me with unease in the mid-dle of a carbolic night, a carbolic life. They say that compul-sive sexual activity, promiscuity if you like, depersonalizes sex, that one who indulges in such activity is a screw-up, an abused child, a fragment of dysfunction, a waif in need of salvation, a person from whom you should run far, far away.

I'd agree with that.

"I'm auditionin' today," announces Bambi to Pedro. He grunts disinterestedly and resumes eating Spaghetti Bolognese from a greasy foil plate. *"Puta,"* he mutters under his breath.

Ole Hank was hustling the bitches like his life depended on it. "Girls! You got a half hour! I want house fees now or I'm sendin' you home!" The doors opened at twelve and the lustful wandered in, the bitches were primped up, and a new waitress stood uneasily in the corner.

"How you finding it?" I ask. It's curiosity. I ask because I know how she's finding it. Like I found it. Like Bambi found it. It's a house of fucking horrors, but curiosity, money, and the pornography in our souls led us there, kept us standing holding that drinks tray, dropping that dress. She looks at me with enormous eyes.

"It don't pay so good. They said if you want money you have to go in the Champagne Room. How d'you get guys in the Champagne Room?"

"You flirt with them."

"Oh."

Pause.

"But whadda you have to *do* in there?"

"Dance."

Pause.

"Dance—you mean like those girls are dancing over there?"

I nod. Her eyes strain open as she entertains the notion, lets it seep in, reluctantly fondles it, passed from hand to hand, stops, pupils well up, obliterate the iris. Whispers, "I feel kinda *self-conscious* about my body."

"Mimi!" snaps Hank. "I'm puttin' you and Bambi onstage next. Grab a fuckin' shot from the bar. You'll need it."

"How d'you do this job?" asks the girl in wonder. "How'd you *learn*?"

"You just have it in you," I reply.

Hot, wet tang of tequila, the taste of bad sex and worse memories, fanny farts and premature ejaculators. The new girl stands in the waitress line next to Lily and Basia, alternating feet, looking bored. *I feel kinda self-conscious.* I've heard those words before. I think I said them once. Bambi too. We don't feel self-conscious, in truth we don't. Because no one's shy when money's involved.

"How long?" I ask Bambi, and nod to the girl. Bambi snorts. "When she has to pay the fucking rent, that's how long."

"Next song," Hank says.

"Next song," the DJ says over the Tannoy.

"Next song!" squeaks Lily, and Pedro slaps her ass for the hell of it, and why not, it's a nice ass.

Hot, wet tang of tequila, my hand on that brass pole. On that first dance you exist only for these dot-to-dots of sensory perception. From hand on pole to hand on dress, slip dress over head, switch hands. It's not the nudity, truly it's not. It's not the five bored, anonymous gazes, it's not the prickling heat, the first time you see your reflection staring back at you, no, no, *no*. Not the adrenaline, *certainly* not excitement—it's one P.M. on a Thursday afternoon. No. It's the relief maybe. The relief that Raoul isn't here, my parents can't see, Paula's safely tucked up on the council estate back in Wales. I'm alone, and no one knows what I'm doing, what I'm doing spectacularly, magnificently badly.

"You sucked," says Bambi pragmatically.

"Were you nervous?" asks Lily. "We thought you were nervous. You walked kinda funny and you never let go of the pole."

Dolores and Hank are talking as I go up to them, pink, damp, too concerned, too damned concerned about this fucking shitty job where we make money by not caring.

"You're hired," says Dolores. "Go make up a schedule with Hank." She returns to *Us Weekly* and a Baby Ruth bar chopped into a hundred tiny pieces to get past the gastric-bypass surgery safely. I'm like that. Chopped into a hundred pieces to make it through a tied and twisted, restricted, gut. Forbidden the luxury of a duodenum, my pieces slap directly, rudely into the jejunum. One piece, distinct from all the rest, is this new thing, this new person, this fetish creature, this commodity, this Mimi doll.

7

WE'RE ALL B-LIST IN THE CLUB. We're there because we're not A-list in our chosen careers, and to supplement that we paint in the cracks with heavy-duty stage makeup and clear plastic heels. Does it bother us? No. A few drinks, several Benjamins tucked in the garter, one or two compliments about our breasts/face/ass, and we've had one hell of a good day. B-list stripping sure beats B-list waitressing, or B-list bartending, or any other kind of B-list career within our "professional" bracket as—for the most part—illegals, mothers, and oversexed outsiders. Our customers? Yes, they too are B-list actors playing a part in a badly scripted daytime-TV soap that would probably be X-rated if it was ever released. Not that they know all this of course. They always believe that we find them attractive, that they're number one, that they're Tom Cruise in this low-budget burlesque comedy played out relentlessly every day between the hours of noon and eight P.M.

I'm loving this job.

Mr. Tom Cruise comes from Dallas, and his graying tash hangs limply in sharp contrast to the veritable forest of spider's legs sprouting gaily from his nostrils. He exudes the stench of gin, cigarettes, and the pungent, noxious aroma of old-man-divorced-no-kids. I am stuck onstage, while a new English

dancer from Stringfellows (on a highly illegal "working vacation" with two Eastern European friends) has a tantrum at the
bar, thinking, mistakenly, that she is important, and that anyone gives a fuck.

"'Ow the fack am I meant to darnce if I can't bloody eat?
When is my food ready? *Oi!* Bartenda! I'm *talkin'* to you!"

Lolling listlessly onstage for my fourth song, Mark the little
fat DJ mimes me a long, intricate story about his weekend
from the DJ booth. Lily stands by the door with Basia, sour
and acidic. I don't talk to them much anymore, not since the
audition. We're too busy prowling, Bambi and I. Prowling as
we sit at the throne of the bar in our polyester mantles, our
aura of fake tan and baby oil, our smiles, alligator smiles, croc-
odile tears, the emotions of a *Sarcosuchus imperator.* Mr. Tom
Cruise approaches the stage, waves a twenty-dollar bill at me,
and smiles sympathetically.

"Doing overtime up there?"

"Looks like it."

The ugly Russian girl takes pity and replaces me onstage.
Bambi's sitting at the back of the bar with Mafia Joe. It's one
of those days, those languid, early afternoon days when the
heat outside is in stark contrast to the icy chill of the AC blasting the ten girls who bothered to show up for work only because they couldn't get a lift to the Jersey shore. I approach
Mr. Tom Cruise and am shortly in the midst of an erotic table
dance. Next to me a girl sits back on her haunches, her ass
plopped into a guy's crotch, her eyes gazing fixedly, bored into
the distance as he groans softly behind her. Her vermilion
mouth stretches wide into a yawn. Over in Camp Mimi, he
seems to be into it, Mr. Tom Cruise, though he doesn't look

like he has money. Black slacks, the plaid shirt, no tie, no signs of corporate wealth. I ask him anyway, for the hell of it, the token question, "Wanna get a private room?"

And he nods. "Sure."

Jeeeesus. 1:30 P.M. This is my day. I *am* the star of this B-List enterprise, this low-budget movie. And Mr. Tom Cruise is, paternally, asking me what kind of champagne I would prefer, Veuve Clicquot or Cristal? Each costs over a grand. Hey, let's get both! And one hour stretches into three . . .

Mr. Tom Cruise is paying for the act. He knows this, yet pretends not to. He's paying for this B-List girl, Mimi in New York, to act like she's into him, and for fifteen hundred bucks . . . Hey, that's certainly possible. Mr. Old-Man-Divorced-No-Kids is funding his own movie right now, casting himself in the central role, emerging from his chrysalis of "corporate lawyer just stepped off the plane and dressed like a hick" and becoming "Mr. Tom Cruise entertaining Alexis Carrington Colby" at immense distress to his disposable income. I just ride with it, pretend to be the A-list bitch he thinks he's getting, although we all know if he was capable of getting any, he certainly wouldn't be seeking out *my* services.

I emerge buzzing from the Champagne Room three hours later. Hank the manager grabs me before I can sneak into the cockroach-infested stairwell and retrieve the half-smoked Parliament I left there three hours previously. Hank's one of the nicer managers. Likes to pet you, doesn't mind shooting the shit occasionally. Of course your popularity with the managers is proportionate to the amount of money you're squeezing out of the clients. Today I have a smiley face and five gold stars.

"Hey doll, you wanna earn money?"

I nod.

"Go see dat guy wid a leather jacket on gettin' a massage. Say you recognized him from *Law & Order*. He'll love you for it. B-list, you know?"

I'm a B-Lister pretending to a B-Lister we're A-listers.

"Oh Mimi, you're cute, you know that? So what episode you see me in? Was I *good*?"

Kristina, the masseuse, pummels listlessly at his shoulder blades, rolls her eyes, helps herself to Mr. *L&O*'s Jack Daniels, and turns the conversation back to a more interesting topic—herself. Mr. *Law & Order loves* Kristina, who is, in actual fact and contrary to all appearances, not just a twentysomething flat-chested New Yorker, but a top model for L'Oréal and a veteran of over forty movies. But the soundtrack to *this* movie, *this* bad TV drama, is slowing down now, switching off, because it's 7:30 P.M. and the night girls are starting to swoop onto the floor with their fresh glitter sparkling smugly in contrast to our tawdry sequined skin. Slickly oiled breasts eclipse sagging cleavages, and Mr. *Law & Order* asks for my number as his gaze already starts to wander over the shoulder.

I'm in a good mood. Slip out onto the street, a wad of cash thudding against my thigh. Stifling, thick with the stench of burned rubber, the screech of tires, meandering tourists in baggy shorts, businessmen, a thick, damp smog from the June heat. The other dancers, the ones I don't speak to, drift away down Broadway. I stop at the local deli, order pastrami on rye, mustard. A rich corporate dude is in there with a bum, a young black guy, about thirty years old. I watch them without pretending not to, adopting that unashamed New Yorker stare. He walks up to the counter, orders the same as me, pastrami, rye, mustard, lettuce, tomato. Ah. Just buying him a sandwich. He glances around genially as if expecting applause. Just buying him a sandwich, playing the role of the guy who cares, the CEO who's at one with the people, massaging his ego with a token act of beneficence. He looks at me, then back at the little Chinese man behind the counter. "I'm paying for her sandwich too," he says, and smiles at me with a Sweet 'N Low smile, saccharine, bitter, and carcinogenic. He's Humbert Humbert and I'm Lolita, in a Snoopy T-shirt aged 5–6 and too-big jeans. I'm only just old enough to have gotten my period, dressed up in Mommy's makeup, clutching my fucking dimes (earned by sucking Daddy's dick) for a trip to the store to purchase some baby formula for my seven little siblings in Hell's Kitchen. He's loving the drama, this guy trying to save the scum of New York. I let him pay for the sandwich, let him have his badly scripted moment, swirl it around in his mouth, revel in the obnoxious taste of it.

"Whadda you do, baby?"

"I write."

"No, come on—lookin' like that. Whadda you do?"

No answer.

Hollow laugh.

"Whadda you do?"

"I write."

I turn to leave.

"Hey! I thought we were gonna get coffee!"

I turn back, still in the role, my B-list one-liner.

"No thanks, 'baby.' Cheers for the sandwich."

He stops and stares. I know even though I'm walking away.

I feel it. I couldn't help smiling, the comforting scratch of money prickling against my thighs.

"Who *are* you?" he calls after me.

"Baby, I'm the Queen."

The Queen of it all, the star of my little B-list life, my little B-list existence, re-created in words just begging to be made into a movie. Paramount, you reading this?

Because tomorrow, for sure, I'll reprise the role.

Aborted from being me for visa purposes, I write as Mimi, anonymous and sly, and yet every bit myself, more so, something poisonous and rich released from being me-me, so that now I can write like I never could before. I'm loving it. Loving, for the first time in my life, easy cash, waking up every morning, drunk and foggy, to find myself sleeping in large-denomination bills from where I forgot to remove the cash strapped around my thighs. It's easy. It's innocuous, the shots downed, drugs snorted, crotches ground down to dust as their jaws drop lower *Geez, how the fuck you do that* and me and Bambi just laugh, slap hands, don't ever let the roles slip until we're safely tucked up in bed, and even then it only surfaces for that three-hour interval between waking and stripping, sufficient hours to fight back the nausea, the headache, the hangover, step on the treadmill, shower, paint your face back on, go back to the club, slip into the dressing room with the other girls, do it all over again . . .

We're sitting at the bar. We're always sitting at the bar. Makes us feel safe, the ritual of one white wine, two vodka shots, three skinny cigarettes, and a chewing gum before we hit the floor. Bet's telling us about her abortion. She was on the pill, had used a condom, and *still* managed to get knocked up. She was worried the abortion wouldn't work either. It would be born in the Champagne Room with 666 tattooed on its head and roaring in tongues for the teat. Bulgarian Natasha shudders and crosses her legs. Our job was mutagenic, toxigenic, carcinogenic, to fertility. We did not menstruate and children were deleted from our wombs with startling efficiency, or else lay at home cared for by grandparents as Mom became sour and shrunken from the job of providing. Julie the bartender sits down. Used to be a dancer, quit because she got too old. She looks down a skinny, badly sculpted nose at us and pushes her boobs back into their too-tight brassiere. "Are you girls, like, best friends?" She motions to Bambi and me. We shrug and down our vodka shots. In the grand scheme of the club, in the hierarchy of bitches, we are best friends—Bambi and I—despite the fact that after eight weeks of working together, I still don't know her real name. But *in* the club, we work in unison, an efficient bitch-grinding machine, leaping on the unsuspecting, the powers of two pairs of breasts, two smooth asses—one white, one black—a potent combination, devastating for the credit card. We work that bitch (yo'), pump the client of all he has. We are the bitches, yes—and possibly I am more of a bitch than Bambi, for she, at least, seems genuinely to like me. But when it comes down to it, the bitch of the day is whomever we choose to assiduously milk dry of money.

"You tried that guy?"

"No. He don't like black girls."

"You always say that."

"Baby it's true! Somma these bitches ain't never seen a fuckin' black girl before. I said to this one guy, 'You ain't never touched a black girl before have you?' And I was right. He hadn't. Fuckin' tourists."

They rarely see past the smooth asses, brimming like ripe plums from tiny G-strings, the plump, firm saline breasts, the kohl-rimmed eyes fringed by stick-on eyelashes. Rarely believe us if they do ask us anything about ourselves. *Oh yes, I have a degree from Cambridge. I'm twenty-six, I'm a writer.* Their eyes glaze over, or they laugh disbelievingly, because you're just another bitch workin' it, and after all, they're here for the tits and the ass, the attention, the fake caresses, the soft sigh of false desire. *Oh, say dat again in your accent doll. Dat's so fuckin' hot, dat accent.* It's not about you. It's about them. Or so they believe.

Work Dat Bitch, Yo'!

There's something dark, twisted, and insidious in all of us, working the devil (dressed in Brooks Brothers) today, every day, at noon walking down those stairs into the club with no windows, a midnight starting after 11:59 A.M., plunging our befuddled money-grabbing brains into confusion with every replay of the movie reel. We're reveling in the power of our beauty and our youth, collating the stories to proudly tell our grandchildren when we're addled and wrinkled, our breasts have sagged, our teeth stained yellow, our eyes milky and dimmed. We'll get out the photos then, show them pictures of ourselves parading round the dressing room on lingerie night, posing in fake furs for Pimps n' Ho's evening, the managers fondly draped around us, as if our beauty and youth could rub off on them too. In some impossible transformation we become whoever we want to be in this club, leave our degrees and our intelligence and our discretion behind, wallow in the dancing, the glitz, the glamour, the celebrities, the endless Cristal poured down our throats, so decadent we could bathe in it.

Go on girl . . .

When the film reel draws to a close, we're drunk and giggling. Tip-out the House Mom, the old, wrinkled, sour Italian woman in the dressing room who always scowls at me. We tip-out the DJ, short and squat with his Hawaiian shirt, his ready grin, slippery hands, Hitler mustache that he tries to brush, laughing, against our mouths. We tip-out the managers, and they hug us, pet us, kiss us, slip a hand on the waist, the ass, and we lean in close against their boners like we're taught to.

"You OK, *guapa?*" grunts Pedro the bouncer, narrowing his eyes, sunk deep within folds of wibbling flesh, enormous muscles slathered over with a generous dash of fat.

"Yeah," I smile.

It made me feel safe, that question. *You OK?* Yeah, yeah sure, I'm OK. I'm doing OK. I'm surviving. More than anyone else would do in the same situation. I'm doing it on my own. I'm independent, getting there, proud. It makes me feel safe, that question. Though safe from *what*, I reason. Because the glitz, the show, the men, the money, the film played out relentlessly day after day—it's comforting in its familiarity, in its very fakeness, its self-mocking hyperbole, its imperfect B-list sham quality. And that's the thing—something that isn't real can't ever hurt you. You *are* safe.

". . . and then I'd lick you from here to here, and then I'd kiss your pussy, and then I'd slide into you, harder and harder . . ."

(Gasp, pause, lights cigarette, looks at me.)

"Tell me your fantasies, Mimi. Tell me what you'd do with my dick."

Always a question that stumps me. I am not, verbally, the most articulate of people, plus I have a slight problem with the exact realm of impossible fantasy this kind of talk leads one to. I don't think my mental powers are sufficiently strong enough to be able to envision this most impossible of situations—the idea that I would *ever* actually lower myself to be found in bed with someone *quite* so grotesque as Mr. Accountant.

"Erm. Let's see. I dunno. I'd erm, I'd make you play with yourself, then I'd probably make a cup of tea and have a cigarette while you jerk off on your own."

I disappear for another "restroom break" while Mr. Accountant mulls over my erotic response. Twelve hundred dollars and this is what Mr. A. gets for his money. Two flat Diet Cokes, a bottle of pinot grigio and a superior level of sarcasm, coupled with a constantly peeing English girl for 120 minutes of quality time. I sit in the restroom and talk to the attendant, a middle-aged black lady from the Bronx, sipping vodka neat out of a Poland Spring bottle. The girls flutter in and out. Busy afternoon. I leave the bathroom and bump into Bambi. The club's filling up. "You OK baby?" She's obviously distracted, looking around with the look of the hustler. I nod, sip some of her wine. "He a groper? Just masturbate. They love that shit.

Make him watch." She's gone. Twenty-three minutes to go. Pedro's at the front desk, talking to a manager before he goes on the door again. He grins at me sympathetically. He's a good guy, Pedro. Not as dumb as he looks. Sometimes, on a slow day, we'll order in from the deli, sit at the bar, ignore the old regulars sneaking in for their favorite girls, drink coffee, talk, laugh. Was going to school. Left after flunking because he had a kid too early. Lost his scholarship. Abandoned his dreams. But he hasn't extinguished it all. I could see there was something stirring inside him, waiting to get out, just biding its time beneath the big, black, mean exterior, the constant scowl.

Fuck, gotta stop thinking so much. Not drunk today. I can do this. Alcohol makes it a lot easier. Hank winks at me and swaggers past, steering a potential customer into the backrooms with his salesman patter, playing up the Guido-speak— "You see anudda girl dis fuckin' hot in da club? Take her in da back! I'll give you a special price . . ."

I reenter the Champagne Room.

"So Mimi, tell me what I'd do with my dick while you were making tea and having a cigarette . . ."

Wine, grab, drink, drink hard, drink fast, drink as if each swallow takes a bite of time, sharp incisors ripping soft flesh, but hard to swallow. They all say that don't they? Hard to swallow.

Time's up. Back to The Emerald City, as Bambi calls it. "We're in Oz now baby," she'll whisper, then lick her pinkie finger and gently trace the outline of her erect nipple with exaggerated gasps while a client squirms in horrified, aroused fascination. The thick, stale smell of old man crawls in my throat like a wet, feral cat, breathe, breathe cold AC crackling in lungs like dry ice, back among the young and the beautiful again. In the corner a big corporate party has arrived fresh from the office, and the girls line up, giggling and obedient, to dance for them. Not drunk enough. I'm not drunk and high enough to hustle effectively, exude that undeniable whiff of supreme confidence mixed with cheap perfume, not take no for an answer.

I am heading toward the bar when I see the guy in the corner.

Loners. If they have the look of the masturbator they're going to be lucrative clients, but you need a higher level of tolerance than I currently have. This one looks innocuous though. Young. Ruffled blond hair. Strong jaw. Blue eyes. Slightly confused, like he doesn't quite know where he is, what he should be doing. This one looks like a stripclub rookie, like he'll be keeping his hands to himself, like he'll get a hard-on if you give him a look. He's dressed expensively, but thrown together all wrong. He has money, but he doesn't have a woman, that much is for sure. Hank smiles and winks as I walk over quickly. It is a seamless operation. Smooth dress over ass, slide neatly onto the arm of chair, successfully block view of Chanel gyrating gracefully onstage.

"Hey."

He looks up, blinks.

"Hello."

The *vowels*—this guy went to Eton, or Harrow, or some damned place. I can hear it even through the pounding of house music, the gasps of girls, the chinking of glasses, the almost imperceptible rustle of ass against stiff cock.

"You're English."

He musters a comeback. "So are you."

"Yes!" I smile inanely and shuffle into his view again before he can spot the twenty dancers with monstrous silicone boobs ruthlessly working the room and attacking their prey—men in suits. "And you went to Eton, right?"

He blinks, confused. "How the *hell* did you know that?"

We know, we all know. We learn to recognize when they're married, when they're lonely, when they're divorced, when they're new parents, when they're rich and successful, when they're merely pretending to be. This job imbues you with a kind of sixth sense for mankind in all its varying forms—of which, when you're talking about the narrow margin of mankind who frequent titty bars, there are really only about four basic types:

1. Saviours
2. Sex Gods
3. Perverts
4. Rich fuckers

Let's not discriminate, let's not be reductive. Most clients are all these, rolled into one indefinable, belching, drunken, horny, brown-paper package of second-class USPS. It doesn't take much more conversation before I'm slipping off my tasteful polyester sky-blue number bedazzled with plastic jewels and pressing my knee into his cock, my breasts against his face, maintaining that miniscule distance, that all-important distance. I'm giddy suddenly, comparing it to the first dance I ever did, four weeks previously, hamstrings stretched taut and screaming as I crouched and sweated and nearly cried with the physical endurance of holding such intense proximity without touching the man who'd tucked a twenty into my garter with lust-filled care. And now. It's like cleaning my teeth.

He surprises me out of my reverie by suddenly running his hands gently up my thighs, and murmuring with a slightly startled look as if he surprised even himself—

"Come out for dinner with me. I'll take you somewhere nice."

I turn around and gently slip away from him, grind him gently, with detachment, bored, disappointed. *Nice.* Huh. I don't reply to his request. They always ask this. *Will you come on a date with me? Will you? Please? Do you like me? Really? Or are you just trying to get more money from me? Will you come on a date with me?*

Can't, I'll whisper back. *Tonight I have a date with Mr. Benjamin Franklin.*

"What do you do outside the club, Mimi?"

I laugh, shift slightly to avoid a drunken stripper about to launch herself over my clear plastic heels, and gaze out unseeing across the mass of naked, writhing, toned, slithering bodies melded onto men in suits, fresh from their day at the office.

"I write."

I wait for the snigger of disbelief as I turn back around and lower myself directly onto his body, so I can feel his heart beating against my chest. His hands slip up to my breasts and cup them, and before I can pull away he looks at me, oddly sad, aroused, curious. A quiver of something unfamiliar rustles inside me. Then I do a very, very strange thing. Something which is completely, utterly taboo in a place which functions entirely on illusion, which considers sex as nothing more than a transaction. *There's no touching, you see?*

I kiss him.

I finish the dance, gather my twenties, rush away from a confused-looking Eton, when a girl I don't know grabs my arm and spins me around angrily.

"What the fuck are you doing? Don't let guys touch you on the floor. Don't *kiss* 'em. Save it for the Champagne Room. You start doing that shit you'll get fired."

Hank walks over.

"Mimi, doll, I don't want you doin' dat shit on the floor. You hear?"

I stutter out an apology.

"No fuckin' apologies! The other Champagne host Kate wants a word wid you."

I drag myself into the tiny dressing room. Kate looks at me in disgust over her old-lady secretary glasses and frizzy brown hair. The House Mom, huge and resplendent and immovable, tuts loudly and resumes knitting. Knitting was a new craze among the girls. Everyone was knitting. The ugly Russian girl was crocheting G-strings to sell to the other girls. The tiny skinny dark girl was making a jacket for her dog. The House Mom seemed to be knitting for the hell of it, for a break from *Us Weekly* and *People* magazine and naked girls whining for tampons and eyeliner. Kate lifts a decaying hand up to her mouth and places a Tootsie Roll on her tongue, which she proceeds to grind slowly in her jaws like a cow chewing cud. Apparently she's an actress. She'd make a fucking fortune in snuff movies, that's for sure. The dressing room is buzzing with girls fixing their hair and makeup, gossiping and laughing drunkenly. I glance at the clock. A half hour to go. In the background I hear a conversation between Diamond and Desire, two of the older dancers from the Bronx.

"I tell y'all about that fuckin' new girl?"

"No, what happened?"

"So Hank makes me go and fuckin' apologize for tellin' that bitch to kiss my ass. You know what she did? Saturday night, I enter the restroom. She's in there, door wide open, takin' a shit, and it stinks. Fuckin' stinks. So I tell her to close the door and she ignores me. So I tell her again. Nothin'. So I go on in there and tell that bitch she gotta fuckin' change her attitude. I don't see why that wrong. I can't have bitches treatin' me like that, givin' me no respect. I don't wanna smell no fuckin' shit when I go in the restroom, you know?"

"Oh honey that's *terrible*."

Kate fixes me with her snuff-movie stare.

"Mimi, we've had complaints about you fingering yourself in front of guys, sticking your finger *up places it shouldn't go,* moving your G-string aside and showing guys—your *pussy*."

She whispers the last word as if the girl standing next to her currently examining her anus in great detail for signs of excrement might take great offense in the unanatomical name for one's vagina. I sigh and attempt a defense.

"Look, you know that's bullshit. Some fucking bitch is making that shit up because I'm making money. You know I don't do that shit."

Snuff-movie stare again.

"Look Mimi. You're treading a thin line. We don't tolerate that kind of behavior here."

I act penitent, but she sends me into solitary confinement in the corner of the dressing room for a little "time-out" and reflection upon my numerous sins, with the implication that I must, at the end of thirty minutes, demonstrate some obvious signs of extreme and humble repentance. I pick up the House Mom's copy of *Us Weekly* and curl up next to the lockers and a spangly G-string bearing the remnants of someone's vicious yeast infection encrusted across the gusset.

"Hey. *HEY!*"

I'm on the street letting the blissful taste of a cigarette trickle down my throat and cling to my bronchioles.

"Hey Mimi!"

Pedro huffs up to Bambi, Lily, and me, scowls, sweat dripping off his brow from the humid darkness of the city nearing a heat record–breaking summer. Bambi raises an eyebrow. "Don't let 'em get you down Mimi. You made money tonight, right? Fuck 'em. He was hot. You did nothing wrong. I'm going out with some of the girls. You coming?"

I shake my head no. I still don't go out with the other girls, only Lily occasionally, but she's so busy studying for her LSATs that she doesn't go out much either. Pedro scowls after Bambi.

"Don't like that fuckin' girl. Hey listen. The guys was laughin' at you earlier. Sayin' you was one of the girls who does shit in the Champagne Room. Mind tellin' me what's goin' on?"

"It's none of your business!"

He looks at me and his face, big and ugly, softens.

"Hey listen Mimi. I like you. I know you got more in you than this. It's just a temporary thing, right? Until you get your feet back on the ground. Go back to school, buy that apartment, get that job—whatever the fuck you wanna do with the money. Don't go makin' out with these assholes, OK? They just see you as a walkin' fuckin' vagina. I'm just tellin' you. It's a job. You gotta stay in control."

My head is banging, and whether it's the heat or the drink I just want to go home, back to Brooklyn, far from all this Midtown shit, far from where the boundaries between acceptable behavior are blurred by dollar bills fluttering gently onto a stage, those whispered words we're never allowed to use in the club, *hooker, slut, ho*. "Am I a hooker?" one of the girls had asked me once as we sat at the bar and sipped martinis. "This guy gave me a thousand bucks to go out with him after work and hang out in Crobar. We made out. But I only went 'cause he gave me the money." Hooker, ho, slut, stripper— the same thing in most people's eyes. A kiss in a bar is forgivable, but a kiss in a stripclub makes you a ho by virtue of its price. Am I a hooker? Who gives a fuck? I'm Mimi, is that the same thing? A name detaching me from my family, friends, the achievements of twenty-six years of living, which wasn't, it feels, so much. I shake my head, avoid Pedro's disturbingly paternal gaze, hail a cab, weave my way through people pouring out of offices, shops, Broadway shows, diners, bars—the normal bars. All the places without naked chicks, tits-and-ass, twenty-buck dances and a little bit of boob. But when it comes down to it, about the same things. Money and Sex. I step in the cab. The driver, a heavy, graying Russian guy, eyes me with interest.

"Is quiet?" he asks, nodding at the door of the club and pulling out onto Broadway, narrowly avoiding a shuffling bum. I shrug into the rear-view mirror, catching his eyes, black, deepset into folds of wrinkled brown flesh. We retreat into comfortable silence. Suddenly Ole Vladimir starts up again.

"You are not American? I can tell you are not American. You know why? You are nice. New York women are not nice. They are mean, they are like Rocky. You know, Rocky the boxer?"

"Ahuh."

"Not nice, these women. I am divorce. I am divorce for three years. But I do not want marry, because New York women, they are not nice. You know parry?"

"No."

"Parry happen in Brighton Beach. Five women, five men. There is vodka, there is much fun. Maybe two girl Russian, two girl Japanese, one girl Dominican. Is good money, is fun, women enjoy parry. I enjoy parry. I can take you to parry. I will pay you."

The cab crosses the Williamsburg Bridge, turns right at Peter Luger's, the famous steak house, delves into the depths of Little Poland and the shitty loft apartment.

"I'm getting off here, thanks sweetie."

"I give you my number so we parry?"

The door shuts with a bang.

Upstairs, the loft oozes waves of baked, stifling heat, the aroma of ammonia and kitty crap. The musicians were out, leaving a pile of ancient frying pans engrained with burned egg festering in the bowels of the greasy sink, spilling out in burps of dirty cups, filthy spoons, stained bowls scattered over the kitchen table, even the sofa. Raoul was next door, prowling like a prairie dog, sniffing out my sin, ready to rip flesh from my carcass. Lucy was out working in a club called Privilege on the West Side. There's a letter from USCIS. "We cannot approve your visa application until you show us sufficient evidence of funds to support your presence in the States." I throw it in the trash, shut the door. Retrieve the bills from around my thigh—pathetic, two hundred bucks today, and a Thursday at that, usually the most lucrative in Manhattan—scrub the streaks from my face in a sink swimming with long, dark hairs and wads of hardened toothpaste, gulped down lurid blue Gatorade to avoid the hangover. I crawl into bed, music whirling in my head, the eyes of that Eton guy, the slightly salty taste of his lips. I'd forgotten what it was like to kiss a man. I fall asleep almost immediately, yet it's a disturbed sleep, a sleep I suffer alone, pickled by the vulgar heat, wafting in relentlessly through the hole in my window where the AC unit had been stolen by a desperate hipster.

Two days later. E-mail.

> Mimi, Well, on the assumption that you
> are who I think you are? I just started
> reading your articles an hour ago. I feel
> ashamed though, that maybe you didn't
> mean to have someone you met at work
> googling you. Well, slightly ashamed.
> That's a British fucking upbringing for
> you. You danced for me on Thursday at
> around 7.30pm, I was the handsome devil
> with the English accent. You refused an
> invitation for dinner but suggested that
> I come back. I can remember you being
> Welsh, 23 (haha), a journalist, having

trouble with your visa, and writing
articles for the Village Voice. Anyway, I
came by the club last night, but feeling
like a foolish stalker staring at you
working the customers, I took a dance for
something to do and left afterwards. With
my plans frustrated I found the Village
Voice website and did a search for 'Mimi'
which got me to an article about
'Immigration' and even my MS Word knew
the author was you. (Please remember how
easily this can be done if you intend to
protect your identity at work) I don't
plan on going back to your club. I go to
stripclubs about once every 2 years
either with friends for a laugh or, when
I've been without a girlfriend for too
long and fear forgetting the sights,
smell and feel of a woman. More than that
and it's hard to ignore how depressing
the whole thing is. Drop me an email if
you want to hang out sometime. 'Eton'

Perhaps we are all of us, by nature, dichotomous, and it's only
through circumstance, desperation, or innate stupidity that the
other person, that bold, obscene stranger, the Mimi in all of us,
can emerge. I look on curiously, a little admiringly, a sharp in-
take of breath as Mimi coolly taps out a single-word response.

OK.

8

First song, dress on

I MEET ETON for dinner in a Japanese restaurant off Columbus Circle. I want the Kobe steak, but it's ninety bucks a pop, and I don't want to come across as a gold digger. Eton has gold to dig. His family owns an island, a shipping empire, an estate to rival the Queen's. I tell him my name is Mimi.

"No, what's your *real* name?"

Everyone wants a piece of me, a little bit of chili to spice up their lives—until it starts to sting.

"Michelle."

We go back to his apartment. I watch him, expecting the pounce. I watch him, expecting the slap. I like him, but still, I expect it, and I'm tired, and nothing is for free, and it had been an expensive dinner even without the Kobe steak. I watch him. I recognize my watching. It's a class thing, a poverty thing, a *need* thing. I saw a little girl on the subway today, flanked by two huge slabs of Mexican woman. Her mom grasped a box of M&M's tightly. The little girl stood with candy stuffed in her sticky fat hand, and watched, and watched. She watched like a hustler. Every time those doors opened she examined the crowd. She didn't approach just anyone, but when she saw what she was looking for, she darted. She chose women mainly; ethnic women over forty, and kids in baggy pants and caps. She avoided whites, men, and hipsters. Her mother and her grandmother sat immovable, immense mollusks of women, unsmiling, sluggish, and severe, an impressive wallop lurking in those meaty forearms. I knew if I approached her, for a tiny moment there would be that hesitation, a loss of poise, suspicion, confusion. The other Caucasian did it for me. "Honey, how come you're not in school?" The girl's face slammed shut like a clam. They got off at the next stop.

I'm waiting for the slap, the pounce, the question. Does Eton want to be Saviour or Sex God?.

The question comes, after I tell him my story, but it's not the question I expect.

"Would you like me to lend you the money for the visa application?"

21°28'N 27° 23'W

La Bella. The deck drained all moisture from our feet. We did not set foot on any other surface for four weeks, the sensation of that smooth, baked teak sanding our soles and rendering them numb. The Captain's feet looked babylike, soft and clean, but he could have run over hot coals if he'd wanted. It was midday, and we weren't long into the journey, maybe five days from Las Palmas, and the temperature had crept up until our throats shrieked for moisture and our mouths opened, closed, like guppies, swallowing brine air that shattered into salt crystals as it hit our tongues. Shammy the deckhand was below in the cabin, writing the logbook in his careful, puppyish script, and the other two were asleep. The Captain wanted to talk. He told me he'd fallen in love when he was seventeen and she was nineteen. They'd saved their money, moved to the West Indies, bought a scrap of a boat, a tiny thing called *Blondie*, and started to fix it up. It took seven years. Then they left, set sail for Panama. They sailed for two years, but halfway through she'd flown back to England, leaving him in New Zealand. They wobbled uncertainly over long-distance calls and the obligation of a mutual history, and then they found each other again in South Africa, but this time, something had broken. They took the boat back to Tortola, and she returned to England to have his baby, and they were, to all intents and purposes, a couple. Eighteen years had passed since they fell in love. He was thirty-five and she was thirty-seven. He lived on the boat permanently now. She lived in England with the baby. He tried to describe what it was. I don't think it was love, but I could see that it might have been, once, before things grew too tired and familiar, like the soles of our feet, numbed to stimuli.

"You ever fallen in love Mimi?" he asked, and I couldn't see his eyes through the lenses, but his mouth turned down, and he was still, and it was unusual to ever see the Captain still. He grinned before I answered, not that I had an answer for him, but perhaps the look in my eyes was enough. "People like you'n me, vagrants and gypsies, no place for that shite is there?" He hummed, suddenly happy, jumped up, flicked off the autohelm, and changed course. "Time to move Mimi. Let's put up those sails. Time to move."

Second song, dress half off,
top slipped to waist, grasp pole

Eton eats as few people do in the days of Atkins and South Beach: fast food and packaged sandwiches, with pure, unmitigated, unhurried relish and a complete absence of guilt. After a lazy, slow evening of grinding and chocolate, a lethargic morning of eating cock, we go out for eggs and croissants, shrimp and sandwiches, praline spread, crusty brown bread, and hot milky coffee.

"The problem with women," he begins through a mouthful of *pain au chocolat*, "is that you just can't say anything, or give suggestions regarding sex, without them taking it as criticism and getting offended. I always seem to have long relationships with the girls who have too many hangups, and great sex with the girls I wouldn't ever date. It would be good to get the combination right."

I don't ask what category I fall into. It seems prudent not to, and in any case, Eton knows full well the impact of his words, and enjoys keeping me guessing. I made him dinner last night—lemon sole and asparagus—then cleaned his fridge and taught him how to slice an avocado. He looked at me in bemusement. "So you're my girlfriend now, are you?" he laughed, and then I fell asleep on him, but not before whispering, *"Not until you ask me to be."* I don't know what I am. The ambiguity keeps me alive, frightens me with its unfamiliarity, its unwieldy, squishy warmth. It's a strange and elaborate combination of dishes, as opposed to a crappy à la carte, prix fixe menu.

In exchange for the meal, Eton said he'd teach me how to deep throat.

It must be love.

Third song, dress off

"Have you ever fallen in love?" I ask Eton, balancing an aluminum take-out tray of filet mignon from the five-star restaurant around the corner on my knee. I glance in the glassy reflection of the large flat-screen TV, switched off. Face like a China doll, lashes like swallows swooping over pink girly cheeks. Clean, bare apartment. The maid had been in the morning. My bag—full of dollar bills, leaking G-strings and garters and fake hair—spills and tumbles across the floor, a streak of bad taste in impeccable, spotless design.

"Of course. I'm not completely heartless."

Possibly we're both just lonely, possibly I sense that Eton is, like me, an expert at leaving, and after all, Eton lives only ten blocks from the club, in a chic, spacious doorman building on the East Side with an expansive view of Central Park, populated entirely by the over-fifties. It's convenient. We are both of us living a vacuum-sealed, flat-packed, round-edged, abbreviated, alleviated life. Gradually, imperceptibly, from the first day of meeting, we begin to spend most evenings together. "Don't wash off the makeup," he'd say, gazing at me as I stood in his glass-fronted shower. "What?" "I said don't wash it off!" "I can't hear you—the *water*." "I just like you with it on. You look pretty. You look nice."

It made it bearable, being with him after the filth of the day, after the tired repetition of the dance had been played out. Eton was a cunt, I could tell, wielding the flippant arrogance of the rich with the quirks of the misanthropist. People stopped when he walked into the lobby of a hotel, a bar, a restaurant (people respect arrogance, they follow it, believe in it); Eton was arrogant and he was bored. If he could have frittered away his multimillion-dollar inheritance, he would have done it. But it kept coming back. Online poker tournaments, roulette at a charity function, a game of Snap with the stakes at fifty cents, stocks, shares, investments, equities, mutual trusts, bonds—every economic seed planted in Eton's Monopoly life grew fat, juicy fruit. He could have turned Old Kent Road into duplex penthouses, blooming like obscene monstrous peaches in a desert of real estate. He was pragmatic about his success, dismissive, *bored*. Life bored him. Money bored him. Food interested him. Sex. Mimi, with her disregard for convention, her complete absence of self-consciousness, interested him. "Keep the makeup on," he'd order bluntly. "Those jeans are too big for you. They look awful. Take some money. Buy some clothes. Short skirts. Nice shoes. Get your hair done properly. I want you to look pretty."

I refuse the money for the visa but buy the clothes. Cocktail dresses, tiny pointy shoes, slim-fitted jeans, skirts that swing elegantly around toned legs. I wear the G-strings I wore in the club, the heels, the makeup. He likes to dress me, becomes offended and confused when I don't take more money. "I bought you a gift," he says one Sunday, three weeks after we met, when every night was a messy, carnivorous feast of bodies. "Put it on," he orders from his chair, unmoving, unmovable, yet a smile curled at his lips. "I want to see you in it. But don't wash off the makeup."

It was a maid's outfit.

Sex and food. Slow, methodical, delectable consumption, frenzied gorging, satiated nibbling. He takes me to Pastis, Café des Artistes, Nobu, Da Silvano, The Spotted Pig, Mamoun's Falafel on MacDougal Street—the restaurants as varying as his sexual palate. We talk about Greek tragedy and TV programs, about films and French philosophy. When we aren't having sex, we talk about sex, in between courses we relish like sex. He licks his fingers after plunging his huge hand gently into me, as if my juices were a rich and heady reduction sauce, and he watches, fascinated, as I lick his stomach, swallow greedily, go back for more. One time I walk through the door to his apartment late after work, and he peels off my clothes, lays me out on the kitchen table, and proceeds to examine and prepare every part of me, like a chef trussing a particularly fine piece of meat. It is a thorough and exact preparation by an artist, and for the pièce de résistance he slides into me. I covet our lovemaking like an exquisite dessert almost too rich to enjoy, an acid pleasure offset by the tinge of sweet pain, a dusting of cocoa, a crystallized *Physalis* on the side. "I've never met anyone like you before," he breathes in fascination after I tell him a story about sailing across the Atlantic, or traveling in Nepal, or the early days of New York. In these stories hardship is an adventure and Mimi a cheeky little gobshite who always comes out on top, who never cries, who is always indubitably sure of her ultimate success. An edited, repackaged Mimi minus the pain, the story without too many big words, the plot without the philosophy. He never visits my apartment in Brooklyn. He never meets Lucy or Lily or Bambi. He knows nothing of my family life, the parents I speak to rarely. Eton adores Mimi, Mimi alone, and I feed Mimi with the fruits of me, the degree, the intelligence, the ambitions, all that renders our affair acceptable in his world. Almost.

A French bistro on the Upper East Side. Everyone in the restaurant has a degree from Oxford or Cambridge, lives in Kensington, has known each other since prep school, will marry within the accepted circle. It's Sunday, midday. We order steak frites and Bloody Marys. I sneak outside to smoke cigarettes with one of the girls, a giggly, pretty girl with huge bosoms studying law at Oxford. I have the Cambridge background, the ability to act as though I belong. Cling to it like driftwood, lost in this vast ocean of alien society. I don't know what they know about me. We hadn't discussed that.

"Where did you meet?" demands Sebastian of Eton when I return to the table. "Just in a bar," I interject before he can reply, and Eton smiles at me, amused. The conversation grows thin, as conversation does when questions are batted forcefully away like mosquitoes, like flies, like missiles. "I can't *stand* American girls," announces William petulantly. "I just don't understand them. I was talking to one for *hours* last night, and *still* no joy . . ." "You should come to my bar," I murmur. "You wouldn't have a problem picking up women *there*."

Eton chokes on his Bloody Mary, and the pretty girl with enormous breasts giggles slightly. The bill comes. Eton pays, naturally, and we leave his friends and walk back through Central Park. It's early summer and already the heat is scalding, hot toffee on bare skin. "You don't have to be ashamed of what you are, you know," he says to me brusquely. "You told me to behave," I point out. "Yes. I'm sorry for being a cunt." There's a pause and we walk on in companionable silence. "I would fuck you when we get home," he muses thoughtfully, "but I feel rather full after lunch, and I think I'd rather read."

When we had sex he would stop sometimes, look at my face in almost tender confusion, and then spit into my mouth, jam his fingers, long and strong, into the esophagus, smile when I started to choke, run his index finger around my teeth, my gums. "I want to fuck your mouth," he'd say, and when I gagged and brought up the thick, sticky, viscous, clear saliva from deep down in my throat he would smile in childlike pleasure, laugh, hold my head down a little longer.

It lasts six weeks, this Eden, and one evening I knock on his door late, late, late after three hours in the Champagne Room. It wasn't unusual to go to his apartment after work, but I knew by now to be sober when I did so, in control, a smile on my face, conversation easy, light, intelligent, humorous. He hated me drinking, hated alcohol, hated anything that threatened his iron control over emotions, over weakness. He hated it in himself, hated witnessing it in others. He wanted a clean, aestheticized version of existence minus trauma and tears, minus fears and confusion. I know it's a mistake to go to his apartment, but I'm too drunk to get the subway, too lost after working for twelve hours straight, and I never take cabs back to Brooklyn. I'm still saving for that escape route. He lets me in and his eyes fleck amber, angry without precipitation. I sit on his sofa and throw my money on the floor, six hundred dollars in Benjamins and several more in singles. It is twisted and crumpled and filthy.

"What are you doing, you idiot?" he cries, and he grabs my hand, and then kisses me hard, and recoils in disgust when he tastes the alcohol, the fear, the scent of the club. "Get out."

I cry, I cry and I think he sees, for the first time, something underneath Mimi, someone else. He holds me tight then, and says, "You're so lost, you idiot. Don't worry, I'll help you."

But when he looks at me the next day, I know it's the end. Revealing my truth has ripped the illusion to shreds. I guess he knew I needed him, or wanted to need him. We shamble uncomfortably through the next few days, stepping around each other carefully. At the weekend, when we wake up, facing away from each other as we always do, careful to maintain our separate sides of the bed, he clears his throat awkwardly.

"I think we should . . ."

"Yes, I know," I say.

I pack my belongings and leave. "Don't you want to be friends?" he murmurs quietly, his eyes lowered. I cry as I shake my head no, and then walk to the subway bound for Brooklyn. "You're purty," says a little boy while I'm waiting for the J train at Essex and Delancey, and reaches out a hand as if to touch a lone tear slowly rolling down my cheek.

I dance better after that morning, with more calculation, less heart, more simulation, less inhibition. Something died inside me, closed off, shut tight. I dance as if I know there is no redemption, no such thing as love, trust, romance, marriage, the happy ending. I dance like I know the ending, am resigned to it, could not lose myself believing it was real. I dance better, you see, when there's touching without commitment, when it's all a safe illusion.

"Have you ever been in love, Meems?" Eton had asked companionably one day, sometime before I left. When, exactly, I can't remember.

In Bollywood movies, you'll notice that the female and male leads never reveal their emotions in Hindi. "I love you" is always repeated in English, the language of the colonizer, as if to distance oneself from the depth of the emotion by translating it into a language that is not one's own. Perhaps they are merely capitalizing on the frivolity of this cheap and tawdry phrase, which has no equivalent in Hindi, in Devanagari, the language of the gods. Love traditionally had no place in the earthly concept of marriage, that financial and social transaction, except as duty. Perhaps the modern Western concept of romantic love in all its transience can only be rendered by that meaningless English sentence uttered over and over, as if repetition could imbue it with a significance it lacks by its failure to translate, its failure to import any meaning, aside from the futile.

I love you I love you I love you.

"No. No, I don't think I have."

"You still love your wife?" I ask, *grind, grind, grind.*

"She drives me fucking crazy. I even tell her she drives me crazy. Marriage changes, you know? You marry someone for who they are, and you love them for it. They change and become who you want them to be, a good mother, and you still love them for it. But . . . there's gotta be something *more*."

I know what you mean, Mr. Nice. More than a dark club on a humid Manhattan mid-July afternoon, sipping sugar-free Red Bulls with vodka to make the time go quicker, the edges a little less sharp. Maybe it's that desire for more, for something different, which makes us all not-so-nice.

"If we ran away together you reckon we'd last longer than a year?" laughs Mr. Nice. I don't think anything would last longer than a year in my life. How could anything grow in a heart overrun with the weeds of nicotine and New York, sourness and pride?

I dance for a Princeton banker. He's hungry. Maybe you know the type. I certainly do by now. He takes me into the Champagne Room with another girl. She has hard plastic tits. Bit awkward, truth be told. Too many holes, too many rules. Dancing is hard because of the limits sometimes. However, I persevere with lesbianity, take a few restroom breaks, make the obligatory gasps and contort myself into positions suitable for Giuliani's strict criteria ruling (non)sexual turn-ons, and then go for a drink with the guy afterward. Don't ask me why. Curiosity, loneliness. I ask too many questions. *But you love your girlfriend? You would tell her you did this? Why not get an escort? Why go home unsatisfied?*

The answers are always as unsatisfactory as the grind. I kiss him good-bye, and it's a faux-lesbian kiss, sexless, with tongues, for show, like porn. I feel weird, wrong, and nearly call Eton. I don't, instead stand on Seventh Avenue in the humid darkness of early evening, cabs whooshing past, lights blurred,

Manhattan moving on relentless, but me postponed, hovering, uncertain and alone, feeling confused, a little empty.

Eton calls. He tries to play the Saviour card, perhaps to assuage his own guilt, but why he should feel guilty I had no idea.

"Look, your visa situation is ridiculous. It's a mess. Let me pay for a visa lawyer. I asked around, I got the name of a good firm. Call them, they're going to send me the bill, they have my credit card number."

A little later.

"You don't have the money in your bank account to show them and you know there's no money in the club in summer. Let me lend you the money."

There are more messages. I ignore them. Foxy's by this time had sent me to their other club downtown, Baby Dolls, a sordid little hole not far from the (former) World Trade Center, just temporarily to cover for some dancers on vacation. There was no money there, none, but the manager, Anthony, was a relief after Dolores, after Hank.

"You havin' boyfriend problems doll?" he'd say as I sat and sipped Red Bull at the bar. "I wouldn't treat you like that if you were my girl." But he'd smile and it was a kind smile, a father's smile, and he'd look worried every time we went upstairs in a room with someone, and tell us to call, yell, walk out, if things got out of hand. We sit at the bar, the empty bar, and drink Red Bull and talk about life and watch marathon sessions of *America's Next Top Model.* I make no money there, but I can almost believe I am normal. I can almost believe that I've tamed Mimi, made her more domesticated, a purring house cat. I'm happier. I miss Eton.

He calls again eventually, and he says the right thing this time, even though we both know it's a lie. *I got scared. You're everything I want in a woman. I wanted a fling and I got someone I wanted to be my girlfriend. I want to buy you flowers. I want you back. I lo—* No, not quite, not yet, not ever, not for me, not in this life. I know the score. He wants Mimi, he wants me to play along, and as long as I can play, it's game on. I hide my drinking from him. I drink more at work to get through it. He never sees me drunk again.

In the room I must straddle him, usually with one leg over his thigh, the other planted on the floor in between his legs for leverage. He desires that the gusset area on my G-string be directly pressed against his penis, a pathetic and slow-rising slug, sleeping in the depths of his polyester suit pants, which emit a rank, stale aroma from their depths, like secondhand stores, old men's apartments. He holds my hips and he moves me up and down. I am not Mimi when this happens. I am not anyone. I am just there for an hour, repeating this friction, thinking about the money and suggesting frequent cigarette breaks, when I will stare into the distance, and he will occasionally thrust out a fat paw to tweak my nipple, prod insistently at my vagina, cloaked in that G-string, thank God for that G-string. Cigarette finished I will resume my position and get back to work. I will change it by turning away from him, and his hands will be on my hips as he moves me up and down, up and down. Another girl who used to go in with him before she got too old tells me to do this. It is called "riding" and it means you can look away. I do not gasp, or feign pleasure, or whisper rubbish, or touch his bare skin if I can help it; I am just mute, a rag doll, a piece of friction—he prefers it this way. He never comes. He rarely talks. I found out he is an accountant, he is nearly sixty, he is divorced, he has fantasies of violent and unpleasant sex with underage girls. Sessions are tedious. He always stays for two hours, sometimes three. I am not Mimi, I am not anyone. The money is good. Eventually I pass him on to a new, small Hispanic girl. He likes them small, and he likes them to look younger than sixteen. I may have looked sixteen when I first started work here, when he first picked me out across the room and I winked at Bambi, pleased to have snagged a bottle, unaccustomed, yet, to the horrors and revelations the Room holds, still finding it sexy, in a way. Now I do not look sixteen. I have nightmares about this one. I can't tell Eton about them. I wake him up sometimes whimpering pathetically, and I am annoyed at myself, and he snorts agitatedly, turns over, back to sleep, and I lie awake a while longer. I have nightmares.

On my nights off, we add a new pursuit to our repertoire of sex and food: ballroom dancing. Eton pays for my classes, naturally. We cha-cha and salsa, waltz and fox-trot, swing and tango. We spend hours practicing in the apartment until our steps are fluid as mercury, and we stare into each other's eyes as we dance to double time, triple time, faster and faster and faster, until we fall onto the floor, giggling, panting, hot, and then he peels my clothes off, and we grow silent, intense, as our starving souls strive vainly to quieten that gnawing hunger.

"I've noticed that I've gone through rather a lot of toilet paper since you came into my life," says Eton thoughtfully, chewing on a pizza, which was called "bruschetta," despite it being, rather obviously, pizza. A young woman behind us released a terrifyingly horsy laugh. Her date looks around anxiously. I could tell they met on the Internet.

"Perhaps I could make a suggestion that you start to use *three* squares to wipe, and not the usual five or six?"

"I *did* bring you a roll of toilet paper the other day," I say, defensively.

"But that was *single-ply.*"

The significance of this rests heavy between us.

I was still writing, occasionally, lackluster pieces for various magazines and obscure websites that paid next to nothing. I was just existing, languishing in stasis, neither legal nor illegal, still waiting for that visa, patiently counting my money every day, lining up in Bank of America to contribute more crumpled dollar bills to my account. The cashier would give me a suspicious snort and pick up a single between forefinger and thumb with obvious distaste. I'd shrug, walk over the street to Foxy's, line up onstage. Dance a bit. Talk. Take my clothes off. Laugh with Mark the DJ. Laugh with Pedro. Gossip with Lily. Hustle with Hank. Squeeze money from the sad, tired specimens who enter during the day only for the free entrance fee, the air conditioning, the cheap thrills of sad breasts, exhausted sighs.

One day a journalist contacts me, and takes me for lunch and iced coffee in a tiny Japanese hipster café in Williamsburg not far from my apartment. He asks me questions for three hours, questions about the Champagne Room, questions about the men, questions about me, my goals, my life, my past. He's only a few years older than me. I have a better degree than him, am probably a better writer. I find it amusing that I have become a zoo specimen of sorts, painful, but inevitable. I smoke ten cigarettes and he screws up his eyes as I exhale the smoke in his face, but I don't offer to stop, and he doesn't ask.

He comes into the club too, and I feel odd taking my clothes off with him there, though when Eton comes in I have no problem with it.

A month later the article appears in the *New York Times*, the accompanying photograph a dramatic portrait of an anonymous Mimi, face averted, gazing at the Manhattan skyline from a hot, dirty little patch of sand next to the waterline in Brooklyn. Eton looks at it in silence, then glances up at me, confused, as if unable to quite reconcile the fictional-seeming Mimi of this feature-length piece with the reality standing before him.

9

AS MIMI I AM A PRODUCT, real life reduced to literary devices, plots, narratives, chronology, subplots, a catchy title. *If I write a book, it will be called* . . . What *would* it be called? "Girl Behaving Badly"?, "Adventures of an Accidental Stripper"? Something titillating! Something with a hint of youthful flesh, a flash of bosom, omitting the tired dark rings under my eyes, the twenty-a-day smoking habit and the cynicism. I like the Enid Blytonesque tone to "Adventures of," as if I were rollicking through New York with Julian, Dick, George, Anne, and Timmy the Dog, a boiled egg and tinned pineapples in my knapsack, nestling cozily next to the G-string, pasties, and the see-through black baby-doll dress. "D'you think," said my niece, upon hearing that I was writing a book, "we can read Auntie's book in school for class, Mummy?" If it was called "Adventures of an Accidental Stripper," why ever not? Why not hurl it onto the reading list alongside Billy Blue Hat and Roger Red? It's OK! It wasn't deliberate! It was Accidental! It's a fun and frivolous romp by a Girl Behaving Badly!

We're lost, Mimi and me, we're fictions within fictions, social selves delicately seasoned, dusted with sugar, presented *table d'hôte* for your delectation. We are the ultimate biographical conundrum, and this we share with all strippers, those connoisseurs of pretense and false names. On these pages, as in life, we're lost. We're all lost.

Eton was obsessed with monkeys, and in particular he harbored a peculiar fondness for gorillas. His response to the celebratory mood that ensued post-article is pragmatic.

"Let's take a day off," he announces gravely, "and go to the Bronx Zoo. I hear they have an excellent Congo Gorilla Forest."

We eat before we leave, in Norma's on Fifty-seventh, where, it is rumored, there was once a thousand-dollar omelette on the brunch menu. Eton grunts in gruff delight as fluffy waffles and voluptuous syrup, nubile bacon and an orgy of fruit, appear on our table.

"So what will you do now, Meems?" he asks eventually, when hunger satisfied, he prepares to retire behind the *Wall Street Journal*.

"I think," I reply slowly, chewing delicately on a crisp rasher of bacon, "I should write an awful chick-lit book and sell it for a vast sum of cash to all the agents and publishing houses who have been contacting me since that *New York Times* article. And then I'll use the money to write the novel I've been planning to write for the last two years. And perhaps on the back of that I can sell the novel I wrote on the boat all that time ago. And I'll probably do a Creative Writing MFA so I can teach in university, travel to India, and maybe do some real journalism. And after all that, I'll move back to England, get married, and have babies."

He looks at me almost admiringly.

"Good show!"

"And I think I should move out of Brooklyn. I have enough money. I've saved about seven thousand dollars. I'm putting together the rest of the paperwork for the visa as well."

He folds his newspaper abruptly and signals for the check.

"Well, as long as we have that settled, let's go and look at some monkeys."

He was amused that I knew how to navigate the subway up to the Bronx. When we arrived at the zoo it was too hot, an ongoing eructation of heat belching over us with sickly, fetid stickiness. We barely manage to see the monkeys and the reptile house, before admitting defeat and going home for fellatio.

In New York, unlike London, there is no amber light at pedestrian crossings. There is a red Stop or a green Go, and in between a malevolent flashing red hand indicating that between those two extremes there can be no soft, ambivalent, honey-safe amber. The tourists, when they see the red hand flickering urgently, stand confused and wary on the sidewalk, grouping closer together clutching their Bloomingdale's bags, reluctant to cross, unable to decipher that ambiguous symbol. The New Yorkers stride confidently on, having lived with that flashing red light for so long, they are oblivious to it.

My status has been elevated somewhat by entrance to the hallowed pages of the *New York Times*. I'm suddenly subsumed by a whirl of meetings with publishers and agents, journalists and curious onlookers, who just want to see me, touch me, check that I'm real. It's amusing, a relief, the tension in my head and heart slowly leaking out like serum from a blister, a painful, exquisite release. Yet I'm still unable to grasp the possibility that this hell could be over, it could all be over. I may even go back to England if I make some money from selling Mimi's story, I decide. When I could return and be someone, be something, have proven myself, could go back being the victor. Maybe.

I start looking for a new apartment. Find one, with two giggly Asian accountants. Move out without saying good-bye to Raoul, notifying only the anonymous musicians. I move to Midtown, Fifty-sixth and Broadway, close to Foxy's. I don't know why, something about the stark, packaged, anesthetic feel to its gaudy tat appealed, plus I knew the area from having worked there for six months. It's close to Eton. I don't tell the giggly Asian girls what I do—*had* done—for a living. I would succumb to commercialism, sell out, and repackage Mimi in a pink cover and a PG rating. Mimi would pay the bills, as she always had, to fund my dreams. But this time in the relatively innocuous format of a paperback book, pink cover.

The days roll by, quickly, intensely. I have meetings in executive boardrooms with publishers, lunch with magazine editors, a photo shoot with a tabloid. I don't feel like a pariah anymore. Mimi has become almost socially acceptable through New York City's lurid need for dirt, pretty dirt, dirt that speaks its mind and plays its game, knows how to sensationalize itself, when to be quiet. I feed into her squalid desires without making her feel that she, herself, has been soiled. I feel, in a way, as if this were the fulfillment of my destiny. I didn't make it the right way, so I took this route into making my dreams work for me. I'm not grateful for it. I'm not surprised by it. I expect it, in a way, for writing about my life, writing about Mimi's life. I *deserve* success. I knew I would get it if I worked hard enough. I knew it would be painful in the process. I'm relieved it started before it became too painful. I know the weeks off from dancing, the garnering for a book deal, the flagrant manipulation of media, the five minutes of fame will last only so long though. I know I should work again in Foxy's before my savings are sucked up by Manhattan rent, but I can see my way out now. It's within my reach. And at the end of the day there's always him, Eton.

"I'm proud of you, you know, Meems," says Eton gruffly as I fillet branzino in his apartment, the air thick with steamed asparagus, butter melting in the heat. He reaches forward and pushes a tendril of hair behind my ear, his finger lingering on the lobe, squeezing tenderly. "I knew you were more than all that." He smiles, his blue eyes, warm, his blond hair, ruffled, young-looking, incongruous with the stiff Gucci suit. His smile is relieved, relieved that the need for him has been lessened before either of us had to acknowledge it and walk away. It makes it easier to make the decision to go back to the club, this success, this promise of riches, this fulfilment of promises, when before his eyes would darken winter blue in disillusionment and disgust at my flailing dreams. It's just temporary now, stripping, like it was right at the start. It's just research for writing, the actions of a quirky, stubborn, fierce girl who always took the difficult path. I know that people recognize their own kind. People like Eton don't hang out with losers, with people like me. Unless they know, secretly, that one day, we'll be worthy of them.

I go into Foxy's the next day, curiously buoyant, even happy, an unfamiliar emotion in those days. It was seven months to the day that I'd arrived in Manhattan, a month since the *New York Times* article.

"Where the hell you think you're goin'?"

Dolores stops me as I walk into the darkened club, and rises, majestic, a King Crab from the bottom of the ocean.

"You think we wouldn't recognize you in the *New York Times*? That article made a laughing stock out of Foxy's. Get your stuff. You're fired."

I sleep fitfully. I always used to wonder what this was: fitful. I could sleep on concrete floors, in airports, on Indian buses, on boats in tropical storms, on someone's shoulder; I could sleep with thoroughness, exactness, refreshing, simple. Lately, though, sleep is this adjective: *fitful,* a nervous slumber, twitching. Sleep is a tick I can never quite shake. I can hear the giggly Asian girls through thin paper walls as I lie in bed and gaze at the ceiling and wonder whether to call Eton. It depresses me being in this colorless, boxlike cell, the new apartment. It depresses me not dancing. I feel a stirring inside, a desperate flapping, an oxygen-starved wail suppressed by convention, by lethargy, by something that feels close to giving up. I can't write. I feel as if I'm curling up and fading away like a will o' the wisp, a leaf in fall, deprived of all human contact. I miss routine, I miss the clients, I miss Lily and Bambi and Lucy, yet when they call I don't answer the phone. I walk along Broadway every day, anonymous and small and silent. I bump into Lily two blocks from Foxy's, just as summer turns to fall. It has been three weeks since I left the club. Lily gasps and puts her hand over her mouth.

"Mimi! Oh my God! I'm gonna get in so much trouble if they see me talkin' to you! I tried to call you, we were worried, you never pick up. Damn, they're gonna shoot me if they see me out here with you."

"Why? What happened now?"

"No, jus' the article still. They're pissed you talked to the papers, and the girls are real bitchy, and it *sucks* without you. You know Bambi went to Vegas? Everyone's leaving. I saw your friend Lucy the other day. She quit stripping, started school. I'm gonna quit too. Hooters said they'd give me more hours until I take the LSATs. And then I'll just get a job with fake papers until school starts."

"What? Why'd you need fake papers? You're American . . ."

She stops, shocked.

"You didn't know? Why the hell you think I work in that place? Don't be deceived by the accent, Mimi. I'm American all right, I grew up here, it's my home. But maybe I just don't have the papers to prove it. You're not the only one with no green card, Mimi. Listen, call me. We need to hang out again. You need friends."

When she drifts away to start her shift I'm left alone on the sidewalk, and I can't see the sky for all the tall buildings. There's no one to call. I miss Brooklyn and Raoul and the musicians. I feel nostalgia for my previous nostalgia, which was, at least, less lonely than this, less mute, less hopeless, less miserable. I try to write some more. I call my agent. He's enthusiastic about the new chapters but I'm not so sure. The first few he'd dismissed as "not commercial" enough. *More sex, more funny, less mean, less dark.* Mimi was giving me mental Chinese burns about the thing. I watch *Oprah* in the afternoon, *E! True Hollywood Story, The Tyra Banks Show, America's Next Top Model.* I survive on packet noodles as my savings dwindle. The gigglys return bang-on 6:00 p.m. Their punctuality and routine depress me further. They emerge at exactly 8:23 a.m. every morning. They consume a breakfast of Nutella and frozen waffles and/or oatmeal flavored with one-hundred-year-old duck eggs. They leave for the office and return at 6:00 p.m. At 7:00 p.m. they go to the gym, for, ironically, cardio-striptease, or sometimes weekday warriors, classes full of pale, flabby corporate types who avoid the weights due to fear of overexposure to lithe, sweating, muscle-bound forms discussing the latest Jonathan Safran Foer novel in between grunts of satisfied effort. They return at 9:30 p.m., briefly check to ensure I haven't consumed their Gatorade or one-hundred-year-old duck eggs, giggle to themselves on the sofa, and watch HBO in placid giggly contemplation together. "Ah! He is so fat giggly one!" "Ah yes, so fat, so fat." Giggle giggle.

At first I ask them what are your aims? What are your ambitions? Where do you want to be in five years, ten years time? But I grow tired of their automaton-like responses, their soulless stocktaking of life. They exist in a perpetual, self-fulfilling cycle of sameness, never deviating from their path, never seeking improvement, never meeting new people, making new friends.

They are content.

Eton regards me with an air of bored contempt.

"I have no sex drive at the moment."

I pause, consider, and allow a glimmer of fear to well up

and crawl desperately over the sea bass like a survivor from a storm.

"Could it be *me?*"

"Perhaps. I don't know."

We leave the restaurant without speaking, and I walk back to the gigglys' apartment alone. The agent rings. I ignore his call, turn over, and sleep fitfully.

The days start to roll by slower and slower. The money starts to dry up, the interviews, the meetings.

We stop dancing. I start taking yoga classes every day at my local gym. It's cheap. Eton doesn't pay. I take, sometimes, three classes a day. I'm still trying to write. The agent stops calling. In Midtown you never see the sky, I notice. Nobody smiles. I start walking around the city after my yoga classes, willing the rhythm of my steps to beat out the sadness in my heart, the weight, the loneliness. It's unbearable, this pressure, this small, malevolent creature inside me thrashing around. I start to run because walking doesn't work. I smile when I see Eton at night, though I feel, in some strange way, as if Mimi is starting to shrivel up, to starve, and that her well-being is dependent upon mine. I do not call anyone from my previous existence before Mimi. I don't see the point.

I finish the three chapters the agent wants me to write, and when he eventually answers the phone, he sends them off to publishers. I hate the words, they are from neither Mimi nor me. Shortly afterward I have a meeting with an editor who asks me if I could change the book, turn it into a stripping sex guide for menopausal middle-aged women. My demographic: *Sex and the City* fans. Can I make it *sexy?* Like that JAP who writes a blog on the Upper West Side about dating and vaginal excretions? Her words scare me more than stepping out naked in front of a hundred leering men. In the end, I call the agent and tell him to cancel it all. I can't write the book. Words—my words, Mimi's words—mean too much to us, we can't hand them over like an adoption, a retarded child we don't want.

Money is running out. The visa has not yet arrived. I take more yoga classes, walk more, watch TV. One afternoon something happens, what I can't remember, but it's the break, and it comes out, that suppressed wail inside me, and its strength is frightening as it sweeps me, us—Mimi and me—along with it.

I call Eton because there's no one else to call, and there's no variation to the long, unrelenting isolated days, and he doesn't answer. I call and call, and stand outside the Time Warner Building, wrapping my scarf tighter, that wail leaking, leaking, leaking from deep inside. I'm terrified of being alone with her, and need someone to hold me tight, as if I had just woken from an interminable nightmare to find a deeper level to that hell. I see some movie star outside the Mandarin Oriental. Some kids ask her for an autograph and she smiles graciously and I want to punch her, and that wail sweeps me along again and I'm crying for hours, pacing and pacing. He calls me at ten. He'd been taking a waltz class. He doesn't understand why I'm so hysterical. Posthysteria, he doesn't recognize this vacant creature with the sad eyes. Mimi pining away, to leave someone he does not, could not, know. He sends me home, back to the giggly Asians. They're watching HBO.

I go straight to bed. Sleep fitfully.

. . .

On 9/11, Foxy's did not close for business. The managers are extremely proud of that fact, and even four years after the tragedy, they would reminisce about that day as if it were the epitome of pre-9/11 glory, that heady, mythological time all the older dancers talk of longingly, the time of company expense accounts, corporate credit cards, nights out on the boss no questions asked, when money would pour out of corporate wallets like cheap champagne. Foxy's did extremely well on 9/11, totalling, between the hours of noon and eight, twelve "bottles," or hours in the Champagne Room. Indeed, of the six or so girls who worked that day, none went home with less than eight hundred dollars.

When your world falls apart, you rely on what you know. When our twin towers fell, Eton and I, it's what we went back to, sex. In our own little way, like those men on 9/11 who went to Foxy's, sex was our constant, our need, our hook—what we needed to become properly acquainted with disaster.

"Face the wall," Eton would order with an astonished look if I ventured too close in bed at night. "Meems, I'm not joking. Face the wall!" and he'd *harrumph* and turn over with a glare (the indignity! Women!) and he'd check, in five minutes, if I was still facing the wall.

"I think," I say slowly, facing the wall one night as we lie in bed, "I'm going to have to go back to stripping. Just for a short time. To make some more money."

From behind me Eton sounds neutral, bored.

"OK, Meems."

After a while he starts to snore. Still facing the wall and

careful not to wake him, I cry—faux tears, sexless, for show, like porn.

Several days after I've made my decision, I meet Eton for breakfast.

"What did you do last night?" I ask, spooning yolk out of an egg onto crusty bread. I keep my voice smooth and normal, I keep the ache and the waning, whining Mimi from my voice. I had been out with Lucy and Lily the night before, talking for hours about returning to dancing. Lucy was in the middle of her first term at law school and had given stripping up completely. Her parents were supporting her through college, and she had taken out huge loans. She knew how I felt about going back, but she knew what it was to need money. Lily had done the same: quit Foxy's to do her LSATs, and couldn't understand why I didn't use my false papers to get a job in a big corporate firm as a PA or secretary, as she was planning to do once the exams were over and the bills loomed. She was, she said, banking on her boyfriend marrying her and giving her legal status so she could use her law degree. I was shocked when I heard Lily's story. She'd arrived in the U.S. from Taiwan when she was three years old with her family, who'd been persecuted by the Kuomintang. But the U.S. government had refused them refugee status, refused them legality, and she'd been here ever since, as American, to all appearances, as Lucy.

"Mimi?" Eton is looking at me impatiently.

"Sorry, I was dreaming. Yes, so what did you do last night?"

"I met that girl, Sarah, the one with whom we had dinner in Café des Artistes."

"Who?"

"The girl who went to Oxford with Julian and Sebastian."

"Oh. That was ages ago. I didn't know you were in touch. I thought she'd left New York weeks back." I gaze at the headlines of the paper Eton was reading. I squint my eyes in and out of focus, yet still I can't read the words. My head aches.

"It was pretty boring. She talked a lot of crap about bars and clubs, Bungalow 8 or something."

Crack egg open. Yolk oozed thick and rich.

He pauses and chuckles. "We had the worst kiss I've ever had in my life."

I look at him.

"A—*kiss?*"

"Yeah."

I get up blindly and leave, forgetting to swallow, and outside I spit egg-and-bread into my hands, dry retches of nothing clogging my throat. I stumble back blindly to my apartment, sit dumbly in the AC, chilled and numb. Eton follows after he has consumed the remnants of his, and my, breakfast. I ask The Questions. *What else happened? Who called who? Why did you call her? Why didn't you tell me? You had sex with her?* "You don't understand. It didn't *mean* anything. It was just *sex.*" Eton leaves the apartment. It was the first time he had ever been in my apartment. I wait awhile, staring at the walls, and then I walk over to see him.

The bed still smells of sex, semen, cunt, and sweat. Is that mine or hers? How could she not *smell* it? It's everywhere. It fills my nostrils, pungent and heavy and thick—it's a thick aroma. Eton smells it too, the souring of something, the lewd crowing of sick triumph, a score, a strike.

"I never asked you, Meems, about the men you danced for, where they put their hands, where they put their mouths. I was hurt when you said you were going back to dancing. And now I've hurt you, and I'm sorry. I never meant to."

He tries to kiss me.

The images slice into my head like bursts of flame, searing hot, a knife in white heat. The man who touched me. That one who looked at me with those eyes—empty, disturbing, dead. The lawyer who climaxed against my thigh. The banker who whispered *"Oh yeah"* for an entire hour. The many who made me sick. The one I kissed. The sweet and funny graphic designer whose hand I took and led to places it shouldn't have gone. The scent of sex made me feel sick. I could still feel the half-chewed bread mixed with yolk that had lain in little globby patties in my hand from breakfast. I inhale sex (hers or mine?), I smile sweetly, I kiss Eton, I profess forgiveness, my head whirls, and I lead him to the bed, the scent of sex (hers or mine?), I pull him on top of me, and grind against him, and kiss him deeply, before pushing him down, and taking him gently in my mouth. I let my mouth caress him, urge him to get harder with my throat. As the blood rushes down and he sighs in relief, Mimi starts to stir again, to awaken, to smile, to snicker silently inside, to hate.

I bite, hard.

10

ETON THOUGHT he was saving me, like the one before him, like all the others. He didn't realize that the process of imagining himself with Mimi was all part of the drag act, the peep show, the blue movie. He didn't realize that playing the part of Saviour is something they all relish. *To save, the act of saving, rendering one a Saviour:* the fantasy that comes after the other fantasy, which is relatively innocuous in comparison. Take her in the Champagne Room, get her to sit hard on your cock, grind down, *hard,* that rhythm, that pressure, hold her hips so she can't move away, *thudthudthud* you can hear the beat of your heart counterpointed to that long, slow grind, an unrelenting cadence, a courtship you can't stop, can't, can't, so close and when it swells unbearably, bruised and purple and weeping, you quickly unzip, push the tiny G-string aside, wet with her lust, clumsily squash, squeeze, cram into her, and she's gasping in delight and pleasure and that unbearable, exquisite portrait of pain, the female orgasm.

Try this in the room and you'll be met with an obstinate hand blocking all entrances and exits, the imitation of desire, an empty sigh like the tired, bored ghost of pleasure. "That's enough dude," she'll say a little crossly, and if she's long at this game and sick of it, you'll know, and maybe that turns you on even more. If she's long at this game and hungry, she'll negotiate, and maybe that kills your lust. If she's new at this game and stupid, she'll do it for free, and you can smell the fear in the mingled scent of her musk, and you can feel the uncertainty and the disgust in the stifled cry and the face that looks away, and in that moment hovering between rape and transaction, maybe you'll entertain the pleasing notion that you could save her, this little foreign girl, so far from home and stinking of abuse. You could save her (final thrust, a squirt, wince) if you actually gave a crap.

I think Eton thought he was saving me, like the one before him thought, the one before that. Maybe I choose them on their ability to simulate; for someone who despises actors, I do appreciate their importance when casting the main roles.

I don't ever want to hurt you, Eton said to me late one night, words rustling down a phone line laden with static, the carefully orchestrated tremor, the choreographed catch in the throat as palpable as the lies, as empty as the promises. But I knew he would because he already had and I forgave him in advance, or was that retrospect? Monogamy is not in their sex. "You don't understand. It didn't *mean* anything. It was just *sex*." I've heard those words a thousand times, a thousand times, and you see, I *do* understand, because it's my job, it's my livelihood, the distinction is our monopoly, the foundation of our empire, and the basis for a thousand and one lap dances. But secretly I believe they are the same, sex and love. The price on both is high, high, high, astronomical, ridiculous, extraordinary! And I can afford neither.

That is why, nowadays, I never pick up the bill. It's a trick I learned from Mimi, and from Eton.

The phone rings.

"Meems."

He didn't say who it was. He didn't need to.

"Thanks for sending that chapter to me. I appreciate it. But, well, erm, I'm not, altogether *comfortable* with you writing about me . . ."

He floundered slightly. I waited.

"You see, the thing *is,* it's quite horrendous reading about oneself and wondering with dread what's going to come next . . ."

It was late. The hour loaned us an intimacy that erased the months in between the last call, the last touch.

"I'm out of control, on the pages. You have all the power. And I don't understand why you stick quite so religiously to the truth. It's unnerving."

I sigh because Eton has not yet realized that I, too, had no control, no power. It's all about her, it's her story, Mimi's, and while I may have the opportunity to exercise some tiny authorial liberties—exaggerating a nervous tic, attributing bad breath and cellulite to a character I dislike—in the end I'm powerless to halt the incessant, relentless rolling of this story to a conclusion of Mimi's choosing. Even the cover, the title, the marketing that has been discussed in those boardrooms, with those editors—it's all evidence of my frightening disempowerment, her authority. I struggle hard to keep elements from the story that may hurt him, us, but in the end the barest of omissions was the only liberty allowed, and the story still thrashes and weeps and holds its arms out greedily for its siblings, wanting to be reunited with the parts I deliberately and efficiently silenced, even when Mimi stamped her feet and pouted, furious at my intervention.

"I'm only letting you write about me because I know how hard you've worked for this book, Meems," he says, troubled and uneasy, biting hard on pusillanimity, knowing that even if he forbade me to write about him, I would anyway, caught in the thrall of veracity. "But I think you should know, I hate it. I hate reading it."

This book, like her, is morphing horrifically before my eyes, the cells multiplying, deformed, like cancer. They can hurt and that fact hurts me. They are alive, too much alive. *I want to stop your nightmares,* Eton had said once with uncharacteristic kindness, and I turned away to face the wall out of habit, perhaps. When Eton called I only half listened, instead hearing those words. *I want to stop your nightmares.*

I find writing about dancing even harder than the dance itself. The dance, at least, ends with the song and the brisk exchange of hard cash. But this keeps going, grows bigger, more fearsome, more unwieldy, horrendous.

I want to stop your nightmares.

I worship at the altar of Olga. My offerings? Libations of tears, torn from my eyes like the wires ripped from between my legs ("No cry Mammie! No Cry! Nearly over!"), stray hair, plucked delicately with Indian threads, my skin, lost under a haze of Mystic Tan, dark blond roots vanquished by the enigmatic two-hundred-pound Russian beautician—sacrificed to the stripclub.

Mimi is back in business.

When we finally sailed into Charlotteville, Tobago, it was too late to take the dinghy in to locate Customs. We were stuck on the boat until morning, our yellow quarantine flag hanging bored and listless in the humidity of a West Indies evening. Around us were three or four other boats, flickering lights shining through portholes, the comforting swell of other human voices. The Captain said we could swim, and he lowered a torch into the water so the deep emerald green lit up with flecks of jewel-like jellyfish, crystal drops. We drank beer we had saved for six weeks, and we lowered ourselves reverently into a sea that licked and kissed our burned, salty bodies, then we grew braver, jumped off the bow, laughed and talked and joked and drank some more. It ended up just me and the Captain, sitting on the aft deck, feet in the water, talking, drinking, drunk at some unknown hour, for we were still on European time, not Caribbean, even though we were *here,* we were looking at it, what we had wanted, what we had worked for all these weeks. All of a sudden he asked me something, and my face crumpled with the effort of holding it all in, all those months and years before the boat. Too much pleasure and pain for one person to bear, and he held me and kissed me on the top of the head as though I were a little girl. "Could tell you'd done some hard living," he murmured, and hugged me a little tighter, "No 'arm done though Mimi. No 'arm unless you let it."

The next day we set foot on land, white, perfect beaches framed by lush, fertile jungle, chickens pecking and scratching, grinning fishermen smoking joints, small colonial houses nestling gently in the crook of the mountains. I left the others and sat and drank beer on the beach, and it rained, big, fat plods of rain, and I felt happy being alone, happy being Mimi, laden with a past that just added to the intrigue, made it all the more interesting. Made me, in some ways, so much stronger.

Vegas. There are two, one on the Upper East Side, one in Chelsea next to Bungalow 8, Marquee, and Crobar. You belong to one, you belong to both. You're a Vegas girl. It's the best club in the business. High-end. Vegas isn't just a stripclub, Vegas is a scene. Vegas is *Vegas*. Thousands of bored, agitated cheerleaders across Middle America secretly yearn to up and leave Peaceville, go to the big city, and launch their careers in Vegas, because in Vegas you aren't just dancing for overweight IBs and prepubescent bachelors. You are getting paid to sit and network with movie stars, rap stars, football and baseball players, with the full figure, flesh-'n'-blood version of those glossy, air-brushed creatures from the pages of *Us Weekly*. You work in Vegas, you might end up on *Howard Stern*, in *Playboy* mag, immortalized by Vivid Entertainment, glorified by hosts of Americans, male and female. Vegas is where I end up.

"One fuckin' one," snorts Sandy with disgust, eyeing the Yankees game on the flat screen while expertly harpooning a graying slab of gyro meat from his tin take-out plate. "Hey doll, you noo here? I ain't seen you around before. You gotta boyfriend?"

Waiters run past, bartenders stock fridges with Red Bull, a collective wail arises from the girls in the dressing room. "Where the fuck is the makeup artist? I need eyelashes!" A sea of bare, tanned, oiled flesh swamps the dressing room, magnified by the mirrors lining the walls, multiple girls, multiplied girls, breasts and bottoms, the whiff of deodorant, perfume, hairspray. Downstairs the music starts with a heaving lurch and an epileptic frenzy of lights. A girl curls up on the chair next to me, hugging her knees into her chest and balancing her chin on top like a child. Glittering flits of glimpsed girls disappear, reappear, grouping and regrouping.

"The girls aren't very friendly here are they?" I observe, more for conversation than any real surprise at this fact. Dancers aren't friendly. We stick to the known, the tried-and-tested. New girls piss us off. New girls are competition. New girls are fresh meat.

"Nah. They're bitches mostly. You new?"

I nod. "First night. Came over from Foxy's."

"You know what happened to me the other day? It was like, my first night here. I was in the Champagne Room with this guy and he said he'd give me four hundred bucks to jerk him off. So I was like, 'OK,' you know? What the fuck, it's money, and afterwards he gives me four bills. I get upstairs and they're twennies. I can't believe I gave a fuckin' *handjob* for eighty *bucks*. Fuckin' asshole."

I laugh. "How long have you been dancing?"

"Third day. I was just curious to see if I could do it or not, but I love it! Getting paid to party. I'm studying theater at Tisch. I'm gonna be an actress."

The manager signals to the bartender and a round of drinks are dispensed along the bar. Onstage a girl in a metallic G-string writhes deliciously on the floor, dark eyes flashing, her burnished skin shiny and smooth, a huge mass of tight black curls flowing around her slim shoulders. I catch a glimpse of a fiery eye, defiant glance, astonishment, a grin. Almost imperceptibly, Bambi winks as she grabs her dress off the hanger and helps the next girl up onstage. She joins me at the bar and helps herself to a sip of my white wine with a smile that looks almost real in its warmth.

"Hey bitch. What took you so long?"

We laugh a lot at Vegas, laugh long and hard and loud. Bambi and I drink, make money, laugh. Sometimes Lily drops by, sometimes Lucy. They say they're happy being out of it, but they keep coming back. Every night is a party, every night is feast or famine, every night I numb myself to the reality of the next day: a cubicle room, two giggly Asian girls, a man I want to call but can't. I forget about the visa, to tell you the truth. Forget about why I'm in Manhattan, forget about writing. Everything becomes subsumed by the only desire you need to have as a dancer: the desire for money, money as quickly as possible, dirty money, filthy money, money that stinks, money you abhor through acts that smack and sting and bruise, ah! *Money.* Money. Mimi craves the money, craves the drink even more, craves the nights at Vegas with Bambi, because in Oz nothing *bad* ever happens. We crave the money and the attention and suck the sweet nectar of scorn, the opium of disgust. *Mr. CEO, I have no sympathy for you, because you walked into a place where shit goes on. The management are vermin. We're vermin, swarming all over pricks like you merely for your money. People's wallets go missing on a regular basis. People get overcharged, and it's no accident. Get the right girl, pay a little extra, and you're going home with a fourteen-hundred-dollar*

venereal disease. It's your own fault, and as much as I know
what goes on here, what scum are running this place, Mr. CEO,
you should really have learned by now. Don't trust anyone—least
of all yourself.

The nights slip away, dribbling pointlessly, melted butter
dripping, escaping, peaking between the hours of one and five
a.m., then subsiding into an aching, shivering withdrawal until the next fix the following night. Six weeks have passed since
Eton and I last talked, and it's now Halloween. I numb the
pain with the sex of money, with alcohol, with my trip down
the Yellow Brick Road. I have fun doing so, the kind of clinical
fun only the truly self-destructive can understand. I inhabit
this Mimi body almost as if it were mine.

"So, like, my fiancé is givin' me so much shit at the moment. He's convinced that I'm cheatin' on him. He had his
dad, like, tap my phones." We're all in Halloween outfits.
Cutesy policewomen, French maids, schoolgirl dominatrices.

"Why is he so paranoid?"

"Well, he's a little upset. He got a hard-on Friday and it
wouldn't go down. It turned out to be like, a *really* rare condition. He had to go into the hospital. They were gonna, like,
amputate. So he's takin' it out on me. I gotta fly to Texas Saturday, calm him down a little. Hey, you get your SpongeBob
outfit from the housemom?"

Everything is for sale in the club. The drinks, the experi-
ence, the girls hanging off your arm, pressed against your dick.
You can buy hats, T-shirts, calendars, lingerie, shoes, makeup.
For the right price it's yours. The right price is the highest
price. Halloween and they're selling outfits to the dancers.
Wonder Woman, though surely Wonder Woman didn't have a

34F chest and a pussy stripped clean of hair? Spider-Man. We won't even go into *that* one. Nurses and sailor girls, fairies and bunny rabbits. On Halloween girls dress like strippers. On Halloween strippers dress like girls, innocent cutesy girls with monstrous mammaries emerging from skin-tight plastic outfits like huge ripe peaches, tiny G-strings disappearing into ass cracks, stretched taut against pink-brown buttholes, glimpsed briefly—for the right price. Girls cluster in the restaurant, order mashed potatoes, vodka shots, Parliament Lights oozing wisps of gray smoke. One of the managers walks in, three nineteen-year-old strippers (Belly Dancer, She-Ra, Uncle Sam) look up, sipping their illegal drinks, eyes darkening. "Don't get drinks from *that* guy. He *does* stuff. Drugs girls. Takes them in the back. You gotta be careful."

Vodka–Red Bulls are the most expensive drink, so Bambi and I order five throughout the night and charge it to the manager's tab with fake names. *I'm a French Maid talking to Shakira and Snow White.* We're dancing for the owner, the owner's friends, the club's lawyer. The right price for them is a cheap price. Marilyn Monroe brings our drinks. The owner catches her arm, looks around. "Private Room. Now. All of you."

Four girls, three guys. Marilyn Monroe looks like a waitress, acts like one too, but for the right price you can get Marilyn to lift her skirts, because that's what she's doing now, two big-tittied blondes kissing her, licking her, a finger gently massaging between her legs while I grind the owner, his gaze fixed on Marilyn, his hands fixed on me. She comes pretty quick, does a good job, looks real pleased about it too. Very gracious. "Thanks girls, that was *so* hot. I've *never* come like that before." I almost believe her. She'd make it good in the porn industry,

I could see that's where she was headed. Cunning concealed as Marilyn Monroe, concealed as waitress, but for the right price she's just like the rest of us, with our butts out, our sweet smiles. We are sweet you know, most of us. You'd be surprised. We're also expensive, fourteen hundred bucks an hour. But how do you put a price on what we sell? Even fourteen hundred is a bargain.

Texas Jolie turns around and looks at the stage. "Gee, guys, check out this chick onstage. Off the boat, right?"

There's one in every club. The patently shit stripper. The girl who can't speak English, gets onstage, and goes red, covers her breasts, mutters Hail Marys under her breath, prays Daddy can't see her now. To the uninitiated, one might assume she's been sex trafficked, beaten into submission to the evil ways of the titty bar with a large club by a 250-pound Haitian pimp. Yet the simple truth is merely that she's incapable of doing anything else. She spends her days twisting her tongue around the intricacies of American English, that vast convoluted map of grammar. She spends her nights trying to wiggle her sagging, cellulite-ridden arse in a seductive manner and failing miserably. As soon as she gets to Level 3, Intermediate English, she'll leave, get a job in a bar, eventually become a secretary, the relief of prising that white, jiggling body into cut-rate H&M office attire evident from the way she will let her present equilibrium—hovering somewhere between acceptable with clothes off, and the fat bitch you fuck on a night out and kick out of bed at three a.m. for fear the hot chick next door might see you with her—collapse in a spectacular fashion.

Margaret, the patently shit stripper, steps timidly onstage, two sad, gray wings flopping behind her. She trips over her gown and reddens slightly. One breast pops out to her palpable devastation. In an attempt to retrieve it, she becomes entangled with the flopping wings. She has the fluid movements of someone who had been anally raped by a large shish kebab. An ancient version of "Firestarter" pumps out inappropriately from the speakers. Jolie laughs loudly, a horrible sound, wrong.

"What's that bitch dressed as? A fuckin' dead butterfly?"

Bambi gazes at her in awe.

"Girl, she ain't no butterfly. She a *moth*."

The night is slow so we order drinks on the manager's tab. Queen of the Night emerges from the labyrinthine depths of the private rooms. Just as there's always a patently bad stripper, there's a Queen of the Night, every night. Sometimes it's me if I get lucky early on. You can always identify the Queen by her obvious inebriation, the huge wad of notes tucked into her garter, and the fact nothing on earth can destroy the joy of having just gotten paid sixteen hundred bucks for two hours of drinking Dom Pérignon with some rich prick when everyone else was sitting at the bar getting drunk on Corona. She yelps excitedly, leaps onstage, and starts to crawl around while pretending to masturbate herself, much to the confusion of two Japanese tourists elegantly sipping Budweiser out of frosted glasses. She gyrates frenetically with an abandonment born of pure intoxication, and scatters her money haphazardly over the stage. We hate her.

"You tried those guys?" I ask Bambi.

"Yeah. They don't like black girls."

"Those guys?"

"Those guys are fuckin' yeast infections."

"Them."

"Jewish."

Pause.

"Shall we order a bottle of wine?"

Queen of the Night performs an impressive scissors kick onstage and falls on her head. The managers look on fondly. The night passes slowly. After half a bottle of wine, Bambi grabs my arm.

"Look at that bitch!"

"What?"

"That fuckin' bitch! That moth! She's givin' dances to that guy, and that guy, and that guy. She's a fuckin' shit stripper. Why she goin' home with more money than me?"

Queen of the Night lies in a drunken stupor onstage. The patently shit stripper is cleaning up. Bambi and I sit sipping our stolen wine, bitter as lemons, poor as church mice, faces like smacked arses.

And then we laugh and laugh and laugh.

Dad calls to say that they're taking my grandmother out for her eightieth birthday.

"Does she still have those Chihuahuas?" I inquire.

His voice, thick with Welsh, rumbles across the crackling line.

"Oh no, *cariad*. They all died. Did I tell you what happened to the last one? Started having funny turns. Twitching, fits, you know. So your *nain* thought that maybe the dog had a heart condition, got out her angina spray, and gave it a puff."

"Did it work?"

"No. Dog dropped dead. Your *nain* was ever so upset."

We pause, and then laugh cruelly, laugh long, laugh hard, laugh until coffee came out of my nose, and my dad has to sit down, thirty-five hundred miles away but we're right there together.

"How's it going in New York, *cariad*? Got that visa yet? What you doing about money? You should call us more often. Tell us what's going on. We worry, your Mam and me."

I stop laughing abruptly. I hang up, later blame it on a bad line. I could still hear our laughter days later, and it hurt for some reason, but it doesn't stop me laughing in the club. I laugh longer. I laugh harder.

Slowly, seductively, the laughter starts to take over, creeps in imperceptibly like a parasite. I start to shake, and it hurts, and then I find I can't stop, choking for breath . . . willing that aching jaw to close, to gulp back the next throttling sob ready to break . . . and it's *painful,* and suddenly there are tears, and it's not laughter at all, it was never laughter, it was more like bitter, putrid rage, a scream inside, and I can only listen in horror to the bile pouring from me in aching, breaking peals, in that empty dead ring of hollow laughter.

I drink more. By ten p.m. every night, *I'm in Oz.*

Eyes glassy, verging on the brink, slide off his lap and veer, wobbling over to the bitches—I'm in my element when alcohol hits the veins, runs pure, distilled.

"So when I first started working my name was Fema, but I just wasn't making money. Then the housemom took me aside and said, like, 'Sweetie, you gotta change your name. No one wants a girl called after the Federal Emergency Agency. Not when Katrina's just hit New Orleans.' You know, maybe she was *right*. I'm doing *so* much better now my name's Coco."

Ah, whattha *fuck*. In no mood for this shit, not today. I could feel myself transforming into one of them, rotting with frustrated ambition. The bartender turns around and hands me a vodka shot.

"So I wrapped the film Monday. I had to play a stripper at a bachelor party. Geez, I dunno how you do this job. Fucked *up*, man. The guys were *so* aggressive. I was *cryin'*, I was fuckin' *cryin'*. They have no respect."

"So how's the manager?"

"Oh he called me Tuesday. He wants to go on a date. You think that's kinda sick when he has a girlfriend? I said yes."

I dunno how you do this job. The alcohol eases my entry into this sick, celluloid world of fantasy, makes it easier to hear the soundtrack, so when you're dancing to the rhythm you're playing the starring role in your own film, a shitty music video, a Broadway musical adapted for the big screen. I stumble away from the bartender, feeling her drag me down, out of the alcohol fog to where the air's clearer, *fuck it, I want that fuggy no man's land again*—'nother shot and I'm ready to go, exhale, fuck, *breathe*, push real life out of this place for a moment, get back to the Emerald City . . .

I'll take ya to de Candy Shop . . .

Whoops, nearly fell then, hand to steady myself, Candy Shop, yeah sweet as fucking candy aren't we, all of us with our smooth, unblemished, saccharine-sweet bodies concealing the decaying souls within, you know what happens if you eat too much candy, right? *Hey man, how are you? You wanna dance? No, well, I'm kinda drunk, so I'm gonna sit here for a while, talk to you guys . . .*

Never understand why they get so aggressive. *For fuck's sake, you came here to talk about the freakin' NFL "in peace"? That excuses your slur upon my character? Yeah, I'm a slut ass-hole, a fuckin' slut for doin' my job and not gettin' out of your face quick enough for your liking.*

Reaction: Pause, consider: Was that offensive? Oh *yeah?* Well take this: Nice little jab to the jaw. Uh oh, look, there's a manager, he's grabbing my arm in one of those well-practiced manager maneuvers, but hey, my other hand's still free! And I look at it with admiration as it makes a spectacular grab for the vodka-cranberry, the vodka-cranberry makes a sublime arc, crystallizes momentarily in the air as all the girls turn, admire—before it connects. *Fuck.*

Shouldn'a done tha'.

Can't really speak, sllllurrrrinnng. Dressing room, already it's a distant memory. "You goin' home Mimi?" *There's no place like home, just a sublet.* Ah, yeah. Punched someone. "Again?" Yeah. *The usual. Jus' the usual.* "How many drinks this time?" Uuuurrrgh. Dunno. See ya tomorrer. "Door's that way sweetie." It is? *Whe' they change thi' place aroun'?* "You know Dorothy's shoes were really meant to be silver? Like, in the book. They just changed it to red for the movie." She bends over, runs a finger down a slim leg, admires her glittering ruby slippers, winks, flits away down the yellow brick road.

Outside it's dark, midnight in Manhattan, winter coming, chilly, but I have the beer jacket on. And the tequila jacket too.

"Honey, you OK? Someone pickin' you up?"

The tears arrive suddenly like amyl nitrate, brain cells popping, *It's not enough to be here, writing, it's not enough. I need the break, the fuckin' break, but who's gonna give it to you? You gotta get it yourself. Like you gotta make the rent, buy the clothes, find money for the lease, pay the bills . . . where d'you fit the writing in all of this, all of this stress and worry and drinking and dancing? An' when you do all this, juggle it expertly every day, build the precarious Emerald City, what's left of you, your ambition?* Ambition becomes a well-practiced sentence repeated at intervals in the club, more to keep others happy than yourself.

Someone comes closer, couldn't tell you who.

"So what happened?"

"Punche' someo'."

"Fuck, you shouldn't be *doin'* dis job."

He says "job" like *jawb*. I love that about New Yorkers. I love the fact I have to say *"cawffee"* to get the brown stuff, because they don't get my accent. I piece my dreams here together, one by one, plan the construction of my Emerald City. Next—a place of my own. A dog. *Dawg*. I giggle and hiccup behind the tears. Ooh, another brain cell implodes. Headache.

"Your eyelashes are fallin' off."

We're off to see the . . .

The Emerald City's in ruins. Feigning fitful sleep, I plot my escape. All I need are some warm clothes, the laptop, the lucky rabbit my sister gave me. I have three grand, it'll get me by, that's just over one and a half thousand pounds. I could go back to Europe. I could go anywhere. I won't say good-bye. I'm an expert at leaving, a professional of reinvention. Same name? Yeah, Mimi. Doesn't bring me luck, but it seems to fit. Dorothy? Don't get me started. Fuckin' hangover. Could stay, would be easier if I had my own place. Problem: No fuckin' money for lease. Could stay, making money at the club. Problem: Imminent departure advisable after punching that guy in the face. Could stay. Problem: Who the fuck will pick up the pieces? Who'll be there if something goes wrong, something fucks up? Eton? He didn't even make it this far. The Berlin Fucking Wall lay between us in the middle of the bed, subdivided by a yellow brick road. Sun up.

The Wonderful Wizar . . .

It's an altercation with myself, when the film stops every morning at five a.m. What next? Where to? Alone, always alone, that was for sure. To stay or to go, when was enough? When was the break? The break came with the resolution of the confusion ripping me up inside. I speak like an English-American, weaving my clumsy way down the yellow brick road, trying to get out of Oz, trying to find courage, and a heart, and a brain along the way. I'm alone now, always. Have to make that decision to walk the yellow brick road, to the far side of Oz, do it before the Wicked Witch of the West Side gobbles me up.

There's no place like home. I tap my heels together three times.

It don't do shit.

I left *La Bella* in St. Martin. Joined a new boat for a bigger wage. Lied on my résumé to get the job. No one knew me in the Caribbean. I thought. Then I bumped into Jon-jon.

"What's with you?" he said, in his nasty jaapie twang. I didn't get what he meant. I'd been sitting in a pavement café in St. Barts in the Caribbean, sipping a margarita, escaping the boat, work, guests, for a few hours, when he turned up. "I don't get what you mean," I murmured in a monotone, and watched as ash drifted down, down, down onto sun-bleached cobblestones.

"Last time I saw you in France, you were fucking everything in sight, drunk in a gutter and high on pills."

I smiled at him. Maybe it was a sad smile. Maybe it was a sweet smile. To me it was a vapid smile, the smile a baby makes when it's about to burp. Reflexive. "Was I," I said. "That's nice of you to notice. Well, now I'm not. I'm working on a sailboat as a chef for rich, fat Americans, and I'm writing a book." I eyed his uniform, the epaulettes. *Mouth snarled on mine, a hand tugging down flies, the other squeezing, kneading, unknotting my breast. The sound of guests on deck, my name called by the deckhand, an inadvertent growl, an ache.*

"Am I in it?" he asked.

"Yeah, you're in it. So's your brother. Who's on your boat this year?"

"Naomi Campbell. P. Diddy. Usual lot." *Name dropper,* I thought, and sipped my margarita. "Name dropper," I said.

"Yah, you think I give a *fuck* about these stupid people? At least I am not a fucking pill-popping English slut." He grinned crookedly, straightened the epaulettes, stood up, walked off down the port. "D'you think people change Jon-jon?" I called after him.

"Yah, sure. But you confuse me, Cambridge. Too fucking clever to be so stupid. Living too hard. You are interesting, yah, but I wouldn't fuck you again. God knows what I'd catch."

Thanks Jon-jon, I mouthed as he walked away, and made that same smile. Empty, about to burp, hovering somewhere between a reflexive laugh, a refluxive cry, acid and stinging.

I knew I'd been a bad girl when I woke up wearing an unfamiliar G-string with a thousand dollars in twenties scattered around me.

I knew I'd been a bad girl. I just couldn't recall how, or why, or when.

"You were funny last night," Bambi would say, and I'd smile like I remembered. "Laughed my ass off when you punched that black dude, that was fuckin' funny." The bartender'll stop me. "Don't you remember? Managers said no more drinks until you start behaving." Jolie will drift over. "You know last night when we were dancin' for those guys . . . ?" Chloe, the masseuse, rolls her eyes and sighs when she sees me. "Don't you ever fuckin' do that shit again Mimi. I'm tellin' you now, you can do that shit in front of me cause we're friends sweetie, but there's people here who are gonna drag you down, who wanna see you in the gutter, you know? You gotta start watchin' yourself." A man will wink, squeeze my ass, give me a smile, *thanks for last night baby* a kiss on the cheek, turn back to the Veuve, the clients he's entertaining. A girl I don't know (at least, I don't think I know), drags me into the bathroom, the harsh strip lights exacerbating my eyes into huge limpid puddles, a ghoulish moth in the mirror staring right back at me. "Mimi, I heard about Tuesday. Me and you gotta talk honey. You got my number. We can't talk here, but outside. Too much shit goes on here." She sees my face, my pale and trembling face, my face that needs a drink, a slap, a wake-up call. "You remember dontcha?" *You remember? You do remember?* It's a chiming refrain, it's Quasimodo's bells, it torments me, a writhing, malignant devil child sitting heavy and stubborn in my womb, it horrifies me, because I don't remember, I don't remember, *I don't.* I laugh. It's a horrible sound, like Jolie's laugh, wrong.

11

I WANT TO STOP YOUR NIGHTMARES, Eton said, and I appreciated the thought, really I did. I appreciated the effort, him casting himself as Saviour, because it saves me and Mimi the bother of looking for the hero. In the short time we've had together it's been fun, I'll admit. I've felt safe, and warm, and cuddly, and sweet. But then Mimi gets restless. And I walk away again, and I'll start writing, getting it out of my soul, but it doesn't seem to make it any better. *I want to stop your nightmares.* I'm torn between being fascinated by my own destruction and disgusted by it. I'm torn between wanting to kill Mimi off altogether and yet fearing that when she goes there will be nothing left to me. I'm torn between wanting him and hating him, needing him and despising him, because when he holds me tight until the nightmares go, I am reminded that I should not *be* with someone like this. I should, by rights, be with someone who crawled out of the same hole I came from.

She's my enemy, my nemesis, the devil, the fake me, Mimi. But she came to me when I needed her most, when *he* was not there, when *he* failed me. Throughout all this she's the one who did not leave me, who made me earn money, get a job, keep going, survive, *breathe.* That first breath sunk deep, slapped hard my blue oxygen-starved body, and with that inhale came the exhale, the long, hard wail *I want to stop your nightmares,* he said, but how can he stop what I can't even recall, I can't even articulate? How can one eliminate an invisible, impalpable foe? *I want to stop your nightmares* but I don't think he realizes that I need them to keep me alive, to keep me from falling backward, to keep me from assassinating the only friend I have. I fight him, I struggle in calm, capable arms, I punch him, I want to wound, biting, plunging my small, white teeth into his innocent, pure flesh, dirty teeth, dirty fingernails, scraping, licking, tangling, digging, corrupting. I hate him, despise him, loathe him, want to pluck him out of my heart, burrowed deep within my skin, I want to kill him, I want him to leave us, just *leave us be,* festering in our misery, our triumph, our sin. *I want to stop your nightmares,* he said, *Oh shut up! Stop! Enough, no more!* We *need* them, we *need* each other, you must go, *please* just *leave,* I *have* to finish this, get it down on paper . . .

I want to stop your nightmares, he says.

Jolie's a nice girl. She likes me. That don't mean shit, because I know as soon as I see her it's going to be a long, long night.

"Mimi! We gotta talk. I gotta give you the update on my fiancé."

She's from Texas, and the words roll off her tongue with a distinctive elastic twang, softened by the years in New York. She has a sweet voice, gentle, jarring uncomfortably with the huge fake breasts, the sharp ribs jutting out underneath, the shapeless legs that never saw a treadmill, the emaciated wrists.

"So he's been avoiding my calls, and he made this road trip like five hours outta Texas, and he *never* makes road trips, and he got real pissy with me for calling him so much, but you know, after the incident with the *hard-on*"—she lowers her voice, whispers the words for fear of offense, continues in a normal tone—"I get real *worried* about him, you know? You think he's cheatin' on me?"

"Sounds like it. Just dump him."

"Well, he's movin' in with me Thursday—it's like a big commitment. I know he's mean, but I love him. I dunno how I can keep workin' here though. He *hates* me workin' in stripclubs."

"Where'd you meet him?"

"In a stripclub."

There's not a trace of irony in her vapid dark eyes, the glossy lips, the soft words slipping off her tongue in a relentless, unceasing confession.

"So then I met this guy Saturday. Here. And afterwards we were gonna go get breakfast. So I wait for ten minutes on the corner of Ninth and he doesn't show. But I know where he works, so the next day I hang out on his street, and I can't find the place, so I go to a gay bar and get like, *totally* wasted with these drag queens, and then I decide to find where he lives 'cause he said it was nearby, and the first house I go to has his name on the door! So I ring and he jus' buzzes me in. Opens the door and is like, *totally* freaked out and excited to see me. So we're makin' out on the bed, and we're just about to have sex, when he tells me he has a girlfriend, and I freak out and start cryin' and tell him I love him and he's an asshole, and then I storm out. You think he thinks I'm crazy?"

"So—you stalked him, nearly had sex with him, told you loved him after an hour, and reacted badly when he told you he had a girlfriend, despite the fact that you have a fiancé?"

"Yeah."

There's something broken in her, even I can see that. Broken as she lies to herself on a daily basis, stores up the self-deceits for her unloading sessions with me. She looks to me for confirmation that she's normal for screwing cunts she meets in stripclubs, for giving handjobs in the back for an extra fifty, for letting some guy push aside her G-string, get his kicks by plunging his fingers into the moist, warm depths. There's something cracked and wrong, flawed, out of sync, crooked, rotting, decaying inside her. It's almost imperceptible until you've worked for as long as I have, gotten to know the girls, built up trust, shared some secrets. And then it surrounds you, an intangible whiff of souls slowly decomposing as they wait for the slap.

Chloe sits down next to Jolie. The club swirls on, out of focus, somewhere behind us, still early, not that many clients yet. Bambi's onstage. Good job. She hates these girls, blond hoochie bitches, she calls them. Chloe turns around and addresses me, waving a martini in the air.

"So the manager I had a crush on said he'd call and he never did. But yesterday he took me to the back and we made out. He got his dick out and asked me to suck it. I said no."

"Tommy?"

"No, not Tommy. Why, he tried that one on you? Tried it on me too. Said he loves me and I'm the most beautiful girl here."

She flicks her long bleached extensions over her shoulder, whips out a compact, checks her makeup. Jolie slips away as a new group of businessmen walk in, slides onto their laps like a fart.

"I have an audition for this really big film tomorrow. It's

gonna make my career. Did I tell you I fucked this guy for seven hours straight on Sunday? My ex. He loves me. Says I'm beautiful."

The rot spreads, mold covering the sheen of life, dragging it down with cloying, asphyxiating stealth. Little Chloe, blond and beautiful, six years old, laughing as Daddy heaves her onto his shoulders. Chloe, eighteen, sweet and clean, moving to New York to be a model and actress, excited, overwhelmed by the Big Apple. Chloe, thirty, pawed by managers, sucking dick for approval, seeking out compliments like an eager puppy, but waiting, just waiting, always waiting, for the slap.

Bambi disappears in the back with a manager before I can join her.

"Fuckin' manager has a fuckin' *girlfriend*."

Jolie and I glance at each other. We knew that. Chloe knew it too, *should* have known it.

"You upset?"

"So why didn't he call me? Dump her? Why'd he make out with me, try and get me to suck his dick? *I don't get it*."

You don't get it sweetheart, because it's slowly choking all that's good inside you, all that you wanted out of life, out of friends, out of lovers. It's about sex now, sex as currency, sex as validation. Waiting for the slap, biding your time, hungrily yearning for it all along—but! something's wrong. When's it going to hit? When does palm connect with cheek in a swift, sharp movement? *Ah*. You can see it coming now out of the corner of your eye, but you don't dodge. Relief, the expected. You sit there and wait for it.

After a long and sober season in the Caribbean and Central America, I flew to Costa Rica to work on *La Bella* again. We were in Aruba after a long, upwind battle against a tropical wave. Our bodies still ached from the shellshock of the boat pounding against the waves, ferocious and malevolent like the huge playground bully who preyed on the kindergarteners. You are reminded, so often, when sailing, of your own frailty, your own irrelevance. Swarming over deck in the middle of the night dwarfed by waves, clinging to a lifeline as fifty knots of wind tries to claw you out to sea, curled up on the bow next to the gyb watching the sun rise over a vast, empty ocean, working without remittance for a faceless owner who pays you wages to suspend your life to tend to his plaything, his tax-relief, his cruelest lover, his yacht.

We were in Aruba, moving uncertainly through people and a land that didn't tilt and jerk and smack us underfoot. The crew, three men and me, decided to go to a stripjoint. We went to a stripjoint. I sat and sipped my beer and smiled as the whores fluttered around them, old withered women painted like China dolls, murmuring their pidgin-English seductions to sailors punch-drunk from the sea. The Captain disappeared for a half hour with one woman, returned, ordered a drink. His face was carved into a mask of mourning. "What's wrong?" I asked. "Aw, I just went upstairs with one of them whores. Not *for* nothing, just for a chat-like. She was very interesting. From Venezuela, telling me about her ambitions and all. But she started asking me if I wanted to fuck her, said for five dollars she'd do it without a johnny. Five fucking dollars!" He looked at his beer, picked at the damp label, rolled the bottom of the bottle around slowly, his gaze avoiding mine. "I'm a dad, you know that Mimi? Got me little girl back home with her ma in Sheffield. I'd fucking kill meself if she ever got that desperate. *Five dollar, sin condom, sin condom!* T'aint right Mimi." He took a swig of beer and the painted ladies floated past, whispering and giggling, insubstantial will o' the wisps, their eyes blank and staring and unfathomable. "T'aint right."

Later that night I'm on a roll. Private room, seven hundred bucks already tucked into my garter. Buzzing from the champagne, buzzing from the giddy hedonism of earning money so easily. I call Eton, high from drink and money, wanting him to be jealous, pathetically emulating Jolie, all of them. The phone rings out. I return downstairs unsteadily, the cold of the brass banister fogging beneath a hot, drunk palm, my palm. I regard it wonderingly, a laugh, back to the bar, a break before I hit the floor again. Jolie was busy. She'd disappeared off into a dark corner, taking that insidious whiff of rot with her. Chloe was massaging a large, well-dressed man in the midst of a large group, laughing and flirting as if she'd forgotten the cracks threading delicately through her tender heart.

Tommy the manager grabs me before I reach the bar. "Come wid me." I wonder vaguely if another client's in the back waiting for me as he pulls me into a private room. No. It's empty. The door swings shut with a neat, decisive click. My head swirls in confusion, and I giggle as he embraces me, squeezes my ass, hands me a shot. "Drink it."

I do. He pulls his dick out. "Suck it."

I laugh and push him away, the DJ's calling my name and I'll be fined if I don't get onstage, and a pretty, sad girl grabs my hand, helps me up the steps to the lights and the fan swirling our hair around our faces, a giant blow-dryer emulating some sordid top-shelf photo shoot.

"Tommy trying to get you in a room?" she asks, concerned. I nod as I slip into the beat of the music, curl my body around its rhythms, wink at the DJ, slide the top of my dress over my breasts, blank looks from faceless men hovering in the dark.

"You make sure you stay away from him, OK? He does stuff. Drugs, girls." *Like I'm one of them.* I am a good girl, I was not born to this, I am the last person you would ever expect to find in a place like this.

Catechesis, an elementary religious instruction, predominantly oral

—my head suddenly lurches into the present with a contraction of my stomach, steady, breathe, hand connects with brass, hold, hold, something's happening to me. What was in that fucking drink? I stumble off the stage and, then, they tell me later, extract a hundred dollars from one man easily (*Saviour or Sex God?*), smoothly, the art of seduction flaying the carcass of their desire, another wine (*Dontcha remember? Dontcha?*), thick, soupy feeling in head, rapidly blocking the connection between mind and body, ontologically distinct so what remain are vivid flashes of disconnected images in a sea of milky darkness, a sense of unease washed down with another shot of liquor, the liquor burns my lips, I lick it, like wine, like it were the blood of him—

—dark room, a marble table, sitting on a leather banquette he's pressed against me hands greedily feasting on breasts cal-

loused palms scraping clumsily against flesh as he squeezes hard
methodical urgent You know how long I've wanted you? Watched
you? You're fuckin' beautiful baby knock on door, waiter peers in
anxiously, uncertainly, as he leans back against the banquette
flies undone mouth lolling arrogantly arm draped over me—

the Bread which we break is a partaking of the Body of
Christ

—door closes Tommy grabs my head his tongue slithers into
my mouth like an animal smacks hand against head again
harder this time scratch of bristle against face pulls hair head's
forced down knocking-knocking-knocking on the door my
tongue works obediently mechanically repeating my litany my
catechism my prayers for the salvation of the soul departed
the mind and body are ontologically separate *Ave Maria* even
as my mind reaches another level of disconnection and my
body no longer feels my breasts forced rudely out of my dress
do this in remembrance of me a hand head roughly pushing
G-string the tears running the pain I don't even feel *gratia
plena Dominus tecum* wish I could forget this bit but I can't
vague surreal sense of confusion *why-is-this-why-this-is-hap-
pening* I gobble it down swallow every last drop I receive him
in place of God this harsh metallic salty taste in my mouth
and the music starts to penetrate my head aching sore—

Hail Mary, full of grace

The restaurant at the back of the club. Managers. Rows of
drinks. Tommy grabs one and pushes it in my face, and then

kisses me long and hard and laughs and turns around and declares to the room "This one's a writer! Warned me I gotta be good wid her cause she's gonna write about dis!" *blessed art thou among women* No one catches his eye, the other managers sigh and look away, back to the game on the flat screen, some food arrives, it sits in front of me for a while, until he stabs the steak with a fork and pushes it into my face, smearing my lips with blood *he who eats my flesh and drinks my blood abides in me and I in him* prying it into my mouth, and it drops out, because I can't chew, swallow. The corner of my eye is puffy and swollen. I stay in the restaurant all night, I earn no more money *Benedicta tu in mulieribus* I speak to people, apparently *(you were speakin' to people, dontcha remember?)* I can still speak, when the night is over I find my way to my locker and get dressed. *I keep breaking*, I told Eton once. *It's OK, you're allowed to break*, he said, but didn't he get it? Didn't he understand what happens when the cracks and flaws held tenuously together are dropped on the stone flagged floor in front of the gasping, titillated audience, watching the break in avarice, in disgusted fascination? *et benedictus fructus ventris tui, Iesus* I'm broken, I told him, and I laughed and laughed and laughed, broken was always broken, was broken before this, will be broken long after *blessed is the fruit of thy womb* but this, *this*, was what it was to be broken *Sancta Maria* this feeling, fingernails scraping down skin, leaving white trails in airbrushed skin and the dark, greasy sludges beneath a manicure, nails dig harder, deeper, and only then with a pathetic whimper and a sob do you release *Mater Dei ora pro nobis peccatoribus*, in the shower with the water at full blast so the roommates can't hear, and I wonder if what I thought I was before all this was just a role, cast off like a snake's brittle paper skin, until with a rip and a tear you got down to the core, *pray for us sinners now* the molten, raw, cancerous center *nobis peccatoribus* I think of their faces as they bow their heads in prayer, Mam's hand reaching for mine, and mine stuck deep, sulkily into my pocket *peccatoribus* Eton was Catholic too, he took me to Church once on Easter Sunday, shaking his head at my mortal sin, the revelation that the last time I had been was when I was twelve years old *peccavi* I close my eyes.

Amen

Bambi calls me the next day, arrogant, grumpy from the comedown.

"Comin' into work? What happened to you last night? Got stuck talkin' to that dumb bitch Jolie. Chloe was cryin' over that fuckin' manager. I made nothin'. Spent all my fuckin' money on an eight-ball too. Tommy said he'd gimme some shit if I went in the backroom with him and he fuckin' didn't. Went off with some other bitch instead. She probably got him off, the whore. Fuckin' *sucked*. Whole fuckin' *night* sucked. You workin' tonight?"

When I go into the gym I catch a glimpse of a gray, sad girl in the mirror, thin legs pumping listlessly on the Stairmaster, right eye scratched and swollen. Already the wounds are healing, the rot's subsiding back down inside me, the eyes, *you can see in the eyes,* but they're closing over too, a web of scars, like the rest of me. Pure white skin, privileged skin. Puckers quickly into a scab when the blade slices. I grab a cab to work, my makeup already on my face painting over the shame, and then I see the place and the stench is too much, too much, I tell the cab driver to turn round, take me back home again, without even letting him pull up to the curb.

As much as I love New York, it's become too normal for me to extract someone's finger from my ass, pluck a mouth from my nipple, grind against a hard cock, cut off pieces of myself with every shameful dark act I commit. I know that I have to dodge the slap, could see it coming from the corner of my eye. Didn't want to soil myself beyond recognition, join the legions of girls waiting eagerly in line for the crack of that palm. I want a normal life, a dog, breakfast over the *New York Times*, bills, mortgage, 9 to 5. Cooking for my man. Once a year, two-week vacation to some cheap resort. Sitting down at the laptop to write my book, my screenplay, my novel. Not hellfire and damnation.

I think of Jolie, nice but stupid (*oh* so stupid), and I see myself reflected in the empty pools of her eyes. Maybe the slap has already come, it's too late, the air I breathe—thick with pheromones—has already distorted me into a caricature of who I was, like Jolie, like Bambi. I used to look at Eton when he slept, and it was the only time I saw him stop frowning, drop that perpetual shield he has against the decay, permanently dodging the slap. It hasn't gotten him. But me?

After last night, I know the stinging mark of the hand, the imprint of the fingers, the rising welts on my smooth skin, are already discernible.

The next day I wake at midday. I ignore the missed calls on my cellphone. I crawl into my workout clothes—a huge hooded top, sweatpants, scarf, hat. I walk five blocks to the gym; pull the scarf a little tighter against the fading scratches on the right side of the face, the yellowing bruise at the corner of the eye. I find a new strength in my body released from its usual hungover shackles. Exercise until my muscles ache, thighs taut and screaming; face pink, wet with sweat. Lungs vacated of stale nicotine breath, I can no longer hear the insistent murmurs of a vivid memory, an insidious shame from that night. Blissfully numb in the sharp smack of the wind on Broadway; thread my way back to the apartment through tourists clutching bags from Macy's. In the apartment I shower for a long time, check the mirror—bruises still there, but fading. Towel myself dry, and note that my body still looks young, unblemished, seductive, even. I remember, distantly, that I have to write an article for a magazine in England eager for the lurid tales of the ecdysiast. I boil water, make tea. The rent's due, a note from my roommates. Electricity, utilities. Have to work tonight to cover them. I pick up my coat and head out of the apartment for coffee, to stock up on fake eyelashes, L'Oréal tanning gel. I dial voice-mail as I wait for the elevator.

Their voices are pitched wrong, like little broken twigs crackling down the phone. Bambi: "Call me back." Lily: "I need to check you're OK. Something happened." Another message: "Where are you? Call me." Another: "Why aren't you picking up? If you don't call me back I gotta call the police."

I don't know immediately because the voices etch in me the fear, the shame, the disgust from yesterday morning, and all I can think is, *They know.* I remember shaking—I *am* shaking, my breath quickening, note the twisted silver wrapper of gum kicked into the corner of the elevator, stark against the thick brown carpet. The shiny brass of the wall is covered with thumbprints, tiny—from a child perhaps. The elevator whirrs soothingly. I don't want to know, step out of the elevator, confront the stark truth, and when it hits the ground floor, doors opening with a dull, muffled ding, I stand reluctant, fearful of stepping out, knowing that the slap has come; it was now merely waiting for me to register the pain.

I can't remember what I'm leaving the apartment for. The phone rings. It's Bambi, I register with a nauseous lurch of misanthropy, a rising of bile in the throat. *Thank God Ivory, you're OK?* What? What's happened? *It's all over the papers. Dancer found in her apartment. Dead. Stabbed. No names yet.* Who was it though? Who could it be?

Who could it be. I want to call Eton with a want born of need, yet he knows me only as Mimi, doesn't care about the rest. He knew only the person I professed to be, the girl who could fuck him, bend over into twisted imitations and simulations of pornography, that puppet show. He didn't know the twisted soul inside who could commit unspeakable acts (for free!) after a shot of liquor from a manager. My body looks smooth, perfect, complete. The deception is in place, and Mimi assuages my fears with a wink, a smile. The doorman catches my eye and I smile back, without feeling whatever should lie behind a smile. I walk out of the apartment building, catch my breath in the chill wind, walk over to the newsstand outside the revolving doors. Reach for the *New York Post*.

The face staring back at me is softer than I remember. An elegant face. The eyes are fiery and proud, not with the arrogance of drugs, but the stubbornness and ambition of youth. She looks—clean. She looks nice. She looks like a girl I would introduce to my grandparents, sit with in elegant SoHo bars discussing skin-care products and Prada bags, the latest *New Yorker*. Her skin is smooth, glossy, and young, the hair long, silky around her beautiful face, slim neck. But her name. *It says her real name.* Something sour rattles in my throat, crawls into the gullet, sits poisonous and sick. The shame! I clutch Mimi tightly, as if she would ever dare to leave me. A shudder, eyes closed, closed, closed, force it out, force it out of mind. Open. Mimi is entwined around me lovingly, protectively, jealously. We danced together, this girl and I. I recognize her face, the profile, the starkly normal name hidden deep inside the Chanels and Diamonds and Desires. She was not my friend. I can't recall speaking to her, even when I saw her nervous and tetchy, driven away from Foxy's by the cruel looks, the long hours, the unscrupulous management. They hadn't put down her stripper name. That hurt me, that the stripper had stayed alive long enough to tattoo her with indelible ink, and yet she was nameless. She was us. She was Bambi on the slippery ole slope to destruction, starting to use the hard shit after work, smoking it to avoid track marks. She was that Colombian girl who people said started whoring to pay for the crack, died in some fucking shithole a couple of months before I ever set foot in a stripjoint. She was the older girls, with families and husbands and regular clients, the girls who never drink and have it together, who save their money and do this out of need, who don't give handjobs and argue with their men back home to let them work. She was me, lost in a world that sucks the sinews from my bones with a smack of violet lips, a hungry grunt for more. Parents didn't know she "danced." Another fucking euphemism. Parents didn't know she *stripped*.

I take the newspaper, smile back at the doorman, back into the elevator, up to the ninth floor, *ding*, in my apartment, can't remember why I left the apartment. I have to work tonight, I'll call Bambi, see if she's working. And then you sit there, empty, numb, nullified by something that they call grief, but you don't know what it's called, for grief is for someone who is dead, someone gone, never to return, someone who you know intimately, someone who shares your life like Mimi does. One moment changes everything, flicks the off switch. My head aches. I knew it wasn't the dancing that killed her, held that rolled-up twenty-dollar bill to her nose for the last time, thrust that knife a little deeper until it hit the aorta. But I knew that by the time we get to the stage, peel our dresses off, caress our breasts, and twirl around on six-inch clear plastic heels, the damage has already been done.

Call Lily, gotta call Lily. Her cell phone rings out. I don't leave a message. Blindly make some tea, the English kind, hot, dark, the teabag left in for three minutes, removed, a splash of milk, no sugar.

I see myself reflected in the empty pools of her eyes. The death of a nameless dancer whose real name littered the papers like a filthy, execrable word was a tragedy I could not bear *The rising welts on my smooth skin are already discernible.* It was out-and-out pornography, child pornography, callous and sadistic and unbearably, heartbreakingly cruel. Because whatever crap we tell ourselves, whatever clever marketing ploys lie out there justifying and legitimizing the groping and the sex and the abuse, whatever those in power will tell you and our clients will lead you to believe, however strong Mimi is, however beautiful that smile, that glance, that touch, the soul within is corrupt and rotting, because this job is wrong, wrong, *wrong*. I can see their painted mouths leering horrifically, a tongue like a lizard flickering in the back of that artificial mouth and whipping it into a bogus smile. *What do you feel?* a journalist asked me once, and he asked because he felt it too, felt the bitter, corrosive heat radiating off me, warping sheet metal. *I feel like I'm tainted and wrong, like I'm dirty, like I will never fall in love, or have children, or get married, or be normal, or lead a life that isn't twisted with desire and sex and bitterness and filth, I feel like I will die with Mimi on my tombstone for all eternity, blotting out whoever I was before, whatever I was before. I feel like I gave birth to a monster, I feel like that girl, The Stripper. That's what they daubed upon her cold dead chest, her blue body, as they waited for the air to swell deflated lungs, waited vainly, vainly, and then watched her die before she could ever inhale deep enough for a chance to correct them. I don't know how I do this job. I don't know how I've done the things I've done, how I've done the things I never told you about, locked up tight, bound over and over in tight-lipped memory, until they became forgotten, before they could be committed to this page, find their way into my obituary. I don't know what makes me different, what makes it easier for me to have my head forced down on someone's cock than for the next person, for the consequences to be slight in comparison to the gravity of the situation (did I enjoy it? did I ask for it? I didn't hit him, I didn't say no, I didn't walk away) a few tears, cleared up by a hot meal, a trip to the movies, a group hug, the concern that my family do not find out for they could not deal with the shame, not like I could, not like I can. All I know is what makes that girl in the paper like me. We share things, similarities, understanding. Not that we are dancers, strippers, whores, sluts, hos. Just that we* did a job because we felt we could cope with the consequences, the sheer weight of our apostasy, the nuclear fallout, not realizing that the half life would be for all eternity, and that the job would be what we were known for whenever we entered a room, someone whispered our name, looked over and glanced into our face, closed and guarded.

What do you feel?

He had asked again, more insistently this time, and I took a drag of my cigarette, looked distant, bored. *Hungry,* I said. *I'm fucking starving.*

I have bad dreams.

The phone rings-rings-rings. Rings out.

The phone rings-rings-rings. Rings out. *I walk as if under water, everything muffled, not really existing until I have my three drinks, my cigarette, keep my date with Mr. Benjamin every night, step onstage with an almost audible sigh, watch as my body melds, pulsating, with hers, a lilt like an orgasm, a spasm, death. It will be OK.* The phone rings. *Dualism is a philosophical concept where the mind and the body are considered ontologically separate, yet the separation between Mimi and me rents this body in half, in quarters, in tiny, wretched pieces. This renders dualism, to me, an inadequate concept.* The phone rings. *I've been here before, it's OK.* The phone rings. *It's all going to be fine.* She soothes me, holds my hand, gazes into my eyes, coos at me like a mother. *Astonishing! I have never seen her like this.* The phone rings. I answer.

"Mimi."

It's Eton. I register this with a faint twist of displeasure, a worm of fear.

"Mimi, you left me a message the other night."

"What?"

"I'm sorry I didn't call sooner, but you were totally incoherent. I could barely figure out what you said. And then I did."

Eton speaks again, his voice unusually tender, measured, resigned almost. He sighs and barely audible, the vowels concealing the exact emotion, murmurs:

"Mimi, I'm at home. Just come around."

The walk to his apartment is only ten blocks. I wrap my huge scarf tighter around me, stuffed red, chapped hands with a perfect French manicure into jacket pockets filled with balled-up tissues shedding lint. My cheek still smarts, my eyes feel swollen and old. Manhattan seethes and bubbles, a witch's brew. A bum is comatose on the street, just outside Duane Reade on Fifty-seventh and Broadway, his penis sticking out of his fly, obscene and swollen, a long trail of urine streaking down the sidewalk. Ladies in elegant kitten heels smartly step over the river. Steam rises from manholes in the street. Hot dogs, warm, spicy. The bonfire scent of huge, salt-covered pretzels. The doorman in Eton's building greets me warmly, all smiles. Javier. He likes me. We speak Spanish occasionally. In the summer I'd bring him iced coffee when I did the morning breakfast run on Saturdays, still warm and sleepy from Eton's bed. I step into the elevator with the little old lady who lives on the third floor. She bows her head in recognition. She walks the same route, unwavering, every day. Eton once helped her, last year, when he'd first arrived in Manhattan and she slipped in the snow. She's tiny, wrinkled, shrunken. She's all there, completely *compos mentis*, it's merely her body that betrays her. Loves Eton. Smiles at him. He always talks to her.

I knock on the door. It swings open and for a moment he stares at me inscrutably. I walk past him into the apartment and over to the window, where I light up a cigarette, stick my head out into the chilly air and blow smoke into the wind. Eton sits in his chair and waits.

"So what happened?" he asks levelly.

He dwarfs me, like I'm a little girl, he's Humbert Humbert and I'm Lolita curled on his lap, *goddamn fucking Lolita*, I'm always a fictional character for someone, except it wasn't meant to be like this, with this *need*, the dialogue of sex disintegrated by pity as I burrow into his shoulder and cry, and he just strokes my head softly, and whispers, "I'm sorry. I'm so sorry."

It strikes me, with acute irony, that this is, perhaps, one of the few genuine moments we've ever shared, when the heartless waltz between sex and love, seduction and betrayal, power and powerlessness, is destroyed simply by (*picnic, lightning*) life. And that makes me cry even more. Because he has a heart, the proverbial heartless bastard *has a fucking heart*, and he's holding me and telling me he cares, and with this curious and unexpected admission comes a new truth, one I'd tried, like everything else, to push back into the darkness and paint over with the thick, caked layers of my stage makeup, to deny and to beat into submission with my shameless act of seduction, my Mimification of the truth, contorting and wrangling reality until it becomes as illusory and indistinct as the identical figures wrapped around identical faceless men in the darkness.

The undeniable, ineffable truth *the connection between palm and cheek* that we just don't belong together.

IDENTITY IS A FUNNY THING. We don't really think about it until others start writing their own versions of us. And then it becomes so intensely, frighteningly important.

Women are complicit in the rewriting of my truth as fiction. They come to me, these writers, dribble into my inbox, led there by a paper trail of words, grasping reporter's notebooks and clunky tape recorders vomiting spools of brown, tangled tape. I trade my history for hard cash, give them my bad dreams for a check, but the dreams remain, and what appears in glossy print bears no resemblance to what I had whispered to these career women, these cockroaches of human suffering, these journalists. *I love it! I would never leave dancing! It's so empowering! I feel all woman! I used to be a geek and now I'm a sexy stripper!* Why is it that women clutch desperately, urgently, needily, to this fiction that this is erotic, glamorous, and in any way a "triumph" for our sex? Why do they revise my history, persist in drawing out my words, and then casting them aside, censoring them with the crude blanks and beeps of war-time love letters to pretty, innocent sweethearts protected from the trenches? I am a heretic for disavowing the dogma of my sex not once but twice: first, in becoming a stripper; second, in refusing the doctrine they attribute to me to make how I earn money all right, OK, *normal*. Normal. Not for me, for *them*.

But then there are those other journalists, those other writers, those other people I meet who insist, more terrifyingly perhaps, that it is not Mimi, not stripping, not sex they are interested in at all.

"You were a geek?" the journalist asked, incredulous, clutching a woman's magazine proffering tips for enhancing orgasm to twelve-year-olds alongside a glossy grinning picture of some silly *geek-girl-turned-sexy-stripper!* and I sucked on my cigarette, eyes tilted to the night sky, watching the smoke dissipate (acetone, cyanide, aluminum, DDT/dieldrin, ammonia, ethanol, arsenic, formaldehyde, benzene, hydrogen cyanide, butane, lead, cadmium, methanol, carbon monoxide, nicotine, carbon dioxide, tar, chloroform, vinyl chloride) and thinking hard before replying, untruthfully:

"No."

BillyMark's. We stood outside, the journalist and I, barely touching, a prophylactic gesture on my part, though the breasts, plumped up with a too-small bra and bursting plush and juicy from a tiny dress, took no heed and engaged him in conversation even when I did not. I leaned against a sticky wall perspiring with the sugared gum of the bill-slapper. Always, eleven p.m. on a Wednesday, they'd change the bills outside BillyMark's. "Sometimes," I said, and traced my finger down the damp, gloopy adhesive oozing from the wall, shining eerily in the hot darkness, "I think I'm going insane." He gave this statement more attention than I would have, awarded a merit to my pragmatism I did not wish for. Talking is merely to expel the emotion from our soul, remove it far from the source, place madness into a context that soothes us with those empty signifiers, words. We kept talking, a delicate fox-trot around the real issue—what real issue, we didn't know. "In what sense, insane?" He sounded concerned. "The nightmares?"

I gestured toward BillyMark's as my answer, and I love that bar, *love* it, it's part of me, who I was, who I am, who I had become. They call me Mimi behind the bar, Billy and Mark do. I'll go there after I finish work, shoot pool, hang out with the bums, the pimps, the hos, the hookers. I institute madness, like I instituted Mimi, into my soul. "And how are things with this man you mentioned, Eton?" the journalist asked suddenly. *"I think I'm losing it,"* I whispered, ignoring his question, brow furrowed with effort and then I laughed cruelly, knowing that this laugh would sear through him with coruscating force, blacken what's inside, but I intended it to hurt, because he was a threat to my Mimi, my alter-ego, the only lover who's never left me. I didn't want to hurt him, but I would, and if I didn't she *certainly* would. It was as if I were powerless to pray for my own redemption.

I threw my cigarette butt into the gutter and went back in to order another beer as he followed me with his damn tape recorder, looking confused, out of place, a little sad.

18°10'N 76°30'W

Whenever the boat was still, I would write, the new laptop purchased with months of slicing, baking, grilling, frying, sautéing, fricasseeing, souffléing, all at forty-five degrees in the Caribbean basin, in a galley the size of a closet. The boys would *humph* suspiciously, look over my shoulder, squint their eyes, rub diesel fumes from out of their sweaty eyes, and retreat back into the engine room. "When's it finished Mimi?" the Captain would boom cheerfully, ignoring my wince at being slapped out of my writing reverie. "Coming down the pub? No? You all right love?"

And they'd go, and I'd be left on the boat, a warm, soft wind whooshing in through the cockpit, kissing my salt-dried hair. I'd write some more, knowing that we would be moving again soon, and when we did, there would be no time.

She's sitting in the corner, hunched up with a backpack vomiting shoes and makeup and fake tan and thin, Lycra slivers of dresses. Girls dance around the cramped dressing room in a ridiculous burlesque, pulling tired, sagging, snagged clothing over stitched and butchered bodies.

"You ain't workin'?" Bambi demands.

She looks up.

"Got fired."

"You got *fired*? Whaddya do? Dontcha remember?"

She waves a hand listlessly.

"Usual. Drunk. Punched some guy. Can't really remember."

Bambi floats away vaguely, disinterestedly, drags the ironing board weakly into the middle of the room, and starts to butcher her dress into a semblance of acceptability.

A small, ugly girl covered in acne scars launches abruptly into a topic of more interest.

"So, if you ain't workin', you two wanna go out tonight instead? I can get us into Marquee. I scored an eight-ball too."

She addresses the question like it's an option, a flippant, enticing prospect, but really it's a desperate plea, cloaked and concealed, like the acne scars. She starts to talk, her words running out like viscous phlegm.

". . . you know I got suspended at my last club, got so drunk I kept forgettin' who'd bought me drinks, so I'd go and give a guy a dance an' the waitress would turn up and say 'Who's gonna pay for this drink?' and I'd forget who it was, and then one day my fiancé came in and found me . . ."

Bambi saunters back over, dress in hand, pupils already stung into oblivion, arrogant and insincere, suddenly concerned as if this was news to her, despite having been in possession of the facts for a good ten minutes. "Girl! Don't leave us! You can't leave!"

The girl looks up, takes another cigarette, flips a lighter, inhales deep, feeling the tar roughly caress the bronchioles, lull them harshly into narcosis.

"Got no choice. I don't want to leave either."

It's obvious—so obvious!—that she's doing it all wrong. She's too proud, too stubborn, too angry, too indignant; she yells if someone yells at her; she stamps her feet at injustice, throws herself headlong into situations, cares too much, cares too little. She's tough, the beaten puppy dog finally grown up, a toughness grown from suspicion, from hatred, a gentle naïveté pulped into submission. Pathetic naïveté. She's unforgiving; she looks at those who haven't suffered with a prejudice born of pain—her own. She's isolated, because the fire driving her is raging out of control, in contrast to the trimmed wick deemed acceptable—acceptable! Standards and rules in the home of licentiousness! Seductive. When she talks to you, leans in confidentially like she's known you for years, talks with the delinquency and warmth of her training, your anger thaws, dissipates, and a stark pornographic image flits across your mind, *fuck, push that thought out.*

She's sitting on the empty stairwell when I leave, trying to get away from the chaos of the dressing room, yet not ready to go home and leave her aborted night in the Emerald City behind. I pass her and walk on. She doesn't look up but she knows I'm there. If she'd asked me to stay, I would have, but she doesn't. She's still puffing away on those damned Parliaments, depositing little piles of ash onto the cold concrete floor, swirling them around aimlessly with a cigarette butt. When I come back later, she's gone. All that's left is her dancer name spelled out neatly in ash, over and over and over again, as if, I thought curiously, she were trying to convince herself:

mimi mimi mimi mimi

My visa arrives a few days later. I can leave. Walk away. But when I try to reach that clawed hand forward, buckled and tangled with the weight of strained ligaments, I can't. I have no money, and too much sadness weighing me in place, sitting heavy and suffocating on my heart. I begin to write about the dreams in which Mimi flips and twists inside like a devil child strapped in the thick, white cotton of a straitjacket. It's as if we have no choice, a Groundhog Day, constant, wearying repetition, our own liturgical ceremony performed with expertise if not reverence—the ceremony of fucking up. We have to see this through to a logical—or maybe *illogical*—conclusion, both Mimi and I, together. I go back to the cathedral of the club, pulse a little stronger, eyes a little brighter, walking toward whatever's calling me without resistance, my own mythology, a martyr to the dance. Yes, there's a choice, at every step of the way there's a choice. But I feel as if I have to walk through burning coals again to find what I'm looking for. I'm compelled to, I'm obliged to, I owe it to her, to force a conclusion to her story. The third intifada.

43°34'N 7°4'E

Arriving in a new port was never exciting. It was merely different: the comfort of feeling sturdy, solid land beneath feet, land that didn't rock and punch and tilt, land that didn't heave and lurch and swing. It was a relief to be somewhere that had a landscape, details to set your eyes upon, distinguishing features, an absence of monotony. It was fun to go to the pubs, order pints, talk to other boat people like us, whom we had never met before but felt we knew just the same. And then after a week or so, we would crave it, the boat. Back to what we knew, in all its glorious, unvarying monotony. The same old. Even if we never saw our friends or our lovers, our families, our children, going back to the boat was a relief. Setting sail again was a relief, anxious hearts dropping back down dry throats to sit in the pit of our stomachs, swollen on jerk chicken and blackened catfish, Red Stripe beer, and dark, sticky rum. It was safe.

I left the boat in Aruba, flew back to France to take another boat from Golfe-Juan to Florida, via Antigua. The new boat, like the old, felt like home.

They never speak to the other girls, just stand and twitter in strange tongues, looking like children who had raided Mom's makeup when she wasn't looking. The garish hot pink flush of communist Revlon, electric blue eyeliner, Chernobyl-frazzled hair, rolls of puppy fat squeezed into Day-Glo polyester. The new club is full of them, it reeks of them, their stories strangled and asphyxiated by a lack of language, the cold, hard slap. This new club feels like home.

"Where do they get them from, Ruby?" I ask the makeup artist, a pretty, goofy girl with long, ratty dreads.

"They get 'em from the agency. The agency sends 'em over. Picks 'em up at night in a big black van, takes 'em home. I used to hitch a ride in the van at night, until they started chargin' me."

"They off the boat?"

"They off the boat all right Mimi. Bran' new off the damned boat."

They're keen, I'll give them that. The other girls eye them with distaste, us immigrants who had been here long enough to say "*cawffee*," who had spent so much time trying to fit in here, we had forgotten where we came from. Identity, identities. With the cloak of our Mimis as a funeral shroud between us and our shame, you think we had time to care for these bitches? Who never paused for drinks, didn't push a straying hand from between their legs, ease a ravenous mouth from their breasts? These girls were here to work, to pay for their tickets, their freedom from whatever post-communist, post-colonial hell they had arrived from. Ambition? Buy a car. Get an American boyfriend. Purchase hair extensions, Seven jeans, Cartier watches, Prada bags. We despise their ambition, we English speakers, we post-immigrants, we who had proven, if only to ourselves, that we could survive, even if that survival meant repackaging ourselves in polyurethane as a Mimi, a Diamond, a Chanel, a venomous creature, at once a friend as much as foe.

"Excuse me plis."

The girl looks at me beseechingly from beneath an untamed mop of mousy brown hair, cute freckled face, no makeup.

"Excuse me plis, how is working in Manhattan? I have worked only in Queens."

I flash her a glance, drink it in, all in. First time. Needs money. Not yet hardened. No clue. You wear the makeup long enough, you start to play the part offstage as it seeps arrogant and drunk into your being, blood flowing alcohol and Mimi. She's too nice. She's too *normal*.

"It's cleaner than Queens," I say slowly.

"You have to take dress off in pri-vett rum?"

"You do. I don't."

I smile at her and disappear, glass in hand, to imbibe more alcohol and smile my fake smile. Later, and four hundred dollars richer, I catch her again, gazing dolefully into the mirror of the dressing room while Ruby and the housemom smoke Marlboros and swig pink zinfandel from polysterene cups. A haze of smoke. Her eyes are red as she stares at herself beneath the lights dotted around the mirrors, then looks at the other girls, embalming themselves with baby oil, perfect slut-look in place.

"Here."

I grab her and steer her to the mirror.

"Sit. You make money?"

She shakes her head no, hazel eyes blinking rapidly. I take over. Foundation, layers of foundation over the brown, young skin, set in place with powder. The eyes. Dark, smoky, thick rings of eyeliner, long, lush plastic lashes. Little white under the brows to open the eyes up. Concealer over dark, hopeless shadows. I lock her in with powder upon powder, seal that tomb with a ghostly dusting of MAC. Ruby sits up and chokes pink zinfandel through her nose.

"Damn, girl! She look like a fuckin' stripper now!"

The whole room starts to take interest, the memory of our own transformations stirring us into curiosity as we all partake in this deliberate erasure of the past. We haggle over a new name for her to replace the name she already had. We decide on "Michelle." We debate on what precise shade of platinum will suit her best, suggest she purchase a lapdog for company, give her the name of a phone store where they don't demand a Social Security number to get a contract phone, and if you sign up with a five-hundred-buck deposit, they give you a bright Pink Razr phone for *free,* just like we all had. Then we lose interest, and when a fresh wave of men surge in and litter the floor with the debris of other people's marriages, we wander listlessly downstairs, flicking hair over shoulders, holding stomachs taut, gently rubbing the icy-cold glasses of our liquor against soft, fleshy breasts, goading them to stand erect, puckered and alert.

I walked through Union Square one day. People swarmed excitedly clutching megaphones and drums and banners as they marched onward and upward for immigrant rights. There were Mexicans and Chinese and Bangladeshis and Indians and white people from who-knows-where. Some new bill proposed, Senator McCain shooting his mouth off once again, pissing off the GOP. I stood and watched them awhile, but really I felt nothing, aside from a little tiredness, and a thirst for Ketel One, soda, lime, crackling ice. I went into work early. I had nothing else to do, and I was bored of my own company.

Venus examines a nipple intently, turns back to the bar and motions for a top-up of vodka in her glass.

"Last night I got so fucked I kept calling my vagina Al Pacino," she says.

"Why?" I ask.

The new girl strolls past, whippet thin, long, striped hair in anorexic, braided worms surrounding an angular face. A "butt-fuck, give-it-to-me-in-every-orifice, cum-on-my" face. I wonder what my face looks like, I wonder idly, even though I stare at it every day when I walk into the dressing room, twisting the lightbulbs around the makeup mirrors to reveal stark, ghostly features. Etched with tragedy, the ones who want to "save" you always say, ignoring your yawns, the glance toward the wallet. No, not tragedy. Just life.

"Mimi, when you teaching yoga bitch? I wanna come to one of your classes. Fuckin' *love* doing yoga after some weed. You know, my son's into that shit. I'm getting worried about the little faggot."

Venus cackles, and through the round, suggestive hole of her dress, her belly quivers and shakes like a jelly, a brown-lined jelly with silver stretch marks delicately threading around the belly button like a slug's trail. I finish my drink. Ketel One, soda, lime, crackling ice. I nod to the Puerto Rican bartender for another, and I turn to Venus and we laugh and laugh and laugh for no damned reason. I suffer every time I wake up with that scratchy, ratcheted throat clawing its way to the sink like a creature alien from the rest of me, but I don't ever drink less.

Derek Jeter scores again, and the bored DJ sitting alone in his booth starts to play bad rock music loudly as strippers twitter and yawn, and we chink our glasses together, look into each other's eyes, beyond them, and I try not to think about the yoga class I have to attend tomorrow, with the inevitable hangover. *Maybe*, you're thinking, *nothing's changed. Nothing's changed at all from six months ago. She's still here, in a fucking club, getting drunk, plotting an impalpable escape, trying to inhabit the body of a fictitious bitch called Mimi she made up for the hell of it.* No, things have changed. They've changed all right. Bear with me, because I'm still taking you on my journey, and as you've probably noticed, nothing's black and white. Having swallowed this great lump of darkness, I'm still spewing it out before I find the light. I'll explain in good time. Bear with me, please. Bear with me.

"You never fuck with a ghetto bitch" says Venus darkly, and belches, her belly quivering like aspic.

"No, never." Colette the masseuse, a tiny woman with a massive slab of silicone pork fat in place of breasts, nods sagely.

Venus winks and slips me a fluorescent-green martini shot.

"You know the problem with these fuckin' bitches nowadays Colette? They're fuckin' career strippers. It ain't no fuckin' career. We used to have fun in the old days. There was drugs, there was shit goin' on. The dances were dirty and we played it dirty. And nowadays there's these fuckin' Russian bitches and some goddamned Disneyland legacy from Giuli-fuckin'-

yani. It ain't no fuckin' career. I'm here 'cause I'm too fuckin' lazy to get a real job. I'm here because I'm a fuckin' waster. I'm a stoner. I'm a fuck up, and I have been for eighteen years. You know my ex-husband slips me money when his wife ain't lookin' 'cause he feels so guilty I'm still a fuckin' stripper? I'm here 'cause I ain't ever figured out a way to get outta this place. I'm here 'cause I ain't ever tried."

Venus grabs her silicone tits and grins broadly, proudly, and Colette nods her head, and the thin layers of skin hanging from her neck flap together with a gentle clapping sound.

"It used to be *fun* in the old days."

Walk of Shame, the walk of shame across the empty floor to the two chairs occupied by men-in-suits, the perfunctory, dismissive glance, sizing up breasts, face, ass, potential for "extras." It's so much easier these days. After the slap something changes, hardens and softens in you all at once. You learn, the sadness sinks into your soul, coal black, but then there's diamonds formed from coal, but mostly it just sits there, waiting to get burned. Drinks imbibed, you wear the layers like they're part of you. After a year they are, kind of. I know people more, I know people inside out. I care more, strangely. I care for the people like me, who talk about getting out, actively use the money strapped around our thighs to daily purge our souls, bade farewell to the yellow brick road, have a normal life with normal, educated, kind people who aren't sex workers. I care about people like Venus who will never get out. I care more. I know people more. Men.

I sit down. Guy looks at me. He looked older than me, exhaustion smoothed onto skin that had crinkled through smoking and stress and too much alcohol and no one to make him smile for the right reasons, but he was young, twenty-eight I guess. I guess right. English I guess. I guess right. Finance. Large bank. *But of course*, mi amor, *but of course.*

"What the hell are you doing here?" he asks, as soon as he catches my eyes laughing at him for being so predictable. I was never predictable. I am never predictable. No one would ever have predicted I'd be good at this, I'd still be here eighteen months later, I'd find something so predictable in every predictable fucker's questioning of my unpredictability. And then he looks uncomfortable and asks again, his question hanging in the air as if he'd traced it with a Sharpie at the precise moment the song ends, so I could hear his voice clearly for the first time.

That accent, those vowels. It was Eton all over again. Something digs deep into my heart, past the layers, the scarring, the alcoholic sharp-tongued defense, the jewel of sense I keep hidden in the back of my skull that allowed me to keep dodging the same slap I once turned toward. A shift in the guts. *Get your money and run, don't tell him shit, don't open up again.* "So what are you doing here?" he asks again, more curious this time, and my eyes shut down. Same question every night. *It's a long story, let's not go into it. Just show me some fucking cash.*

"I'll do better than that. How about you help me fix up my friend here, and we'll have some fun together?"

He knew, he could tell, he played his role perfectly, and because he did, I could play mine. I laugh long and hard and sincere. "Champagne, two sluts, and some drugs?" I lean over and stare right into those eyes, let a smile touch my lips, let my lips slyly brush his, retreat.

"Perfect!"

The Russian bitches peel off, blistering like burned plastic, howling and charred and bitter because I'm stealing the money they need for poor Ole Grandpapa's cataract operation back in fucking Kiev. Champagne Room. The English guy hands over a bundle of notes to the sluts—my colleagues, I should say—handpicked because I know who the sluts are in this place. They disappear with English guy's friend. But English guy just wants to talk, helped along by the drugs of course, courtesy of the waitress who kindly reassures us it's not cut with glass.

English guy. So predictably predictable. English from jolly old fucking England, Mummy caught with those porcelain talons generously digging into the crotch of one of Daddy's old college buddies post-sundowners one evening. Daddy understandably doesn't want the scandal so the divorce is quick and generous, and somewhere, lost in alimony, are the two little blond boys so impeccably tutored in buggery by their parents that really the prefects at boarding school came as something of a relief. Little, lost, lonely English, life a whirl of Aspen, St. Tropez, St. Barts, the Hamps. Had a few friends at Oxford, but never seemed to go down well with the girls, though he tried to make light of it. Little, lonely English. Parents superbly and aristocratically indifferent; he's only just starting to bond with Daddy, who finally told English he loved him when he discovered the prostate cancer was in rather an advanced stage. Little, lonely English.

The drinks keep coming as we curl up close on a leather banquette in a small, windowless room in the back of the club, but then, something—strange. My dress doesn't come off, and we huddle close, talking, laughing, conversation improved by amphetamines, and when the slut comes into the room to see if my guy wants "servicing," he says no. No. A simple no.

I curl into the nook of his armpit discussing London fields while my colleagues bust a gut behind a thin partitioned wall getting his drunk friend to spurt pathetically into a limp Trojan. *Stop trying to save me—go for them. I'll get out, I'll do it without you. Hey, I may seem like a drunk, coked-up bitch, but I'm training to be a yoga teacher. I have friends who probably work alongside you. But the ones on the end of your cock—you think they have any chance? They need your help, your unconditional offers of money, jobs, contacts, but never love. When you don't come back, don't call, don't think about me, deliberately slice me out of your mind as if the memory was a tumor, I'll still get out. Not them.*

I didn't expect to meet a girl like you here.

Yes, but you did. Get over it.

"Come back to my apartment?" he asks at two a.m., after 1.5 grams of the alkaloid formation of *Erythroxolon coca*, or cocaine. And I say yes. He entered this place like a blustering cunt, paid for whores, and leaves holding my hand like a lamb. And when we arrived at his apartment (eight thousand dollars per month) he made me tea, draped a soft blue shirt around my shoulders ("This cost seven hundred dollars. Can you believe I spent 350 quid on a facking shirt?"), and then drew me to him. His arm wraps around my shoulders, cold and thin. Wasted. I touched his cold hand with my warm finger, let it seep into him. He doesn't try anything else.

"It feels so—*comfortable*," he observes wonderingly.

Maybe it's the drugs tapping into the emotions, exposing

the pathetic, lonely reality behind the empty, huge apartment, the seven-hundred-dollar shirt, the nice guy acting like a cunt, sipping Earl Grey, talking about his best friend's wedding in Oxford, his once-a-week yoga class, Daddy dearest's undignified anal probes.

"Don't try and save me," I said. "Don't try and date me. I don't date very well. I don't do boyfriends."

He looks confused.

"But it's hard *not* to when you need help."

Little, lonely English. Tonight he gives a shit because he found a girl who could be his therapist, and in exchange for emptying his wallet of approximately nine thousand dollars, I'll let him believe he can save me—that he *wants* to save me, instead of bending me over for sodomy like he's been taught. Once I did. Need saving. Once I needed to crawl into Eton's lap and sob and take the pain away. I needed my own gruff Daddy with a million-dollar estate and advanced stage of aggressive cancer to fork out the money for my rent and living allowance so I didn't have to dress up as Lolita for Humbert Humbert every night. I needed a grownup to tell me what I was doing was right or wrong. I needed to feel that every choice I'd ever made, every spectacular exit, every sleeping body I'd left curled up in sheets was inevitable. That I was playing out my fate, my karma, what I *had* to do because whoever was behind the control panel was making it that way, making my life shit, turning me into a victim, a puppet on a string, God's little fucking lapdog.

The shirt feels soft and cool on my skin, but the apartment looks too empty for one person; unread books lining shelves, an empty fridge, a guy my age who wakes up in the night and needs to smoke to have something—*anything*—to assuage what's hotwiring his brain into nervous action twenty-four hours a day. I don't think I *do* need help, lying there, my brain subsiding into an alcoholic fuzz, the vacancy of a comedown, temporarily soothed by entering someone else's loneliness and confusion, trading it for my own. He does not sleep, he has bad dreams most nights he says, and smokes a cigarette, and I hold his hand and whisper, *"I want to stop your nightmares,"* and he looks at my pale, limp palm with disinterest, the pulse of the comedown pulling him into a private purgatory I shrank from in horror as too similar to my own.

"I'm going to work," he announces at 6:30 a.m. and smiles, and it's the uncomfortable smile of distance. I can feel the smudges of black hollowing out my eyes, skin translucent and pale, blond hair in a halolike fuzz around my thin, expression-less face. A mousy face, devoid of glitz, of sex. A young face. "Stay, sleep."

I don't stay. I let myself out without a note, knowing I would hear from him again. I liked him. I have a thing for English cunts. He'll probably be pissed, kicking himself for missing out on the Brazilian slut, opening up to a dumb fucking stripper, believing her stories. But he'll still come back. So much loneliness in Manhattan, besides my own.

When I leave at 7:23 a.m. for the walk of shame, it's curiously gray outside, darkened shop windows reflecting empty cobblestone streets. Designer names mark this area as elite, alienating. *Chanel, Steve Madden, Burberry.* SoHo. No idea where I am. Not my New York. It's chilly, a day before the heat of Easter weekend sets in and wakes the blossoms into spring. The weekend will be warm, brunch with friends in the East

Village, coffee and eggs and daffodils. But now, midweek, it's cold, unfamiliar. I have a curious feeling that I'll turn off West Broadway and onto Kensington High Street, but rounding the corner there are no black cabs, just an early morning yellow taxi swooshing by, grinding to a halt. I step in, my jaw still aching from gurning for twelve hours. I'd forgotten what it was like, the walk of shame, senses numbed, a dull contemplation born of nerves frazzled into sheer exhaustion, clothes damp with cold, stinking of the night before.

I call Eton. He doesn't pick up.

13

OK, I'll ADMIT. This one made a difference, coming as he did so late in the game when I'm winding down, still bruised, a heart cracked from my longing for Eton, my need, my lo— when I'm ready to hang up the shoes and the dress, coolly contemplate the assassination of my bestest friend. I think he thinks he's saving me, as he reads these words over diligently and holds me in the grip of my nightmares until I wake up with a choked cry still coiled in my throat like a small viper. *Eton* never does that. "Face the wall," he'll growl indignantly. "Meems, we've had this conversation before. I'm not joking. Face the bloody wall!" Now *this* one. Ah, this one. I think, in all honesty, he believes he's falling *in love with me*. The late-night phone calls and the planning-our-lives-together and the symbolic and extravagant gestures, the smileys carefully chosen (Crying Face! Happy Face! Bear! Heart! Flower!), planted in between effusive cyber-kisses—ah, sweet love! But when Mimi goes, I doubt he'll be happy with what's left—this shell, this husk, this crust.

I do wonder sometimes if they could be defamatory, my words. An invitation to former clients and workers, friends and fucks, to behave tortiously, to embroil me in the vicious vocabulary of law suits, the grandiose performance of legal battle? Yet the privacy invaded, the horrendous disclosures, have been mine, and mine alone—or Mimi's, depending on how you look at it. I received an e-mail from someone recently. Someone who had found their way into my nightmares on these pages, someone who expressed concern at my intentional disclosures, my lack of regard for his privacy, my obstinate and stubborn habit of re-creating, exactly, what I had once heard whispered in my ear, caught and registered at a dinner table, stolen maliciously and stored, gloating like a Golum, in my words. I lost patience, found myself goaded into a fury. What about what *I've* lost? What has been stolen from *me*? What about how people view *me*? I've defamed myself in spectacular fashion, I've inflicted intentional emotional distress upon myself all my goddamned life, can *I* sue *me*? Can *I* e-mail *me* with a fancy lawyer cc'd, the barest hint of a threat in grave and polite legal language, a malicious intent to maim in the only way possible, stealing from me my words? Me me me me, but what about *me*?

I wanted to slander him, face to face, scrawl it in brass rubbings, steel tomes, diamond obscenities, to defame him for all eternity, for all to see, I wanted him to know how much he'd hurt me, in my life, in the time we knew each other, but also now, when I am trying, trying, *trying,* to stop these nightmares, in the only way I know how. I never asked for anything from him, and yet Eton wants me to retract my words. I e-mailed him back a polite refusal, and when we met up that evening he never mentioned it.

I want to stop your nightmares.

.   .   .

He looks concerned at my outburst—no, not Eton, the other one, English. He watches me hiss and spit and curse, and then gathers me to him, distressed, and I want to punch him, kick and scream, fuck him, because what *good* could he do me? An empty gesture of prolixity? The closeness of his heart assuaging my erratic beat? He wasn't Eton. *I want to stop your nightmares.* But then I realized I had stopped, and had started to doze off as if I had been drugged, and he's rocking me, his mouth pressed tightly into my hair, his eyes—I knew even though I could not see—closed as if in prayer, as if willing to draw the demon out of me, extinguish it once and for all.

"You remember the time you lost it?" I ask, nursing my drink (Ketel One, soda, lime, crackling ice) as I recline against the bar and eye the Knicks game on the flat screen. Suddenly you're an "older" girl at the ripe ole age of twenny-fucking-seven, you're hanging out with the older strippers, talking about how it used to be, talking about the past. It's comforting, reaching back to that vague repository of memory, even as you swallow a hard gluey knot at the thought of six months stretching into twelve, into eighteen, into today.

"Oh yeah. I was seventeen. I waited until my third dance and I was still fully clothed. My friends stood at the bar and yelled, 'Venus, you gotta get naked! It's a fuckin' stripclub!' Everyone told me I'd be a pro at the end of the week. That night I cried, 'cause I'd lost my innocence. And then, by the end of the week, I was a fuckin' pro. Way I figure it—once I got molested for Smurfs, and now I do it for hard cash."

I chuckle and let the vodka sink into the pit of my stomach, clench my bowels involuntarily, force the contents to stay there, to soak up the alcohol as I enter phase 2 of the ritual of anesthetization. Derek Jeter scores a home run on the big screen. It's 9:45 p.m. and girls flutter listlessly sipping foul pink drinks from martini glasses, waiting for the Monday-night perverts. Always perverts on a Monday. What kind of retard wants to look at tits on a Monday? Mondays, deathly Mondays, quiet Mondays, boring, hopeless, waste-of-time Mondays. I just want to go home. It gets boring pimping Mimi out every night, especially when there's no one to pimp her out to. I just want to go home. Stop thinking, drink. Ketel One, soda, lime, crackling ice.

"I just wanna go home," sighs Venus, and she's thirty-five, and she has a fifteen-year-old kid, and has been dancing for eighteen years, and home is a two-bedroom brownstone complete with two small, brown yapping lapdogs, a home just like normal people, and she looks at me and I know what she means. It's one long hellish Yellow Brick Road, and every time you think you're getting nearer to your destination, something else happens. Something else drags you back.

I wonder if she'll ever let me go, this Mimi creature I love and loathe. *I want to stop your nightmares.* But she is my nightmare, night after night, every chapter I write, as if the very process of giving her life on the page makes her stronger, more potent, more terrifying, more destructive. She gnashes her teeth and wails like a banshee in my dreams. Yes, I may leave this place, this hell the club—but whether Mimi will leave, now that, *that* is another story.

I can't be with you, I tell him lamely, enjoying his discomfort. She'll never let me. Go find a nice, clean girlfriend you can take home to Mummy.

Later I call Eton, spend the night facing the wall, our backs barely touching.

I arrive at my yoga class ten minutes early, nod to the girl on the front desk. She takes my curled-up ten-dollar bill with a visible sneer, refuses to meet my eyes, waits until I walk away before surreptitiously wiping her hand on her saffron yoga pants. I roll out my mat. The teacher starts talking about the need to be flexible, adapt, change—some bullshit about welcoming the destructive power of Shiva into your life in order to make way for the new. Lady to the left of me farts and tries to disguise it with a cough. The room twitters and hums in expectation. Silence. I need it to balance out the anesthetization, to feel something different from what I felt onstage, which is dark, giddy, exhibitionist pleasure. Here no one looks at my mat, my body. Class starts. But sometimes they look at my soul.

I call my dad more often now, but we never speak of how I survive in Manhattan, what my life is, if I have a boyfriend. *Come into Downward Dog.* He asks about the writing, how the great American novel is coming along, and he says the same thing before he hangs up. "Take care love. Mam sends her love. Something will turn up. You've worked hard." But what's love without the accompanying check? What's love without a Get Out of Jail Free Card, someone to sit you down and say, "You're fucking yourself up irreparably baby," What's hard work without the rewards? *Extend the right leg into the air, bring it forward and place it in between your palms.* Maybe no one says it because I talk such a good game. I'm doing OK, writing a lot, totally learning from this experience. I talk it to the infrequent date I take home and whisper sarcastic noth-ings to, until at five a.m. I churn them out like sour butter so I can sleep until midday, make that daily yoga class before the ritual starts up again—me and Venus and Colette, girls I've seen before in Bambi and Lucy and Jolie, seen before, and before that even, will see again and again and again in every bitch like me who walks into that dressing room. It goes around and around on an interminable hamster wheel. *Take the left leg forward to meet the right.* My distant family on an echoing phone line, my distant dreams fading.

I'm on overdose. Overdosing on life, and you can't tell from the tone, but I'm loving it. *Fold down over your legs, uttana-sana.* The dark way I paid for my purity tapped into something that was more me than anything else—ridiculous, fierce, dirty, and wrong. The labels adopted here are more soothing than any I've had in those forty other countries, lives and times, coalescing in that two-syllable word—Mimi, me-me—more me than anything else, more me than she from before. *On the inhale float the hands above your head to meet in a high prayer.* I'm gloriously, fantastically tainted by cheap vulgarity, reveling in it. *Bring the palms to meet in front of your heart, namaste.*

Namaste.

I have my own apartment now, paid for by numerous hours in the Champagne Room. It's on the Lower East Side, right next to that dive bar Sixes and Eights, part owned by the two black punks you can buy coke off if you don't mind them doing lines off your nipples. *Inhale your arms above your head.* I have books I bought lining shelves I bleached with Clorox from the deli on Stanton. I have friends who call me and ask me to bars and restaurants and movies I can't go to, because at eight p.m. on the dot I'm in that club, smaller than the others, less interesting, just as dirty, just as pure. *Exhale, swan dive over your legs.* I have yoga clothes I drag to the Laundromat on Second Avenue between Third and Fourth every Tuesday and watch churn in the washing machine while I read Flannery O'Connor and Machiavelli and Iyengar. *Step back with the left leg.* I have hangovers and comedowns, and I have sober days when I read books, stare out of my Lower East Side illegal sublet, and gaze at the small snippet of blue sky I can see above the fire escape. *Take the right leg back into Downward Dog.* I have moments when I can laugh like I did back in the beginning, but more moments when I laugh like I did with Venus. *Inhale forward to plank.*

Breathe.

When I come home from yoga I play music from the club—hard, electric trash echoing tinnily from my laptop. Before I step into the bathtub to scald off the sweat and the confusion, I stare at myself naked, luminous and shadowy under a twenty-five-watt bulb. The precise pure moment when I slip the clear plastic heels on and pose in front of my audience of *Blattella germanica*, tiny roaches daring to grow more bulbous and foul with each passing day, the exact second the old dude with no legs in the wheelchair on the street slides a needle into a vein, the girl next door screams her orgasm out loud, someone's phone rings, a baby mewls—I realize. I stare hard hard *hard*, harder than I do with the vacant gaze born of the anesthetizing ritual, harder than that pathetic glance begging myself for sympathy, harder than puppy-dog eyes into a soul pleading for forgiveness for fucking up the last eighteen months, *Harder*.

I realize I did this shit *because it gave me a fucking purpose when I had none*. I wanted something impalpable—experience, life, knowledge—without even knowing what that meant, not knowing that I wouldn't even recognize when I had it because it would hurt so damned much. *Not having what you want gave you a purpose* (and I can't help noticing the left boob is marginally bigger than the right, and that bikini line needs tending, and maybe a French polish isn't amiss). And now I have the apartment, the ambition to write more ferocious than ever because I have the words and the darkness, and every writer needs that darkness, I have the money pouring in from a source that no longer claws and rips my pathetic heart open until it becomes intolerant of sympathy because it's numbed already. I had embraced my atheism, there could be no redemption, the soul was lost, I had nothing left to lose. I have the hours free to write my great American piece of high-brow pretentious crap, the yoga classes all happy-happy, clappy-clappy, *Hare Krishna Hare Om*. Deep down in that sour, addled heart, simmered and stewed until it cracked right open and poured the soft pulpy interior onto the page, I had all I ever wanted, my life's ambition, my dream. Maybe it wasn't the way it was meant to be, how it should have been, no. But maybe it's all Mimi and I deserve.

If you want aesthetics, leave now. But if you're still here, reading this far into the story, aesthetics was never what you desired, was it?

.   .   .

BillyMark's. Billy-Fuckin'-Mark's. Of course it's where I ended up, that bar. Every damned night after work, every damned night, and I stopped caring about life, stopped worrying about what Mimi was up to, I just went to BillyMark's.

Ceiling fans wafting the dark stench of sweat oozing through cheap polyester; six ripped black motherfuckers staring at you with blank faces and an air of pugilism; a slim, tired blond bitch with a poodle perm sitting quietly in the corner. We sit, play pool with the *whoosh-whoosh-whoosh* of dilapidated ceiling fans slicing through warm, melted butter air, caressing our bodies like the soft whistle of the Dominicans—sour, sweet, curdled. "You looking at my ass?" I ask the biggest motherfucker. "You wanna mess with me bitch?" and they fall about laughing. The blond bitch sighs, and it seems like with the exhalation something moves, stirs inside her, just as quickly dissipates in the hot summer air. "Got a cigarette?" I ask, and we go outside, lean against sticky, gummed-up walls perspiring with the blanket dark.

"They think he's my pimp 'cause he's black," she says with the lethargic twang of Atlanta, Georgia. She spoke so soft you had to lean in close, before you realized you were almost touching her head, her soft, badly permed hair, her limpid brown eyes with pupils so huge they wrestled you lazily into pity if you stared too deep. "He ain't my fuckin' pimp. I'm a dancer. He's my boyfriend. I used to escort. Still do when I need the money. But I like dancin'." The fake hair's trailing off my shoulders, eyes crayoned into a caricature of a ho's, I look like a ho, a ho at two a.m. in Billy-Fuckin'-Mark's. I look like a stripper. So she knew, and she told me this shit. *Dancer*. We're not fucking dancers. When, in the history of time, has grinding cock ever been dancing? In the world of the fucking American club, that's what. You go into a club, a bar, some shithole on Twenty-seventh and Tenth, you see all these bitches with their Prada handbags grinding cock on the dance-floor, and they call that dancing. They'd be offended if they knew what they were doing was being done on the opposite side of the street for a lot more fucking Benjamins.

"You thought about working in Manhattan? Like, at Foxy's or Vegas?" I ask, and the smoke from my cigarette puffed out as I spoke, hot breath, loaded with tar and decay.

"You work there? You'll help me get a job? I need money. I don't like escort work. It's kinda boring, lonely. I gotta two-year-old son, I need money."

And it hangs there like the smoke we exhale, distilled and loaded and heavy in the front of our faces like a mask of death, or maybe just Manhattan, but I take her number knowing I won't call, and we go back in and we sit at the bar, two blond bitches waiting for their men to finish playing pool.

"Hey Mimi, he your boyfriend?" yells the bartender, and I shrug, shake my head no, and the old Puerto Rican lady married to the young dude from Cuba starts singing, her addled hands floating elegantly around her face as she mimes along to Patsy Kline on the jukebox, and the big black motherfuckers stop for a second, and everyone pauses, holds their breath, and it's kind of beautiful in this fucked-up lunatic place way out on the West Side, filled with pimps and hos and people like me who just came along for the ride. Kind of beautiful, a lotus growing from crap, and when the old Puerto Rican lady stops singing, the blond girl starts texting her friend, the black motherfuckers pick up their pool cues, my guy takes a swig of

Jack, and the old Puerto Rican lady stands, smiling beatifically, shining like she knew there was applause even if we couldn't hear it, and she sits down again, downs another shot of tequila, and then goes outside to cry, because it was too fucking beautiful not to.

"Call that girl again?" he smiles, cradling the pool cue as the Puerto Rican lady sobs and her husband dressed in one-piece camouflage gear slowly peels the label off a Bud bottle, rolls the paper, sticky, damp, in his hand, so I pick up the phone and call my black bitch up in Harlem, Bambi. "He ain't pickin' up the damned phone the Fat Fuck," she screams, even before I say hello. "I can't find him. Listen, if you guys want coke or weed, that's easy, but this shit ain't going down well. There ain't no one in Manhattan beside that Fat Fuck, and he won't get off his fat ass to fuckin' deliver." Waves of cheap beer are coursing through me, and the guy's talking to Billy at the bar, or maybe it was Mark, or maybe Billy. So I get another beer, go outside with the blond bitch again, and dance salsa with the Puerto Rican lady in the lewd heat of a Manhattan night, dancing like we're lovers, laughing and cussing out the menfolk.

We wait until the next day. Order a take-out of diesel to keep us going, hand delivered straight to my apartment by some dude I stare at like a child, my eyes glazed by too much liquor, too much sex, two straight days of drinking. I call in sick. "You ain't working? You gonna get in trouble girl. You left early Thursday night too." I left early because my time was running out, the story was drawing to an elegiac conclusion, an arabesque of destruction, me and Mimi. "I can't give blow-jobs," one of the girls said to me last week, a bitch from London, and her eyes widened with horror at the thought. "I can't even imagine puttin' that thing in my mouth. Fucking disgusting. My friend told me to imagine it was a lollipop, but I can't. It's just sick." And then she looked over at some guys, slipped elegantly onto their laps, hand slid between thighs, a gentle lick on the ear. I left.

The diesel's working its shitty little magic as undulating waves start to wrap around me, claw down the thoughts, and replace them with that sunken, smacked feeling of disconnection that comes from being so connected, so in tune, it's almost unbearable. *"I'm so fucked up,"* I whisper, and he just smiles, and there's a moment when I have a twinge of something— horror? fear? fear and loathing in the Lower East? *Is this right?*—and then it's so right you don't need anything else, just the warm, intense, safe pressure of prolixity and from somewhere the tinny prick of the music worming its way into your brain, and the waves just keep rushing, and rushing—

We end up several hours later wearing different clothes, in the club downstairs. "Call again," he says, and I do, someone different this time, and it's the same answer, so I use the tricks I learned back in France, I used nightly at Foxy's, at Vegas, at Jack's, and I stand and watch and wait and talk shit on the street, and hit the jackpot. Inside he's sitting waiting on a black cracked-leather chair with a bottle of Veuve Clicquot on a Formica table, two plastic flutes smudged with fingerprints, and the black dude who owns the place slides into the booth next to us.

"This little white bitch cracked me up man. She just stood outside and came straight out with it, 'Can you sort me out?' in that hot little accent. I don't do it for everyone, but I looked at her and *knew* she was special. Gimme eighty bucks. I'll sort you out."

So he does. The club's filling up, and there's a bunch of Hispanic girls, their asses hanging out of teeny-tiny skirts, there are too many girls, a lot of girls, and the music's old school, riding somewhere between Bob Dylan and hip hop, not even eclectic, just fucking wrong, and I love that too. When the waitress comes over she's sad and listless and Russian. "What's your name sweetheart?" I ask. "Michelle" she breathes sadly. There's something between her and the black guy. We don't know what, and are too fucked up riding the waves to even care. And then the other guy comes back and we're led into the backroom, sigh, exhalation. I love this shit, loved it, left it, and now it's back in NY to haunt me, another fucked-up night in shit city. We're in a black room in the back of a club and the manager's chopping out lines of something with a sharp, metallic stench, free drinks, we're flavor of the fucking month. The place is full of trash, we're trash, white fucking trash, middle-class trash playing it dirty because it's the place we feel at home, we feel ourselves. He doesn't know my real name, doesn't care, and I like him for it, like him for not being Eton, like him for the mutual using, like him even more for knowing that tomorrow he'll be gone. I don't know his real name. And then that blissful, fucked-up tsunami of chemical endorphins blasts into your system, and your ego expands so painfully it's like you're going to explode, and I look over at him, playing drums in the middle of this fucking shit-hole in Manhattan we found without looking, and he looks up and just smiles. Smiles at his little white trash fuck grinding along on the dancefloor with some fat dudes and loving it, feeling the inevitable, inexorable pump of chemicals coursing through the system and melding indefinably with the memories of times past, the beat of something you've known before, that sweet, orgasmic pleasure of living in a way you really shouldn't, and loving it, *loving every damned fucked-up minute*. He gets up and he starts dancing with a slim, tanned girl, hotter than me, but that's cool as well, because he's not my boyfriend, I don't do boyfriends, never have done. The end of the night approaches, but it's still not over, even as we're locked into the club and fed Red Bulls to pump our over-hyped, exhausted, frazzled souls into something even higher, and we go back to my place with the tired, sad Russian girl and the two pimps, drink Stella and black tea, smoke some weed, and the sad Russian girl leans over to me, and I clutch her hand, cold and unloved, and she asks me if I'll help her, and I slip her my number, and the black dude smoking shit slouches against the wall, his eyes rolling in the back of his head, and the guy I'm with laughs, and when they leave, we lie in the bath, let the music assuage our abused bodies, let ourselves drift gently down and into each other as the water trickles gradually down the plughole, The Drifters play on . . .

He leaves at midday, by which time I've forgotten his name, deleted his number, gone back to bed, alone. Eton calls a few hours later. I don't pick up.

I start to vomit the darkness crawling into my soul back up on the page. Summer rolls on, intense and unforgiving. It's all the same to me now. I just write, fill up the void with words, scrabbling and feverish, urgently seeking the combination— the perfect combination—that will unlock the door, swing it gently, cleanly open, show me the end.

14

ENGLISH USED THE WORD *"girlfriend"* the other night.

What a repulsive term, so redolent of playgrounds and hot, sticky childhood paws stinking of cheese and onion crisps as they scrabble, disgustingly, for your hand. *Girlfriend?* I thought, vaguely after I'd recovered from the initial distaste, *that should probably be in the plural,* but I've noticed, lately, Mimi's aversion to his (highly suspect) charms. When men are around, Mimi is around—the two go hand in hand, *men-Mimi, men-Mimi,* like a merry-go-round, swinging back and forth. Yet that disarming smile, the English charm, and that good-natured optimism of his—all traits I abhor yet find mildly tolerable— seem to make her bristle agitatedly, walk silently away in a pouting, suspicious sulk. She does not trust him. I don't either, but slowly, irritatingly, I am beginning to slip as each day brings me nearer to the conclusion, as my words begin to peter out. If she had her way the story would go on forever—but I've noticed her rages are becoming interspersed with periods of sad, quiet calm resignation. Could it be the end? I feel almost guilty. And then the rage again, the rage as she demands more attention, more time, another story—*but don't you remember that time . . . ? And did you put that in? And what about when he . . . ?* We argue a lot, nowadays, I have to say.

He listens in confusion and not a little fear when our petty squabbles froth out into a tumbling tumorous mass of obscenities. I oscillate between me and Mimi, veer frighteningly between hatred, and—something I have never felt before. I'm loath to give a trite and specious term to what is, after all, just the need for a little companionship, something a little different from the perverts and the pedophiles and the creeps. Someone to fill up the ever widening gaps in between my feasts with Eton. But then we tumble into bed arguing vociferously about stoic philosophy, American politics, the crisis in the Gaza Strip—something to flaunt our young, intelligent minds, display their full pretentious arrogance—something far removed from all of this, something that reminds me I still exist in a world outside the contingent realm of my body. I laugh as his hand gently, deliciously, traces its curves with a tender reverence and the good humored battles melt into a buttery pool by sucking, hotness, taste, thirst satiated, hair and mouths and limbs melded and fused in one long kiss so my body is his, his mine. And yet—would you believe it?—we have not yet done the deed . . . "sealed the deal." . . . I feel dizzy, a little sick, a little scared . . . *It's just a pleasant distraction from an otherwise unfortunate period of my existence.* I don't do boyfriends.

Mimi, of course, disagrees with his presence, would have me rewrite the story with a sunset ending in Mustique on Eton's opulent yacht. *I can't do that,* I tell her. I do have a little smirk when I exercise what little power I have, but then I have a duty to record some semblance of truth, surely? It's not cruel to insist on the truth? It's just journalism, good scholarship, conscientious objection. We do agree on one thing, though: no boyfriends. No, no boyfriends. I have always followed this policy, and I have yet to suffer the ridiculous acrobatics of a broken heart, the inevitable Judas-like betrayal. I have yet to drag the carcass of a relationship upon these slim, toned shoulders, and with osteoporosis in the family, I have no plans, as yet, to do so.

I have bad dreams.

I wonder if, when I leave this place, they'll go, or if they're like cancer, always lurking somewhere in my malignant soul.

I walked there barefoot, and the sidewalk felt molasses warm and sticky. Everything feels surreal in 110 degrees, and the skirt barely skimming my ass, the black soot etched onto neatly manicured soles—these are merely details swimming around in a fishbowl of heat—magnified, syncopated, irrelevant. Cold pink feet on a warm black sidewalk, the only thing catching me from falling right off that freakshow merry-go-round called Manhattan.

I put the shoes on right before I step into the restaurant, curl a tendril of dry, bleached hair around one finger, skirt too short. Want it to feel right. Doesn't feel right. The whole night, place, time doesn't feel right. It's anal without the Astroglide, dead babies at a wedding, foreskins at a bar mitzvah. It's disconnected and jarring, and slipping those black soles into silver mules adds another layer of unwelcome detachment. I want the sidewalk, foul and syrupy; I want to revel in the dirt, engrain the city onto soft pink soles, scour it into the white cotton of my appearance and wear it like stigmata. I give it up for silver mules, a chichi joint, and swinging away from the intimate embrace of the night into the slap of arid AC.

An angular vegetarian restaurant with sneering waiters and a man with a blank face and an air kiss. I sit down. We talk. My head swirls from no food and three sips of wine. I can't remember the words, just more careless details muffled by the heartbeat in my head. The phone rings. I don't hear it.

"Your phone's ringing," he says. It's the Fat Fuck.

"I gotta go," I say gratefully. "Wait for me." I stand outside, just out of site of frosted pale glass. Heels hurt, top buckle grating across the thin layer of veiny flesh. Damp is pooling in the soft pits under my arms. Stand on one foot. Stand on the other. The Fat Fuck was a while. Couples walk past. It's one of those nights every bad writer will describe as "balmy," as if you could stick it in a tube and sell it as ChapStick. Balmy. A balmy night, aromatic with the scent of dog piss, exhaust fumes, masturbation. Masturbation. Life, one big futile exploit to jerk off our souls, our ego, who we think we are, who we want to be, who we profess to be, who we construct with the latest electronics and condos and exotic sexual positions and fucking underage kids. The climax is a little death, that long awaited, never-talked-about spatter of liquid dissemination. The Romantics called it a little death. Maybe the quality of orgasm was better in those days. Maybe I'm dating the wrong guys. I take my shoes off again, making sure I'm out of sight of the guy. Feel ridiculous in the dress, those damned silver mules. Feel surreal, doggy-paddling in the soupy heat. My head swirls nauseatingly. The Fat Fuck turns up eventually, and I can feel the tension from the guy inside even though I can't see his eyes, maybe because I can't see his eyes.

"You ever thought of bachelor parties?" the Fat Fuck asks,

a drawl somewhere between Harlem and Atlanta, Georgia. "I can hook you up. They always want white girls. Always askin' for white girls. Hard to get white girls. They don't wanna get intimate with black guys. You have a problem with black guys?" In his hand a plastic bag, dripping. He has on white yellowing Chucks, no socks. I keep eyeing that damned bag, wondering when he'll shut the fuck up, nodding, agreeing to whatever the hell he says. He has my chocolate-coated mushrooms on ice, wrapped lovingly in a Gristedes bag, drip-drip-dripping onto the sidewalk, teardrops evaporating instantly on asphalt. Right now I'd agree to suck off his damned dog if it got me those fucking mushrooms, two weeks late, so I don't even want them anymore but paid him because someone else would pay me more. So I stand outside barefoot while the guy sits inside encased in his BlackBerry bubble of burned enthusiasm. Some fucking pride. Seven blocks and two avenues barefoot, hiding the evidence in silver mules, a push-up bra, the cool, leveled gaze of someone used to standing outside being assaulted by waves of heat waiting for a Fat Fuck to turn up and deliver Class A's. My life sure as hell sounds better than it feels.

The Fat Fuck leaves and I have to put those damned silver mules back on, push open the frosted glass door, brace myself for that wasteland of a conversation. His mouth is a round O when I throw the mushrooms at him. It's an inauspicious time. You know when you feel the tide change, start to drag the debris, the driftwood, the treasure, back out to sea, snatch back what it vomited up on the shore? That's now. Somewhere between the consumption of a pesto green soup and the pickup of chocolate-covered mushrooms lovingly wrapped in a Gristedes bag, now dripping over plastic vinyl chairs. "So what's wrong?"

I ask eventually, when the pulse in my head threatens to make me scream. You have to ask three times, like calling the devil. "No, what's wrong?" You're getting there, you're getting closer. "No, just tell me, what's *wrong?*"

"You scare me," Eton said. "There's something very dark in you, Meems. You've changed."

I look down into the pesto green soup, look up at him again, and then I kiss him on the cheek and leave abruptly, the buckle of those damned silver mules grating horribly against raw flesh. There's an art to leaving, a perfection, a symmetry, and it's taken me twenty-seven years to learn. It's a superb exit. I wait two blocks and then I kick those damned silver mules off, grab tight, tight, tight onto the railings, feel the sidewalk firm and solid and comforting beneath my bare feet. You probably couldn't tell, or maybe you could, but I was scared that if I didn't hold tight, I'd fall right off.

BillyMark's. Hot fingers against a cool bottle, the same Puerto Rican lady at the end of the bar, but this time she isn't singing and there's a wise stillness in her nut brown eyes as she gazes at me and smiles.

"Where's your boyfriend?" asks Billy, or maybe it was Mark, or maybe Billy. "Thought you said you had a hot date with someone special tonight? Future husband? You guys have an argument?"

"He's not my boyfriend," I say.

"Aw, you guys have an argument? You ain't talkin' no more? I ain't never met this one either. How come you never brought him here? You guys'll get back together again, guarantee it."

The old Puerto Rican lady gazes at me steadily, her addled, spotted hands resting gently on the bar.

"No," I smile, and stare curiously into her deep, pure eyes, so beautiful, so alive, set back in sagging folds of brown crepey skin, and "Goodbye Yellow Brick Road" is playing on the jukebox.

28°28'N 16°20'W

I was falling, falling, falling, but couldn't remember the jump, and the bottom seemed to be evasive. So I tried a little harder.

"You never said good-bye," B said, calling me in Palma as we prepared to sail across the Atlantic.

"No, I didn't," and I hung up, called the next one. "Meet me tomorrow night."

Kept jumping right into the next addled day sodden with alcohol and the echoing, stark numbness of a beer-sodden soul still reeling from a chemical high and the smack of the night. I forget every man, but I remember every morning, my eyes wide and vacant, unable to speak. I'd sit at Bar Toni, down espresso, and nod to the French guy with the curly hair and the dirty, long, yellow fingernails who sold me shit I'd sell to tourists for twice the price. I left my men like I left my boats: abruptly, before I got kicked off for turning up for work at six a.m. with no sleep and a jaw locked tight, clenched shut—whether through drugs or something else, I couldn't tell. Still can't.

C came with an unspectacular yelp like a small dog while his wife roamed the streets for him, calling a cellphone that beeped uselessly beneath the bed next to the suitcase and the flip-flops.

"I'd leave her for you, you know," C sighed, and he would, I knew it. He'd jump, knowing that the fall would be swift and clean and the result a carnival of crushed and splintered bones, intestines oozing like reptiles across a baked sidewalk.

When I got to Gibraltar he'd left a message for me. I ignored it. And then we sailed to the Canary Islands—which island I forget—and it rained, and we sat in a bar sipping Baileys staring at the masts of sailboats kissing dirty gray clouds. He called me again.

"I want to leave her. I've decided. I'll meet you in St. Martin."

But I hung up, and when the Captain looked over to ask me what was wrong, he caught my eye and smiled, and he knew, having mastered the exquisite art of falling, falling, falling for all eternity, without fear or retribution or spilled blood—ours, at least. I time them to perfection, my leaps over that cliff, waiting until the bow of the next boat noses close to mine and I can spring over in a perfect arc, clearing saltwater licking at my heels, fall to safety, fall on my feet, hit the deck cleanly, half wishing I could feel the same sting that everyone else gets from the impact of earth punching body.

I'm always on my way out, ready to jump. Bag slung over shoulder, moving on, ticket in hand, a flight, a boat, a train. It's a solo occupation. On reflection maybe I never mastered my vertigo. I just lived with it until it became part of my soul, and every night was just jumping again and again, senseless, exalted, perfect. I don't know if I can give it up.

When I first saw her, the eyes weren't so much lobotomized as scared rabbit. Rippling folds of baby pink flesh nestled beneath buds of breasts—dangling like a suckling cow too young to be reproducing but forced into it by the cattle market. She was scared, this bitch; scared beneath the thick, black lines painted round blue depths of inane youth. When she danced, it was with a fixated grin boring into your face to distract from the body she doesn't want to show; the body her parents probably think is still covered up with cheap H&M even as she sends back the big fucking dollars to pay for their post-communist rent, their American beers. "How do you dance, plis?" she had asked me, and I just shrugged, nodded to the vodka clasped in my hand, the glass misted from the heat of my palm, ice crackling and fizzing, emitting little puffs of gas into the arid, chilly air. She took the drink and she grimaced, the little rolls of flesh rippling up from her baby stomach up through her baby breasts, into a face whose cheekbones sank beneath prepubescent pudge.

"Listen sweetheart," I said, and I leaned in urgent, like I gave a fuck, grabbed her hand, stared into those pretty blue eyes, felt my hand tighten against a round, pink forearm, saw my skin ghoulish, white and taut against this fucking honey-blossom oozing the nectar of nineteen and new in Nueva York. "Get out. Get your fucking money, get back to Russia. This place isn't for you. Drink what you need to do the fucking job, keep your wits about you, don't suck cock, and you'll be fine."

She looked scared, now I think about it, but her brain was still working because the pupils contracted as she shrank away, disappeared to a corner, thought about the cash, got back to her pathetic faux-grinding in midair. That same fucking grin, the blond hair, dark roots delineating the stark white flesh of her scalp bobbing up and down in the white light, the disco flashes from the sad glitter ball, there since '83. Familiar. She was always there, in her corner when the lights tracked across the club. Another crappy dancer. Kind of gawky, kind of cute.

I didn't give it another thought, just turned up for work, saw her around. Didn't notice that shy, sly smile slowly flailing like a weak sapling beneath the cancerous weeds of something sicker. I started skipping work, hanging out with deadbeats from BillyMark's, but the money ran out, so after a couple of weeks I went back.

But it was all different when I went back. Different because you get away and you become the person you were before, the person slowly asphyxiating beneath the thick, caked layers of Mimi. You become what you aren't when you're in that place, caught between the rapid beats of bad house music like a heart patient on amphetamines, the jarring, listless gyration of the dance. The two never meld, surprisingly. You'd think if you spent forty hours a week in this place you'd get some fucking rhythm. Just a discord. A discord like the sour taste from too many cigarettes counterpointed against no food for a week, the dark stench of alcohol roaring out of your mouth like a sewage drain, drenched in Orbit sugar-free. She was the first one I saw, but now the pretty blue eyes were lobotomized with the scalpel of money, hard fucking cash, and she led the old dude with the bad breath up the fucking stairs to Never-Never Land, 'cause I'd never been there and I didn't intend to go, the *private* private rooms, more private than the others, where your dick up her peachy ass costs 300 bucks, and ramming the back of her throat will go for a Ben Franklin, and straight-up pussy probably about 250. And you wonder what it was like for her—the first time. Whether it was as bad as her stage show, as transparent as the scared rabbit eyes that were a glass mirror right into her fucked-up little Russian head, allowing the sense to leak out like a soft-boiled egg cracked swiftly open. It seeped out as easily as that dress peeled off, that spangly, glittery G-string curled up in the corner of the room like a dead spider, that dignity was shed.

What's your name sweetheart?

Me me, she breathed.

You must listen to this, said English one evening, *d'you know the story behind it?*
When he felt he couldn't give anymore, he stopped.

He spent those twelve years rediscovering the craft— obsessing over the score, the scales, the obsessive dotted rhythms of Schumann, the lilt, the exaltation of Bach. And after months rehearsing, in May 1965 he announced a recital.

People lined the streets outside Carnegie Hall, unheard of for a classical musician. His wife, Wanda (so it's said), handed out refreshments to the queues of people desperate to see the reclusive pianist, isolated from his public for over a decade.

He was late. Terrified, as usual, by the task he had undertaken, the task that simultaneously drove him and destroyed him. He stood in the wings and refused to step out into the lights, his nerves strung to a pitch outside the human range. The manager was eventually forced to push him onstage.

You can hear the doubt, the confusion, the self-flagellation, in the Bach-Busoni Toccata. He feels his way into the music with the reckless execution of an artist discovering a terrifying impotency, virility painfully seeping out through the dribbling keys, dropped notes. He slips . . . the audience gasps . . .

But he keeps playing.

He slips again—and the audience is astounded, horrifed— afraid that he was right. *He had no more to give.* I used to stand outside Carnegie Hall sometimes, when I worked in Midtown at Foxy's, inhaling the shocked scent of the audience, the tang of fear, and then the relief.

He recovers. He moves into Schumann, into Debussy, and finally, Horowitz finds his element in Scriabin's Sonata Number 9, which he releases with an ecstasy born of the devil. Nothing this good could ever come from Heaven.

Before the night was over I went quietly upstairs, past the girls drunk and waving cigarettes around in the locker room, talking about their asshole boyfriends from the Bronx fucking bitches while they earned the rent. I dressed, scrubbed the crap off my face. I didn't say good-bye to anyone. But I wondered as I walked home through the East Village, the warm night pouring onto me with damp, false caresses—I wondered if it was all worth it. If staying someplace, trying for what I wanted—or not even wanted, something I had to do, *have* to do because it's all I know—I wondered if trading in ignorance for this unbearable sadness, this knowing, this dull, deep ache, was ever going to mean anything besides poverty, a Bob Dylan song, spending my last twenty bucks on a six-pack and some cigarettes, sitting down and doing what I know best. Ratcheting it up from my dark, boiled heart as the AC whirrs and Manhattan starts to slowly wind down in preparation for the reprise, which continues regardless.

. . .

When the phone call came I was sitting on the fire escape, expecting it. It was nine a.m. and my eyes were still wide and spanked with coke, and I clutched a cold bottle of Corona in my hand. I'd been at BillyMark's the night before, shooting pool with some guy. Doesn't matter whom. He wasn't my boyfriend. The phone rang and I answered it and hoped my credit didn't run out and we talked for a while and I brought out the Mimi doll, just for show, the fading euphoria of the night lulling me into a conversational mood full of flamenco grandeur, braggart lifts and twirls, steps that made you inhale quickly, sharp, in sheer, giddy amazement. I became a writer that day, officially, on the record, with a publisher's advance. It was, nonetheless, a transaction. A transaction that pleased me, though secretly I believed that what they were buying from me was not the original, not the real. They were just buying another artifice, a meme, another simulation, while the words I wielded would release her into a terrible life of her own, divorced from mine. They wanted me, naturally, to write as Mimi. No one is really interested in the girl underneath.

I didn't celebrate that night. I was bored of BillyMark's and the club, bored of sex with strangers and cheap, bad drugs, bored of Eton, English, British cunts. Instead I purchased a six-pack of Corona and a half a gram of coke, and wrote some more. I gave myself two weeks to limp lamely through the rituals of dancing. I don't know why two weeks. I don't know why I just never went back. Maybe I knew that I needed to wean myself off her first before plunging cold turkey into a Mimi-less existence.

I seduced English later that week. It was almost an act of obligation more than any real desire, a reflex ingrained in my soul, like a hand reaching for the rosary, a litany repeated,

mechanical and efficient. But his clumsiness, sweetness, ten-
derness, made me laugh, normalized the insanity of a clinical
act and imbued it with something more, some meaning,
some—*faith*, perhaps. It was enough to make me halt, disturbed, before either of us experienced the little death. We
curled up together and slept so soundly, so comfortably, so
safe, that I did not have nightmares. It was if my sin were
merely venial, and not mortal.

That sleep aggravated me. I did not face toward the wall.
Who had seduced whom? I felt powerless, longed for the safe
transactions of the stripclub, seduction without impunity, seduction with necessary penury. A frugality when dealing with
emotion, a laissez-faire when it came to the extravagant, ridiculous circus of pouting and posturing, giggles and sighs.

When I seduced him I did not plan to let it go so far. I
waited for the slap, waited in anticipatory pleasure and need
for it, and yet he regarded me quizzically, curiously, with gentle, nonjudgmental amusement. He knew that I was writing
something that made me sleep badly. He knew that I would
disappear at night for hours without him, hours that stretched
into days, nights, weeks. He knew not to ask certain things. I
think he knew not to take it, me, too seriously, expected me
not to stay too long. He knew that I still lov—well, he knew.

"Has it changed you?" English asked with an interest that
was too casual, too smooth, too light. I lay wrapped in clean
white sheets and he sat at the bottom of the bed, wrestling
with a corkscrew, a bottle of Chianti. I sighed, deep and long
and low.

"You have no idea." I smiled. And then we kissed.

· · ·

I recently met a publicist who was interested in marketing Mimi to her fullest potential. He took me to some chichi restaurant and I was on my best behavior as my eyes glazed over in boredom at the prattlings of inane celebrities at the next table. I looked around for a waiter to fill my wineglass, which he did with a chilling obsequiousness. "So should I call you Mimi?" he said, after the wine had served as social lubricant and he became fatherly, friendly, jocular. I stared at him as if he had suggested I strip naked for him. The cheek! "No," I said coldly, and excused myself to go to the bathroom, narrowly avoiding a skinny starlet with a Botoxed face, rigid, unyielding, frightening.

I want to stop your nightmares.

"I don't know if I can give it up," I tell English at seven a.m. after a night of hard drinking, and ash from my cigarette spilled like wine onto my lap. "I think that even though I want a normal life and clean living and everything to be nice and what it's never been, I know that at some point I'll get back to the top of the cliff, and I'll want to jump—or Mimi will push me over." It felt weird saying it out loud. But he was the one who told me about vertigo. And he said he mastered it by jumping, so that's something, at least. That's something.

"It's OK," he replies, and I can tell it really is. "If you get to the top, and you want to jump, I'll jump with you."

I wanted to say that wasn't the point, but then it occurred to me that maybe it was. I thought some more. All I said in the end was, "Thanks." But I think he understood.

. . .

Three a.m. and a warm wind blew. My bags were packed, the apartment bare and clean, life disposed of in shipping boxes and black plastic garbage bags. After three years, it was surprisingly painless to leave the city. When it came down to it, I doubted New York had even registered my arrival, let alone noticed my departure. On Houston cabs crawled past, slowed, perhaps by the hour, the bliss of a cool morning wind after the treacly heat of the day. A bum emerged from behind a parked car, wandered incoherently over, sat down next to me on the stoop. I recognized his face.

"You leavin' Manhattan? I seen you around this street, with the English guy. I do work in this block sometimes for Fer, you know Fer, the super? Yeah, I know everyone on this street."

His breath was hot and festering, a wet, dead rodent in the heat. "What are you doing up so late?" I asked quietly, a smile that didn't reach my eyes, glance toward my watch *where the fuck is this car?*

His eyes glimmered, glanced at me sharply, then the focus dimmed and the voice went low, intense.

"I have nightmares," he shrugged. "Dreams, images, call 'em what you want. I have nightmares, most nights. Keeps me up."

"What are they about?" I whispered, and Manhattan was never so quiet as I waited for that answer.

"Things. Violent things. Sad things. I don't want the nightmares, so I don't sleep no more."

He threw back his head and laughed, and in that black, burned mouth the bitter charred stubs of teeth emerged and the stink, the *stink*—it was unbearable, like the laugh. "I have nightmares," he repeated, and he laughed again, longer this time, harder. The car drew up. "Should I tell him you left?" he called after me, as the bags were thrown in the trunk. "He's gonna miss you, pretty little thing that you are. You said good-bye?" and when I ignored him he let the laugh turn into something that sounded like a stifled scream. We drove off quickly down Houston.

There's an art to leaving, a perfection, a symmetry. While Mimi squirmed and howled and thrashed away inside me, the exorcism, that ritual purgation of words, was performed almost seamlessly. She left quietly—too quietly—as if one day, she might be back.

Sometimes I miss her, the ole Mimi doll. I miss being raped by a focusless gaze, the anonymity of being the centripetal force in a roomful of dicks, of being the other woman, that faceless other woman we females all fear, the bitch who makes our boyfriend/husband/lover drool and cower and snicker and groan, balls heavy and leaden and loaded with lust for the something more, the something more men always want because monogamy is just not in their sex. I want to be the high-carbohydrate, benzene-loaded, phenylalanine-fizzy smack laced with aspartame and bursting with sugary, acidic cancer agents. I want to be the snack that fails to satisfy, the food for hungry ghosts with empty holes where stomachs should be. After all the plots to kill her off in spectacular style, I want to be Mimi. I want to be Mimi again, for all the good it does me, did me.

Sometimes, I miss her.

Acknowledgments

Thanks to the wonderful David Godwin and all who work at DGA—Kirsty, Sophie, and Kerry. Thanks to my editor, Carole DeSanti, and everyone at Viking for taking on a manuscript that needed so much work. Thanks to Eton for the maid's outfit and the dinners and episodes of *Lost*. Thanks to Scarlett for the Bassett hound pictures, and Nicola for the spare bed and food. Thanks to Amy for telling me her story and everyone I met campaigning for immigrant rights. Thanks to everyone who helped me be illegal. Thanks to those who helped me get legal. Thanks to Paul Carr. Thanks to the yogis who never judged me—Sarah Tomlinson, Emma Canarick, and Allison Bonanno. Thanks to Paul Berger for writing the fateful article that started the ball rolling. Thanks to all the women I worked with in the stripclubs of New York City. Thanks to the (very few!) men I met there who had respect and kindness. Thanks to everyone who believed in me, read the blog, and encouraged me.